Carnival and Culture

DAVID D. GILMORE

Carnival and Culture

SEX, SYMBOL, AND STATUS IN SPAIN

Yale University Press
New Haven &
London

Set in Sabon type by Keystone Typesetting, Inc.

Printed in the United States of America.

Library of Congress Cataloging-in-Publication Data
Gilmore, David D., 1943–
    Carnival and culture: Sex, symbol, and status in Spain / David D. Gilmore.
        p.   cm.
    Includes bibliographical references and index.
    ISBN 0-300-07480-8 (cloth : alk. paper)
    1. Carnival — Spain — Andalusia.   2. Sex role — Spain — Andalusia.
3. Andalusia (Spain) — Social life and customs.   I. Title.
GT4262,A55G55   1998
394.25′0946 — dc21   98-16185
                                                                        CIP

A catalogue record for this book is available from the British Library.

The paper in this book meets the guidelines for permanence and durability of the Committee on Production Guidelines for Book Longevity of the Council on Library Resources.

10 9 8 7 6 5 4 3 2 1

This book is dedicated to my family,
for whom it's carnival
365 days a year

Carnival, in order to be enjoyed, requires that rules and rituals be parodied, and that these rules and rituals already be recognized and respected. — *Umberto Eco, "Frames of Comic Freedom," in* Carnival!

That which we are capable of feeling, we are capable of saying. — *Miguel de Cervantes, "El Amante Liberal,"* Novelas Ejemplares

The metaphor is probably the most fertile power possessed by man. — *José Ortega y Gasset,* The Dehumanization of Art

Tú eres el Carnaval, lo que tú quiere que seas, el Carnaval será. (You are carnival: whatever you want to be, carnival will be) — *Official motto of 1995 carnival season, Fuentes de Andalucía*

Contents

Preface

Ten years ago I wrote a book about the role of aggression in Spanish culture. I apologized then to my friends and colleagues in Spain as well as to my readers for concentrating on things that made people sad or uncomfortable, for emphasizing the culture's negative aspects: annoyances like gossip and slander, malicious nicknaming, backbiting, and scapegoating. By way of exculpation, I said that someday I would make up for it by writing a book about the things that made people happy. This is that book. Nothing makes people happier than carnival.

The study is based on material collected on numerous trips to Spain between 1971 and 1995. During that time, I visited and revisited the inland areas near the cities of Seville, Cordoba, and Malaga and attended many carnivals in the provincial *pueblos,* or rural communities. I witnessed the Spanish village carnival for the first time in 1973, and most recently in 1995; this span of almost a quarter century was a pivotal period in modern Spanish history, bridging the Franco regime and the new democracy. I am mainly familiar with the following towns in western Andalusia and their respective festivals: Fuentes de Andalucía, La Campana, Ecija, Estepa, Osuna, and Marchena, all in Seville Province, and Montilla, Aguilar, and Montemayor in Cordoba Province. A Spanish assistant, María del Carmen Medina, also did some interviewing for me in the towns of Las Cabezas de San Juan, Pedrera, Aznalcóllar, Los Corrales, Gines, Alcalá de Guadaira, and Cazalla de la Sierra, all of which are in Seville Province.

I must issue a caveat about the translations of the carnival songs and other verbal material from the original Andalusian-accented Castilian. All translations are mine, including both the coplas and the published works. The carnival poets, or *"maestros"* ("Meistersinger" is a possible gloss), are often illiterate, but their words are sometimes taken down by scribes or by literate friends and printed on broadsides (*folletos*) for sale during carnival. In this way the poets earn a few pesetas as well as a measure of local fame. I collected some of the lyrics in this way, by buying them on location, or making recordings made during performances, still others through recompiling them from listeners' memory. Many carnival poets, especially Juanillo "El Gato" and his son Manolo Benítez, did me the honor of sitting down with me and reciting their otherwise irrecoverable lyrics over glasses of sherry. None of the songs, printed or otherwise, are copyrighted. I thank all the poets for their patience and their help and for sharing their work with me. Like so many Andalusians, the carnival maestros are generous to a fault with their most prized possessions.

My translations of the poets' work are admittedly prosaic and pedestrian. Wordplay, tropes, and puns in the original Andalusian Spanish are of course mangled or lost. I have also ruined many jokes because of the inevitable failures of transcription of localisms, idioms, and parochial allusions. In some instances, I had to sacrifice literalness to achieve an analogous sense or mood in the English version. Throughout, in translating the coplas, my goal has been to render substance rather than style, and besides, unlike the maestros, I am no poet. So I apologize to my readers and to the composers themselves for the infelicity of the English versions. I hope I have done their meanings justice if not their art. All lyrics are transcribed verbatim, complete with misspellings and solecisms.

Finally, let me make a note on the "ethnographic present." There is no "present" here, ethnographic or otherwise. I collected the lyrics between 1972 and 1995, but the songs themselves date from various times between 1900 and 1995, so this is a generalized work of twentieth-century texts. But most of what I have to say here about behavior in bars and homes, and during carnival too, describes fieldwork in Spain between 1971 and 1995; in that sense the field data, but not the songs (which are eternal), are wedded to the late Franco years and the early years of democracy. I have added a chapter on the evolution of carnival, which describes changes in the festival between 1982, when free elections in Spain assured the restoration of full democracy, and 1995, the time of my last experience with the carnivalesque. The ethnographic present, then, may be described as the second half of the twentieth century.

My field trips to Spain were supported at various times by generous grants from the following agencies and foundations, public and private: the National Institutes of Health, the National Science Foundation, the Wenner-Gren Foundation, the H. F. Guggenheim Foundation, the National Endowment for the Humanities, the Program for Cultural Cooperation Between Spain's Ministry of Culture and U.S. Universities, the Council for the International Exchange of Scholars, the American Philosophical Society, and the Research Foundation of the State University of New York.

Acknowledgments

I am very grateful to so many people in Spain that their names would fill an entire book by itself, for the Spanish people are the best hosts in the world, and the most generous. But a special word of gratitude must be extended to the following men and women whose warmth made my time in Spain so memorable: Salvador Rodríguez Becerra, Alfredo Jiménez Núñez, Isidoro Moreno Navarro, Antonio Milla, Manoli Fernández, Paco Fernández, Antonio Siria, Cristóbal Martín Lora, Sebastián Martín Lora, José Martin Ruano, María Aurora Ruano, and Manolo Benítez. In Seville, Salvador Rodríguez Becerra, perhaps the leading expert in Andalusian folklore and culture, also assisted me in my attempts to decipher some of the more obscure references and Andalusianisms in the often garbled texts. I also wish to thank María del Carmen Medina, who administered the carnival questionnaire throughout Seville Province in a most competent and efficient manner.

Back in the United States, a special debt of gratitude is due to Anne Jones Weitzer, who provided masterful editorial assistance, turning a lot of academic jargon into readable English. I am also indebted to Gladys Topkis, anthropology editor at Yale University Press, who provided so much encouragement and direction, not to mention some splendid lunches on Lexington Avenue. The following friends and colleagues also deserve thanks for reading and commenting on various drafts of this book: Daniel Bates, Stanley Brandes, Alan Duben, Jill Dubisch, James Fernandez, Michael Herzfeld, Timothy Mitchell, and Robert Paul. Again, as always, I want to thank Ruben Reina for his guidance and support throughout the fieldwork experience.

I also want to thank the editors of various journals for permission to reuse some of the material published earlier. Parts of this book appeared earlier in different form in the *American Anthropologist,* the *Journal of the Royal Anthropological Institute (MAN), Ethos, Ethnology, Anthropological Quarterly,* and the *Revista de Diolectología y Tradiciones Populares.* An earlier version of Chapter 9 was read at the symposium "Anthropology and the Mediterranean," organized by Anton Blok, Christian Bromberger, and Dionigi Albera, which was held in Aix-en-Provence in May 1997. The proceedings were published in their edited volume of the same title (Paris: Editions des Sciences de l'Homme, 1998).

Introduction

Nature yields nothing without ceremonies. — Ernst Cassirer, *The Philosophy of Symbolic Forms*

Like nature, society reveals nothing, certainly not its deepest secrets, without ceremonies. This book is about how Spanish society yields up some of its darkest secrets through ceremonies and rituals. The secrets in question are those which affect the people deeply and shape their social relations: secrets about sex, gender, and status. The revelatory ceremonies themselves are diverse and of varying orders of magnitude. They include rituals of the February *carnaval:* not only the masquerading, burlesques, and song lyrics that are our main focus here but also more mundane events involving table manners, bar etiquette, olive picking, buying a drink, building a house, having sex, baiting one's mother-in-law, and the quotidian household routines we have come to expect in books by cultural anthropologists. As Cassirer does in the opening quotation, we could lump all these patterns together and call them nature, in the sense that they represent the little structures of daily life that give meaning to the flux of the world. Here we are interested in a small part of that world — the southwestern corner of the Iberian peninsula, called Andalusia — and in a specific series of rituals that people there practice to their mutual delight and everlasting joy.

A typical "Mediterranean" region, Andalusia is Spain's deep south, a land of vast olive orchards and vineyards, golden wheatfields and endless rows of sunflowers, lush gardens with manicured citrus, fig, and tamarind trees. It is a country of breathtaking beauty, blanched by a torrid sun, slaked by autumn downpours. With its shimmering blue skies, white-walled villages, wailing flamenco music, bullfights, and thousand varieties of sherry, Andalusia is well known to tourists. But it is also a land, I hasten to add, of deep class divisions and grinding poverty (equally Mediterranean legacies), which are perhaps less well known to outsiders. Its popular cultural traditions, rarely glimpsed by foreigners, are unsurpassed for richness in Europe. Sometimes in this book we will detour to discuss the Mediterranean world of which Andalusian Spain is a part. When the material warrants, we will make comparisons and contrasts with other places farther afield, but our focus remains this western extreme of the Latin Old World, where the festival of *carnaval,* even more than Holy Week and the summer fiesta, anchors the yearly cycle of rituals. In analyzing carnival in Andalusia, a festival that the poor say "makes life worth living," we are interested in some specific cultural conundrums, which carnival sheds light on in surprising ways.

The first of these themes is that of sex and gender, a category that I broadly define to include all the ways in which men and women relate to each other in and out of bed. By "gender" I mean the ways in which men and women interact in the social encounters of everyday life, and by "sex" I mean the erotic and reproductive side of life. I therefore differentiate sex and gender semantically, as do most feminists (see Ortner and Whitehead 1981b), using the former term to mean anatomical/biological differences and the latter to mean cultural (symbolic or arbitrary) constructs. Both can be subsumed under "male-female relations."

Our second theme is that of status — again, broadly defined. By "status" I mean not only ideas about the inequities that separate people in general, but also the invidious distinctions that separate men from women. In these two obviously linked domains, sex/gender and status, we are dealing with notions of *difference* and *separation* in human relations. Status includes not just differences in wealth or prestige but also feelings and attitudes about them, the ways in which people frame the injustices of social class, and their moral tenets about human hierarchy and democracy in a general sense — that is, how people appraise one another according to local criteria of inclusion and exclusion, superiority and inferiority, dominance and submission.

The third, and final, theme is that of ceremony itself, specifically *carnaval,* and within the context of the Spanish celebration, a genre of oral versification called the *copla de carnaval,* or carnival ditty. We are interested in how this quintessentially Mediterranean fiesta (for it originated in classical antiquity) provides a screen upon which the themes of sex, gender, and status are projected, negotiated, and understood through verbal representations. By analyzing the lyric genres of the Spanish carnival, and what these oral productions say about sex and status in Spain, we may discover some of the worthwhile secrets of the culture. Why are sex and status so often debated and fought over in ceremonies? Why is ceremony so often a matter of sex and status? Why do people celebrate so *furiously*?

It is the thesis of this book that Andalusian ideas about sex, gender, and status are best and most accessibly expressed in the rituals of the February carnival, or the *locura de febrero* (February madness), as people sometimes call it. Such an argument, holding up carnival symbolism and ritual as constituting an anthropological Royal Road to understanding of cultural "deep structure," has been made by others working in Europe — recently by anthropologists (Kertzer 1988; Mintz 1997),[1] historians (Le Roy Ladurie 1979), and literary critics working with historical materials (Bakhtin 1984). But the idea has special utility in rural Spain, where carnival is above all a license for the expression of powerful feelings and impulses normally kept in check by a repressive moral code.

The capstone of the creative architecture throughout rural Spain, but especially in the south, the February carnival provides the masses with a "crazy" (that is, ludic and subversive) but also preternaturally sane mechanism by which they can experience and negotiate the conflicts and contradictions that trouble them deeply and that demand some sort of psychological release. In the part of Spain considered here, western Andalusia, the villagers perform this "collective therapy," as one Spanish ethnographer puts it (Checa 1992: 68), mainly through the vehicle of the carnival copla.[2] The copla is a narrative poem, usually of four or five verses, sometimes much longer, often but not always in couplet form, which is performed publicly and reacted to en masse by the village population assembled in the streets. Governed by few rules, these festival representations break through normal barriers of reserve to convey and "unwrap" messages about sex and status that frame the deepest secrets of culture, thereby making these secrets public and accessible to the people as public performances.

Alternately scatological, defamatory, and laudatory, the carnival songs initiate a diverse series of moral dialogues between singer and audience, between self and other, between the concepts of high and low, between notions of good and evil, between categories of people: men and women, rich and poor, adult and child. The copla metaphors are stories the people invent that "define themselves to themselves" (Geertz 1983:58), their whimsical messages sometimes critiqued in riotous, obscene skits that may accompany the song cycles. Thus, carnival rhetoric within its madcap ritual context has much to tell us about the inner workings of the "structure of sentiments" (Fernandez 1972:43) in this part of Spain and about how the people experience and perceive their society and its traditions as elements of the felt life. *Carnival and Culture,* then, is an essay in the dialectic of culture accessed through the dialogue of poetic texts.

While I do not pretend to propound a new theory of carnival or to shed a new light on folk ritual or oral artistry in any general sense, I do suggest that previous views of the Latin carnival have been too one-sided and need ampli-fication. Most prior students of European carnival have seen the festival in the light of Marxist and, specifically, Gramscian models of political conflict, cul-tural hegemony, and proletarian resistance in which carnival rather narrowly reflects a radical oppositional consciousness. For these observers carnival is above all a political event, a "contrary" or "revolutionary" assault against the ruling orders and normative structures (see Kertzer 1988:144–146). Applying Antonio Gramsci's ideas about the workings of the "contradictory conscious-ness" of the proletariat (1929–1935), most Marxists see carnival as "a con-trary image of society," as sublimated "class struggle" (Le Roy Ladurie 1979) —that is, as a contested event pitting the upholders of the political status quo against their working-class opponents (Cohen 1993). In other words, carnival is proletarian class conflict in the realm of the imagination (Scott 1985). This view is found also among some quasi-Marxist postmodernists, who, arguing from a similar viewpoint, see status inversion and proletarian rebellion against elitism and hierarchy as the essence of the carnivalesque.[3]

This political view is valid for Spain, as we shall see, but it is only a partial truth, and like all half-truths conceals much. In the Spanish case, the February madness is morally inversive and politically subversive, to be sure, challenging the high and mighty, indicting capitalism and elitism, ridiculing authority and extolling a utopia of human equality as a political alternative; but paradox-ically, Spanish carnival is also reversive and restorative. Although its verbal genres subvert the status quo, they also subvert their own status and sexual subversions, negate their own negative. Thus carnival rehabilitates the tradi-tional order. In Spain, carnival capsizes the noncarnival world, but it also restores the upside-downed hierarchies to their former place, upholding and even glorifying them. Spanish carnival is both revolutionary and reactionary, subversive and conservative at the same time.

In my opinion, only the Russian semiotician Mikhail Bakhtin (1984) has fully grasped and appreciated this defining paradox of "praise-abuse" (1984: 416) in carnival lyricism toward the constituted authorities. The true sense of

carnival rhetoric in medieval France, he notes, is that "it was essentially ambivalent; it closely combined praise and abuse, it glorified and humiliated" at
the same time (1984:418). In Bakhtin's view, carnival is never pure negation:
"We must stress . . . that the carnival is far distant from the negative and formal
parody of modern times. Folk humor denies, but it revives and renews at the
same time. Bare negation is completely alien to folk culture" (Bakhtin 1984:
11). Those who see the carnival spirit as pure negation, as one-sided dissent
and undiluted revolutionism, and who have invoked Bakhtin's work to support this view, are mistaken; they have badly misread both carnival and
Bakhtin. Terry Eagleton, for example, writes: "Bakhtinian carnival . . . at once
cavalierly suppresses hierarchies and distinctions . . . and at the same time does
so as part of a politically specific, sharply differentiated, combatively one-
sided practice—that of the lower classes" (1989:188). Taken at face value,
virtually every word of this sentence is misleading.

Carnival is of course lower class (except in places like Rio and Venice, where
the rich participate), but even when it is fully a working-class event, as in rural
Andalusia, it is above all *ambivalent.* It is two-sidedness, dualism, equivoca-
tion, not suppression or negation alone, that Bakhtin speaks of as the essence
of the celebration and the wellspring of the folk culture that gives birth to it, as
both a past and a permanent process. It is this contradictory, inconsistent, and
protean nature of carnival, its "deeply dynamic fusion," and its "complex and
contradictory combination" of affect and ideology (1984:23) that best captures the meaning of the Spanish festival today. "The people's ambivalent
laughter," Bakhtin writes, expresses neither a monotone of rebellion nor one
of acceptance but "the point of view of the whole world; he who is laughing
also belongs to it" (12).

In the anthropology of modern and contemporary carnival, one of the few
to have captured this essential dualism is David Kertzer (1988:144–150).
Looking at the political consequences of carnivals in southern Europe, Kertzer
notes that the European festivity can be both revolutionary and conservative
at the same time (1988:146). More than most carnivals, and for reasons to be
explored here, the Spanish festival exemplifies this paradox. It is my objective
to expand the debate about ritual, carnival, and carnival politics by describing
the contradictions and dualisms in the Andalusian case. I do this partly as an
antidote to pre-existing dogma, but also as a way of appreciating the richness
and complexity of working-class Spanish culture and folkways.

Bakhtin's ideas about the ambivalence of folk culture are relevant to Spain
also for an important reason having to do with the strikingly bifurcated organization of carnival performances and song genres. In southern Spain, unlike
most other places, carnival texts take two distinct forms, each with its own

traditions and history. The first of these is the familiar ludic form: satiric, comic, and nihilistic. Such verses are sung by bands called *chirigotas,* jokesters or comedians. Very different are the *estudiantil* minstrels (students or scholars). Incongruously solemn and dignified, they sing of tragic, sentimental, and other serious themes. In Andalusian carnival, there are no symbolic markers between the two groups; they perform simultaneously, some bands even switching identity during the festivities. In tandem, the two genres obviously symbolize and personify the human condition, like a twin Greek chorus, both condemning and praising.

This thematic parallelism exemplifies the inner contradictions of the kind Bakhtin identifies as energizing the folk imagination in the world of Rabelais. Although I make no claims to any kind of historical continuity, or to relevance outside Spain, I argue that Bakhtin's analysis hits on timeless truths about the carnivalesque in contemporary Spanish culture and about Latin carnival in a more general sense. In the Andalusian festivity, as others have noted (Mintz 1997), the impulse to degrade the high and mighty exists alongside a paradoxical reverence for tradition and hierarchy, as it did in early modern French celebrations; denigration of womanhood coexists with a powerful veneration derived from Marian worship and a matrilateral family structure. Fierce anticlerical feelings commingle with a deep, though heterodox, Catholic spirituality; and a political revolutionism of a particularly violent and nihilistic kind alternates with a strident conservatism. Lower-class attitudes about sex and status in modern Andalusia are also highly ambivalent and sharply contrasted, for they are based on the splitting and polarization of affect that occur in most cultures of the Mediterranean region; but oddly, such feelings are not necessarily ambiguous. Marked by stark opposites, such a balance of *ambivalent but unambiguous* forces is inherently unstable and produces a dynamic subsurface movement that, as Sigmund Freud (1905) argued with regard to wit and humor generally, finds expression in such outlets as festival ribaldry, ritual, and art. As a period of unfettered creativity, carnival provides both the license and the opportunity for the release of a therapeutic energy in the realm of performance art, what Timothy Mitchell calls "festive canalization" in Spanish folklore (1988:2).

A dynamic ambivalence about key issues in life such as sex and status is by no means unique to Andalusia or Spain; affective ambivalence appears in virtually all cultures, as well as within all individuals as an integral part of normal mental functioning. And although this emotive ambivalence similarly seeks release or reconciliation in ritual elsewhere (Victor Turner, Mary Douglas, and others have made this point before), what is unusual about Andalusian folk culture, as the astute Mitchell (1991, 1994) has argued, is its unusual degree of tolerance — in fact, sympathy — for cognitive dissonance. The two-sidedness of affect in this culture, this emotive ambi- or bivalence, appears with little modulation or blending. Rather, like the two carnival genres — the comedic and the scholarly — and like praise and abuse, symbolic oppositions in culture appear simultaneously, in juxtaposition, but remain in discrete and vivid contrast.

This ongoing dialectic created in this way ("counterpoint" might be a better word since we are basically speaking of musical compositions) yields what the Andalusians call "the spice" (*picardía*) of life. This effervescent zest, which is the sparkle of juxtaposed antitheses, is what they say provides the energy for carnival and, as it finds pleasurable expression in festival laughter and earthy merriment, makes their otherwise drab lives "worth living." As we shall see, it is at carnival-time that Andalusian culture openly mingles its internal contradictions, laying them side by side, forcing together oppositely charged magnetic fields, and thus pushing them into consciousness and initiating a response in the cathartic process of folk art. Thus the people "tell of themselves to themselves" (Geertz 1973:448).

The "spicy" contradictions of Spanish rural culture, which furnish the soul of the carnival spirit, also express themselves at other times of the year, producing a piquant broth of colors and moods, all culminating in February. This will all become apparent as we move on to the empirical data, but suffice it to say at this point that Andalusian carnival is the major pretext for the communication of the culture's dual signals. Carnival is, however, only part — even if the most important part — of the cultural mechanisms by which competing meanings come to dialogue and get worked out. Other social contexts, equally prominent and equally unstable, also serve as theaters as our drama unfolds.

The first of these secondary venues is the domestic setting, the family or household. In this bounded, sequestered world of home and hearth, where men put in only a fleeting appearance, the women command and the men obey. Otherwise subject to male control in public affairs, women thereby enact a reversal, in micropolitical terms, of the "normal" situation of male dominance. Not to put too sharp an emphasis on it, the matriarchal home is thus, metaphorically speaking, a carnivalesque parody of the public patriarchy.

The second venue is the world of the neighborhood bar, tavern, or bodega, which, restricted by convention to men, creates an all-male world apart. Likewise bounded and defended, this café world is a place of male bonding and sanctuary, equivalent to men's secret societies or men's houses in other places (Vale de Almeida 1996). Here the men, fleeing from the woman-dominated home, establish an alternative society, separate from and equal to that of the feminized home. It is here in this refuge that the men, in a reversal of a reversal, find a compensatory kitchen sovereignty. And it is here, too, that these re-empowered men engage in their life-enhancing rituals of manhood, the give-and-take that define their sex: tournaments of tippling, competitive treating, toasting and boasting, carnivals of drink.

Our third venue is the wider context of community space. By space I mean, simply, the way people use and interpret their built environment, the spatial architecture of everyday life. This includes not only the division between male "public" and female "private" space but also the rules, taboos, and boundaries that define the use of public places according to sex. These prescriptions, too, undergo a series of inversions, reversals, and transformations throughout the year, culminating in carnival-time.

In each of these venues, the carnival copla, like a portable Greek chorus, provides moral commentary in the form of declamatory lyrics, which are remembered, repeated, and ruminated on for literally decades after their maiden performance. So I believe that carnival, much in the way anthropologists have argued the role of myth to be in preliterate societies, is the clue to the inner structure and workings of this society as a whole, and the most accessible, as well as the most entertaining, way of approaching its defining contradictions. Carnival ceremony not only illustrates but *is* the "movement of the whole society" (Mauss 1974).

We begin with a historical account of carnival in its many national guises: carnaval, carnivale, Mardi Gras, Fasching, belsnicking, mumming, and so on. Then we move on to discuss anthropological interpretations of this protean festival, and then to the Spanish coplas.

2

Carnival in Spain

Carnival is the people's second life, organized on the basis of laughter. — Mikhail
Bakhtin, *Rabelais and His World*

Carnival is the popular festival in Catholic countries that takes place in mid-
February before the Lenten fast. Widespread geographically, the holiday is
known by many names: *carnaval* is the Spanish and Portuguese variant.
French speakers knew it as *carême-prenant,* or more commonly today as
Mardi Gras ("Fat Tuesday"), owing to the custom of eating up all the fat in the
house before fasting. For Italians it is *carnivale,* although Pisa has its *Car-*
nelevare, Naples its *Carnolevare,* and Sicily its *Carnilivare* (Rector 1984:39).
Homologues, cognates, and synonyms abound in the other Romance languages (Caro Baroja 1965:27). Latin carnival is equivalent in calendrical
terms to the late-winter *Fastnacht* or *Fasching* in Bavaria and Austria and
other German areas, and further afield, similar to mumming or belsnicking
observations that take place in the English-speaking Caribbean countries at
about the same time of year.

A secular event not condoned by the Catholic Church, in fact condemned by
its hierarchy as pagan, the Latin carnival begins on Shrove Sunday, the Quin-
quagesima, and continues until the following Tuesday before Ash Wednesday.
Then it abruptly peters out, often to the accompaniment of ritual floggings,

wailings, and lashings or other ironic lamentations, such as the burning of "Signore Carnivale" and "Don Carnal" effigies in Italy (Silverman 1975:157–161) and Spain, respectively (Caro Baroja 1965:22). Goya's famous painting *The Burial of the Sardine* depicts one such terminal ritual in Madrid.[1]

At this point, the licentious gaiety of carnival is suddenly and inevitably replaced by the solemnity and sacrifice of Lent. With its wild abandon and obscenity, carnival is obviously a refuge from everyday life and from self-control. It is one of those events that anthropologists have identified as belonging to a class of "time-out" behaviors that overturn the rules of the workaday world and provide psychological relief to the masses.

The origin of carnival in Europe is lost in the mists of time, of course, but the Greeks already knew it by 1,100 B.C. (Rector 1984:39). It is perhaps the oldest of all Western pagan festivals still observed today. Carnival also may be connected historically to the Bacchanalia, Lupercalia, and Saturnalia of classical antiquity (Bakhtin 1984:8). The Bacchanalia were the celebrations observed by the ancients, both Greeks and Romans, paying homage to Bacchus and Dionysius, the gods of wine and debauchery. Not surprisingly, these events came over time to be associated with licentiousness, drunkenness, and orgies. Lupercalia were festivals celebrating the god Pan or the faun, and usually held in the middle of February. The Roman Saturnalia, observing the day of the god Saturn, were held in mid-December. The King of the Saturnalia was a satyrlike figure who became king for a day during the festival and then was symbolically killed off (Rector 1984:39). All of these holidays probably contributed to the medieval European carnival marking the onset of the Christian fast.

The word carnival itself probably derives from the medieval Latin *carne levare,* or *carnelevarium,* which means to take away or remove fat or meat, indicating a day of gustatory excess before the Lenten deprivation, although there is some debate about the actual etymology of the word.[2] (For an account of this and other arcane semantic matters, see Caro Baroja 1965:28–29.) But whatever its name or setting, carnival is a period of licentiousness for participants, a wild bacchanal in which the popular classes unleash the pent-up frustrations of the past year by dancing lewdly, singing, carousing, and generally unraveling to the mad accompaniment of musical entertainments.

Carnival is therefore equivalent in the mind of the common people with *celebration* itself as a generic thing, a temporal parenthesis in which the people oppose the moral and sexual license of holidays to the moderation and oppressiveness of everyday life. Carnival is, above all, inversion of the world as it is (Caro Baroja 1965:47), a turning upside down of things, a revolution in systems and order. It is therefore a time for liberation, surrealism, intoxication, hysteria, impulsiveness, defilement, debauchery—a capitulation before the resurgent id, or what Ernst Kris calls "a holiday from the superego" (1952:

182). Carnival is thus relaxation in the most literal sense of the word: a sudden removal of repression and external pressure, as from a coiled spring. The people's pent-up energy is discharged.

Because carnival in peasant villages in Europe historically had a wild and often proletarian character, local elites — landlords and nobles — either have not fully participated in the raucous events or have done so circumspectly. Normally kept in check, class antagonisms and political resentments can rise to the surface during carnival, along with sexual impulsiveness, harmless aggression against social equals, and regressive obscenity. Once unleashed, one passion can easily veer into another: "Significantly, aggression against peers can become aggression against authorities," as Daniel Linger (1992:52) points out in describing a series of violent rebellions in Caribbean carnivals that began as peer-group confrontations. Because carnival overthrows the normal order of the world and turns morality upside down, letting loose the emotions of the masses, the rich have historically realized its explosive tendency and have always braced themselves for a period of mischief and disorder (Kertzer 1988). Moreover, because the celebrants all wear masks (carnival being above all a masquerade) and in this way obscure their identity, hoi polloi merge into a faceless, anonymous mass, including criminals and miscreants, all losing their individual sense of shame and whatever minimal inhibitions they may have had.

Throughout Latin Europe, therefore, the celebration has often historically included not only such innocent pleasures as masquerading, transvestism, and sexual horseplay but also, and more ominously, contentious skits and mock trials, status reversals, anticlerical tirades, scatological satires, staged uprisings, violent abuse of lords and masters, and all manner of revolutionary theater (see Bloch 1920; Cox 1969; Gaignebet 1974; Bakhtin 1984; Eco 1984). David Kertzer (1988) provides some truly hair-raising instances of murder and mayhem during early modern festivals in southern Europe, as does Emmanuel Le Roy Ladurie (1979) for the specific case of the French town of Romans.

Scholarship aside, we know intuitively that as a time of mass action, Latin carnival has political implications and dangers. In some cases, the rulers and elites throughout history have also acknowledged this and, appreciating the value of "letting off steam," have permitted the proletariat to ridicule symbols of authority and generally "get it out of their system." Long before the anthropologist Max Gluckman (1963) wrote about the conservative functions of "rituals of rebellion," a sixteenth-century French lawyer wrote of carnival: "It is sometimes expedient to allow the people to play the fool and make merry, lest by holding them in with too great a rigor, we put them in despair" (cited in Kertzer 1988:144).

This permissive, or perhaps self-protective, view echoes the Roman saying about bread and circuses and probably can be found wherever there is sharp sociopolitical stratification or inequality and where rich and poor live closely together, especially in overcrowded towns in southern Europe. Latin carnival, however, often went beyond mere ribaldry and merriment to take on more dangerous, even revolutionary overtones, threatening the very order of society: "Carnaval fut aussi révolte" (Faure 1978:92); that is, carnival also made for rebellion. In the French town of Romans in 1580, for example, as reported by Le Roy Ladurie (1979), the festival turned violent, pitting artisans against the elite; many were killed in the ensuing class warfare. France has a long history of carnival insurrections in which the authorities were either symbolically or actually attacked (see Kertzer 1988:146–150).

In Italy as well as France, the tendency of carnival to degenerate into a symbolic or real jacquerie has a long history. In 1647, for example, the rabble of Naples used the pretext of carnival to rise up against their autocratic rulers. The rebels assassinated their class enemies, beheading them and dragging their bodies throughout the city in a grisly rite of rebellion. As if to remove any doubt about their intentions, the leaders of this revolt placed placards proclaiming "Traitor to the People" on the gruesome remains of each victim (Kertzer 1988:145).

Carnival in Spain

Although this widespread and colorful celebration has faded away in many areas of the Iberian peninsula owing either to the forces of modernization or to government repression (Francisco Franco banned carnival in 1937 during the Civil War), the traditions of carnival are still strong in certain localities.[3] It remains vibrant in parts of Valencia Province on Spain's southeast coast, and in Andalusia, the southernmost region of the peninsula. In western Andalusia, carnival has persisted most notably in the port city of Cadiz, where, however, it has been considerably watered down under government supervision (Mintz 1997).[4] The festival also continues unabated in a few small villages and rural towns in Seville, Cordoba, and Malaga Provinces, some of which are described in this book. In many of these small farming towns, the festivities go on in defiance of government prohibitions (Rodríguez Becerra 1985:118–119). In many towns between the provincial capitals of Seville and Cordoba, for example, after a hiatus during the harsh 1940s, a resurgence in the festival occurred in the 1950s or 1960s, when most local governments turned a blind eye to what had become a relatively peaceful entertainment. In some pueblos, like Fuentes de Andalucía and Carmona, both in Seville Province, the people took to the streets in defiance of the Franco prohibition and paraded for days on end, despite occasional police harassment. In other places, like La Campana, also in Seville Province, the municipal authorities ignored the ban and joined in — one of the earliest manifestations of the growing official disenchantment with the Franco dictatorship that eventually eased Spain's transition to democracy after the dictator's death in 1975. The *carnaval del pueblo,* or village carnival, as it is called, still stubbornly resists management or interference by official meddlers, and continues its merry ways, along with the uninhibited, spontaneous, and revolutionary mass actions we have come to expect as part of proletarian festivities.

Today, in carnivals throughout rural Spain, north and south, villagers masquerade in the streets for three or four days, the men usually in transvestite costume. Masqueraders march back and forth through the main streets, pack the bars, sing gossipy or satirical songs, trade insults, and engage in lewd behavior. Half the inhabitants of any given village may be in costume, the other half in street clothes, both sets of celebrants intermingling and then changing places at various times. There are no set rules about who may masquerade or when. People in small groups may also choose to act out rehearsed skits — many of them scabrous and caustic — at any time. In some villages in Andalusia, there are also more organized groups, usually of between three and ten people, that perform minidramas victimizing deviants or lampooning the authorities.

The high point of the Andalusian carnival, however, is the famous strolling musical band, with its festooned instruments, colorful costumes, and ribbons and bows. These musical groups compose and sing the uninhibited "spicy" songs that are the heart and soul of the festival and which townspeople eagerly await throughout the year. Organized weeks before the festival, the bands are led by a "maestro," a master poet or virtuoso, always a local man from the poorest classes and often illiterate. Accompanying this Andalusian master singer on his wanderings are the troubadours, usually between five and twelve in number, who supply the musical accompaniment and vocal chorus (Figures 1 and 2). The entire band is called the *comparsa* or *coro* in Cadiz Province (Mintz 1997) and the *murga* in the area around Seville. The musicians are called *murguistas.*

After the festival begins, the players issue from their homes and promenade through the streets, beating their drums and chanting their whimsical ditties. In keeping with the aggressive tone of the celebration, their lyrics are alternately satirical, bawdy, and inflammatory. To be successful, the songs, people say, must have the requisite "spice" (*picardía*)). This ingredient of spice is indeed the soul of the carnivalesque in Andalusia; people say that without spice "there is no carnival." By spice of course they mean gossipy, provocative,

1. Murga band. Juanillo "El Gato" in street clothes (lower right), 1973.

and sexually suggestive lyrics. People sometimes sum up this desirable spicy quality as "anything that annoys people" or whatever "ties a can on the people's tails."[5] "Spice" means both stimulant and irritant.

Most people in western Andalusia consider the main entertainment of the February carnival to be the raucous parades of the choruses, the rest being merely window dressing. The lyrics comment wittily on events of the past year, and the composers make liberal use of ribald puns, scatological imagery, erotic metaphors, outrageous tropes, and crass insults to entertain their excited listeners. Thus entertained, the latter reciprocate by buying the singers drinks and throwing money at them as they proceed on their way. In this give and take, whole villages become weaving, waving masses of turbulent humanity united in song and merriment. The anthropologist Julian Pitt-Rivers has called attention to the shamelessness of carnivalesque behavior, when "anything goes" (1971:176). It is a time of license, a time when people expect incitements and challenges, a limbo that can turn vindictive or chaotic: a time for what Spaniards call aggressions — *los agravios* (Caro Baroja 1965:83). These agravios — insults, challenges, and innuendos — are the heart of carnival. Thus one may regard the coplas, with their suggestive lyrics, as displacements of more violent forms of expression, as *symbolic violence*.

Given this belligerent license, the festival in Spain has served many purposes, one of which is social and political protest, usually in the form of leftist mass

2. Murga band emerging at start of carnival, 1991.

action (Pitt-Rivers 1971:176). Many of the murga coplas violently attack the rich, the government, and priests, as well as other perceived enemies of the particular time and place. Since such "controlled disinhibition" (Brandes 1988:176) cannot always be confined to the rhetorical realm, carnival, like other folk celebrations, has occasionally led to open class warfare and intra-community violence in Spain. Edward Malefakis (1970), Jerome Mintz (1982), and Temma Kaplan (1984) cite a number of instances before and during the Second Republic where carnival provocations escalated into insurrection. Because people were sometimes murdered or assaulted when things got out of hand — always a danger with "controlled" disinhibitions — it is no wonder that both twentieth-century Spanish dictators, Primo de Rivera (in the 1920s) and Franco (between 1937 and 1967) banned the celebration, as posing a threat to public order. Indeed historical research shows that the Spanish state has either outlawed or severely curtailed carnival since 1586 (Rodríguez Becerra 1985:119). Emperor Charles V prohibited the fiesta in 1500, Philip V in 1716–1717 and 1745, and Charles IV in 1797.

Yet Spanish carnival is by no means only a ritual of rebellion or political protest; rebellion against class oppression is only one of its themes. The aggressive energies of carnival have been unleashed in two directions: vertically against the authorities and horizontally against peer-group deviance. In this sense, and in one of the purest inner contradictions of Iberian culture, Spanish carnival is culturally conservative or collaborative as well as politically provocative, and its agravios directed as much at the poor as the rich (Gilmore 1987:108). Especially important is the punishment of sexual misconduct and general immorality in a culturally conservative society deeply concerned with norms of propriety: "The songs of *Carnaval* are recognized by some to have been the guardian of marital and pre-marital fidelity" (Pitt-Rivers 1971:177). Voicing both the democratic and the self-punitive impulses of the common folk, carnival simultaneously uplifts the common folk and, wielding a repressive Catholic morality, keeps them down.[6]

Song Styles of Carnival

Traditionally, as mentioned earlier, the bands are of two types — the chirigotas (jokers or comedians) and their opposites and counterparts, the estudiantiles (scholars or academics). Making up by far the majority of carnival singers, the jokers sing the familiar satirical or obscene coplas. Prohibited under Franco, these lewd genres were nevertheless always performed surreptitiously in the bars and alleys by comedians, to acute communal appreciation. Many ethnographers have written at length about these chirigota coplas (Gilmore 1988, 1993; Checa 1992; Mintz 1997).

The second type of band, the estudiantil, equally important although much less well documented in the literature, devotes itself to solemn or tragic subjects. These the estudiantiles treat with sententious moralizing in a kind of sermonizing gravity quite at variance with the regressive jollity of the silly chirigotas.[7] The estudiantil costumes, usually simple tunics festooned with ribbons, differ little from those of the chirigota minstrels, who however sometimes adopt more elaborate fantasy "themes" and disguise themselves as Arabs, soldiers, pirates, medieval knights, monkeys, or palm trees. Often these somber scholar-poets commemorate sad or tragic recent events such as earthquakes, fires, floods, or other natural disasters, expressing sympathy for the victims and warning the complacent of the wrath of God and nature (Gilmore 1993). Other serious bards sing homilies on subjects like sexual exploitation, death and loss, patriotism and regionalism, or extol such "Andalusian" virtues as tolerance, mercy, brotherhood, filial loyalty, or, in the Andalusian Marian tradition, quasi-religious admiration for motherhood. All are virtues consonant with the Castilian Great Tradition and Franco's "national Catholicism" and represent the conservative and traditionalist subtheme in Andalusian proletarian ideology that we spoke of earlier. The estudiantil singers therefore represent a curious contrary theme embedded within the carnal puerility of carnival: serious, tragic, orthodox, virtuous, and dignified in tone, and utterly at odds with the usual madcap hilarity. As far as I know, it is only in Spain that such a strong counterpoint in carnival moods and entertainment styles exists or has existed.

In keeping with the unpredictability of carnival in Andalusia and reflecting its stark thematic juxtapositions, performance style for the "serious" verses of the estudiantiles differs little from that of the comic verses of the chirigotas. There are no markers, musical preambles, or visual clues to alert bystanders about what is coming. Costumes and instruments may be the same for both types of bands. Indeed the very same men may sing in both styles, according to their fancy. Consequently, audiences have no prior expectations as they gather around a marching band, which is as likely to sing an obscene burlesque as a sentimental dirge. My informants say that the people gathered do not know whether they are about to laugh or cry, an emotional ambivalence that reflects the capriciousness of an event celebrating the dissolution of boundaries. In rare cases a drum roll or preludial trumpet blare might announce a solemn subject; this fanfare is apparently the trademark of the singer "El Quico," who is a master of both genres.

Occasionally, an estudiantil singer, especially if he has previously been performing in a burlesque mode, will pause, adopt a grave expression, clear his throat theatrically, and tap a few times on his tambourine to produce an effect of gravity. But no other distinctions are made. In some cases a band simply switches seamlessly from one format to the other.

Because the same troubadours perform in either style, or both, and sometimes alternate between them during a single perambulation, there are no deliberate symbolic or stylistic boundaries between styles. The musicians use the same standard Spanish folk tunes to frame their words, the only difference being that decorous subjects are usually performed in waltz time rather than in the faster sevillana or pasodoble style. Indeed, musicality is entirely secondary in Andalusian carnival. None of the music is composed for the occasion but is instead "borrowed" from popular hits, flamenco forms, and other folk melodies. The tunes and melodies are not important, as any Spanish participant will tell you. A Spanish observer from Cadiz, Ramón Solís, notes that "the music holds a secondary place. The most important element is the lyrics, charged with critical context, and acute yet benevolent satire" (cited in Mintz 1997:xix). Only the poet's words, and of course the audience's interpretation, reaction, and participation, count as matters for later discussion and aesthetic judgment.

Funny lyrics inspire laughter and interaction: hoots of encouragement, heckling, jokes, other forms of dialogue. The serious songs, however, are met with an appreciative silence. Or routinized commentary — "so it is," "how true," "deeply spoken," and other words to that effect — may be addressed to the audience at large. For the most part, the same maestros compose tragic as well as philosophical songs, as the muse dictates, so their identity offers no clues about the coming performance.

I was told in the 1980s, though, that some poets specialize in chirigota comedy only, as a matter of personal taste or ability. One example is the jokester Juanillo "El Gato" (Johnny the Cat), a beloved comic poet in the town of Fuentes de Andalucía (he died in 1989), whose poetry we will sample many times. Juanillo was a rake and cut-up, referred to as a caricaturist, or mime, who felt himself incapable of estudiantil gravity because his face was frozen in "a permanent grin." But other comedians have no such inhibitions. They simply parade around town shifting modes as the mood takes them. One such was Marcelino Lora, who died in 1970, and whose work we will also see in the following chapters.

Only one distinction between comic and serious performances remains sharp in onlookers' accounts. It has to do with the age of the lyricist (not necessarily of the singer, for the two sometimes differ). The men who write in the bombastic mode are generally older than the comedians. Poets normally start out in the chirigota style and only later, after gaining a reputation, do they venture into estudiantil elegies, which, for success, require "deeper" (more mature) sensibilities. Some carnival lyricists remain pure comedians all their active lives, as in the case of the irrepressible Juanillo "El Gato," and his son Manolo, who continues the family tradition. It is true that during carnival many more comic than serious songs are performed. People say that for every serious performance there are five or six burlesques.

Townspeople say also that the point of Andalusian carnival is that it erases the boundaries between people and between things, that it throws everything together in a topsy-turvy promiscuity. So the ethnography of Spanish carnival cannot be framed through the use of criteria that rely on such immobile conceptual or affective bipolarities as serious and comic. As others have noted, in carnival "tragedy and comedy often intermingle" (Le Roy Ladurie 1979:206). Contextual differences between the two genres turn out to be much less important than their ritual conjuncture and interplay. It is important to remember, also, in considering the confusion of styles and emotions, that no distinctions of class or status separate the singers or the genres. The balladeers are and remain a homogeneous group experimenting with two lyrical styles.

In all cases, the poet-virtuosos are solidly working-class males. The composers are never women, and they never have been. The men are always *hijos del pueblo*—that is, native sons, locally born, members of the poorest classes (Pitt-Rivers 1971:18–19). They are often landless laborers, always manual workers—the class that furnished the revolutionaries during the Franco era and before. I must emphasize again (for it will become important later) that women *never* composed or sang the carnival songs. They have always served purely as audience and subject matter. Up until 1995, in fact, the last year in which I witnessed the carnival, women still did not engage—even peripherally—in the writing of lyrics. Nor did they perform songs or skits in public. Carnival verbal discourse in rural Andalusia remains entirely a male preserve; women in no way participate in creative wordsmithing.[8]

Led by their maestro, the all-male murgas meet a few weeks before carnival to begin work on the poems and to select targets. Some of them ad hoc, some consecrated by tradition, these cliques meet behind closed doors, concealing their work even from kinsmen, so that their lyrics are fresh for debut during carnival. Again, no women attend the composition sessions, and even close kinswomen are prevented from overhearing the men at work. In summary, then, rural carnival coplas may be described as purely male and purely working-class expressions. These limitations do not always hold for the larger cities, with their more sophisticated populations. In some provincial capitals—for example, Cadiz—the propertied classes and in rare instances some women participate (Mintz 1997). Participation by urban women is a recent development, however; it has not as yet been duplicated in the hinterlands.

Transvestism

Another salient feature of the Spanish carnival that concerns us here is sexual inversion. Cross-dressing is virtually universal, but male transvestism is especially important. It is a venerable tradition. As far back as observers can remember, Andalusian men have celebrated carnival with rituals of female impersonation; and indeed this tradition in Spain, as elsewhere in the Mediterranean, goes back to ancient times (Caro Baroja 1965) and probably stems from Greek transvestite masques. Caro Baroja (1965:49) cites a Spanish carnival song from 1605 that includes the verse:

La mujer se viste de hombre	The women dress as men,
Y el hombre se viste de hembra,	And the men as women,
Aquí se asan entre cuestos	On this hill men-women heat up
Allí se asan entre cuestas.[9]	On that slope women-men burn.

Today in Andalusia, men and boys almost always dress up as women, as in the past; but girls and women have more choice and do not always choose to parade in masculine attire (Figures 3–10). My fieldnotes for 1972–1985,

3. Mascarones (male masqueraders), 1973.

for example, show that about 80 percent of male masqueraders dressed as women, but only about 15 percent of women dressed as men. Women prefer "fantasy" costumes that are decidedly feminine in a conventional sense: those of television personalities, princesses, ballerinas, majorettes, American actresses, and so on. The women remain "female," even in disguise. By contrast, the *costumbre* for men, very consciously recognized and cherished throughout the 1900s, encourages youths to dress up in their mothers' garments. A few males may imitate priests, pirates, "Moors," or ghouls, but most men prefer to go out in drag and find great amusement and joy in donning their mothers' clothes for this purpose. Men are called *mascarones* (clowns), women *máscaras* (harlequins). We will discuss varieties of costume and mask, and their meanings, later, in Chapter 5.

In the traditional proceeding, the transvestite clowns promenade throughout the main thoroughfares of town, accosting bystanders, making pseudo-homosexual overtures to other men, and screeching lewd witticisms in a particularly shrill falsetto voice that quickly becomes grating. The men spend considerable time on their costumes, waddling up and down the avenues and adding props and padding to achieve the desired voluptuous look. They place fruits in the brassieres that they snatch from their sisters' and mothers' wardrobes, tie down pillows on their derrieres, and cover their faces with weird masks and veils. They complete the drag-queen costume with purloined jew-

4. Máscaras (women masqueraders), 1973.

elry, scarves, facial powder, and any other feminine accessories they can pilfer from mothers' or sisters' inventories. Girls are also permitted sexual license and engage in promiscuous behavior, which, however, is almost entirely heterosexual. Men and women both participate as masqueraders, with the men predominating, in about a two-to-one ratio.

The essence of the male carnival transvestism, for which there is no female equivalent, lies in the concept of the *colcha* (quilt, or coverlet). The colcha is the maternal symbol par excellence in Andalusian culture. In Andalusia, the nuptial bed is always covered with a coverlet or comforter, which of course no one but the conjugal pair ever sees — except at carnival. A functional piece of bedding, this colcha also represents the women's reproductive life and of course is deeply bound up with notions of fecundity, sexuality, honor, and shame. Its cleanliness and whiteness, somewhat like those of the whitewashed exterior house walls, symbolize the wife's moral history, her social responsibilities conflated with her sexual purity, which must be spotless like the bed sheets. In a symbolic sense the colcha-quilt is a portable womb. Interestingly, the same term, "colcha," is sometimes used for the menstrual rag.

Throughout western Andalusia, the colcha is the centerpiece of the male costume at carnival. The young men who masquerade during the festival must, by convention, wrap themselves in a colcha, regardless of what other auxiliary female garb they select. Specifically, custom dictates visible use of the mother's colcha, displayed either pinned as a skirt, or else used around the shoulders as a shawl. The colcha of course may be merely suggested by a similar garment, but to wear the actual item directly lifted from the mother's bedchamber is the ideal. Aside from this nucleus of costume, great latitude is permitted within the bounds of carnival transvestism. The men always cover their faces completely with a mask, either a homemade one or some cheap commercial variant.[10] Most men, however, continue to adopt a simple feature-less white sheet or towel to mask their faces which gives many of the trans-vestite clowns the eerie, faceless appearance: a female cipher, "everywoman" without a visage, and, apparently, without an identity (Figures 3, 5, 6, 8).

Usually, small groups of friends organize shortly before carnival to plan the colcha ritual, which requires help. Each man brings a coverlet to an as-signed place, and the men dress each other in turn. The approved method is a regal wraparound, in which the model rotates in place, while two friends encase him in the mother's ample garment. Once the final touches have been added and the costumes completed, the friends sally out into the streets. The mascarones commence to mince about, imitating women to the best of their ability. They speak in a piercing falsetto squeak, inviting male bystanders to fondle their privates. There is much thrusting of buttocks and "breasts." A typical exchange:

> Mascarón (jiggling breasts): Hey you, there, you handsome man, have you
>   ever seen titties like this?
> Bystander (laughing): Why, no, these are real pineapples.
> Mascarón (thrusting chest): Hey, would you like to touch my titties? Yes? Go
>   ahead!
> (Bystander now fondling admiringly.)
> Mascarón: Ooh, that feels nice. What about my ass, do you like that, too?
>   (Turns and lifts colcha to expose pillow.)

Variations on this burlesque continue throughout the day amidst great hilarity.

Spanish carnival costuming differs greatly from that in Brazilian Mardi Gras and other Latin American and European carnivals (Rector 1984; DaMatta 1991). There is none of the expensive or elaborate costuming that one finds in the Rio festival, for example, in which the moneyed classes participate enthusi-astically. In fact, just the opposite is true. Because Spanish rural carnival has always been a poor man's event, and one avoided by the elite, the objective of the working-class participants has always been to have a good time while spending as little as possible, in the frugal worker style. Costumes are therefore intentionally catch-as-catch-can, and purposely threadbare: a form of sartorial *bricolage* or proletarian rag-picking, of which the local people are proud rather than ashamed. Indeed, it is considered crass and pretentious to wear an expensive costume; such "showing off" is not in the true spirit of this workingman's carnival. As Mintz notes in writing about the equally penniless people of Trebujena, a pueblo in Cadiz Province: "Poverty was an incentive rather than a bar to invention." He quotes one working-class spokesman from that pueblo, who said: "The Trebujena costume — like that of surrounding towns — does not require any special materials, just a few rags that can be found in any house, wit, inventiveness, and cheek. The point of the costume is that besides being surprising, it must stir the laughter of the observer and the wearer at the same time" (Mintz 1997:225). In the towns of La Campana, Fuentes, and Carmona, and in other rural communities in Seville and Cordoba Provinces, the use of rags was a conscious expression of working-class solidarity, as well as a symbolic demonstration of the triumph of wit over poverty, in itself a political act.

The ragged transvestite clowns adhere to two generic motifs: the "mothers," who employ the colcha theme, and the "witches," who wear fright masks to create a different, much more grotesque image of womanhood. Neither spends much money on a costume (the goal being to spend nothing, if possible). Both use castoff clothes, broken-down paraphernalia, and the usual scraps. (I discuss the symbolic meanings of the contrasting styles at greater length in Chapter 5.) The differences between the two are, however, as much behavioral as visual. The colcha clowns, usually slightly older men, maintain some degree of decorum while parading, while the younger "witches" cavort and threaten in an aggressive manner, often manhandling and haranguing bystanders in a way that can only be called combative.

The observer's first impression of carnival in Andalusia, then, is somewhat disappointing in a purely visual sense. Given the crudity of the costumes, their moth-eaten, tattered look, the emphasis on farce and parody rather than style, and the pedestrian facial masks and accoutrements, the overall impression is rather shabby compared to that gleaned in Rio or New Orleans. Soon, however, one begins to appreciate the imaginativeness with which people use salvaged and discarded materials to construct very expressive and colorful masquerades.

Controlled Violence

The final element of carnival celebrations in Andalusia is the eruption of aggression, the "rhythms of violence," that Julio Caro Baroja (1965:47) speaks of as inherent in Spanish carnival. Symbolic aggression is ventilated in two ways, equally controlled, "up-to-a point" threats that never quite break through to actual physical violence and that resemble what Daniel Linger, in his study of Brazilian carnival confrontations, calls "ritualized aggression or agonistic display."[11]

First there is the verbal aggression of public insult, denunciation, or accusation. Being disguised completely and thus protected from reprisal, people search out enemies and publicly lambaste them with premeditated insults. One man in the town of Carmona, for instance, was surrounded by local antagonists and subjected to half an hour of the vilest condemnation, which, by carnival convention, he had to endure in stoic silence. In La Campana in 1970, a young woman received the unwanted attentions of a vengeful spurned lover. Dogging her footsteps, he shouted sexual abuse at her until she fled to the safety of her home in tears. Such abuse is expected and continual, a form of verbal vendetta.

As townspeople say of these agravios, a man or women must not take offense and must not react with anger to any such carnival provocation. "This is the way of carnival," they say, meaning that to break down under such a sustained verbal attack, even to flinch or to react in a visibly emotional way is to lose face. Everything must be endured cheerfully, with a smile. Every person is therefore both a potential abuser and a potential victim.[12]

The other form of violence is openly physical. But this is moderated by custom to barely tolerable limits. Young boys and girls, also masked, sometimes carry long staves or wooden poles with which they whack each other on the back or leg, or on other nonvital areas of the body (never the head). With malicious glee, the young marauders also attack bystanders, sometimes in groups, sometimes singly, occasionally with real enthusiasm. The pole-whackers make their *palos* (clubs, or staves) from a variety of farm tools and household devices, such as mops and brooms. Many of the adolescents carve a long notch at one end of their clubs, so that when the pole descends on someone's back or shoulder, it makes an explosive noise—to startling effect. On first impression, the impact sounds like a gunshot and can be fairly disconcerting; but one soon gets used to the ripping reports. Apparently, this kind of semiserious physical battling using sound effects goes back a long way, at least to the seventeenth century: "Carnival also signified an opportunity to give vent to irrational impulses, to engage in disorderly, violent, and even aggressive gestures, accompanied by insults to passersby, to produce unusual and incongruous sounds with the aid of various devices. It created considerable insecurity in the popular quarters of towns, in Seville, for example, where the women deliberately provoked brawls" (Bennassar 1979:32).

As in the case of verbal abuse, the physical attack is supposed to be laughed off by the pole swinger's victim as "just a carnival thing" (*una cosa de carnaval*). Even if bruised in spirit or body, one must never take offense or show anger. To *give* offense is the purpose of carnival; but to *take* offense is the one absolute taboo. Carnival therefore provides a ritualized "cover" or excuse, as do alcohol or drugs in other cultures (Marshall 1979), under which people may give vent to their aggression and display other normally forbidden passions with impunity. One typical carnival verse, following a particularly caustic series of insults, puts this command in perspective:

Entérate, no te vayas a enfada'a,	Understand this, you must never get angry,
Porque estas son las cosas	Because these things we do
Que trae el Carnaval.[13]	Are only for carnival.

In this way, the Andalusian festival of today differs from some other Latin carnivals, for example, in parts of urban Brazil, where carnival often coincides with deadly physical violence.[14] Uncontrolled violence, usually of a political nature, did sometimes occur at carnival-time in Andalusia during the Republic (1931–39) and in earlier periods, but real fighting died out entirely after the Civil War and is unheard of today.[15]

This brief outline of the main features of the Spanish carnival describes the festival as it existed from 1900 to the present, that is, during most of the twentieth century. We have taken a quick glance at the expressive genres of carnival, its masked clowns and harlequins, and its dramatis personae. We can now place the Spanish carnival in the context of ritual and performance, an anthropological task that will occupy the following chapter. After that, we move on to a close exegesis of the texts, the spicy coplas.

Carnival, Ritual, and the Anthropologists

The contrast between play and seriousness is always fluid. The inferiority of play is continually being offset by the corresponding superiority of its seriousness. — Johan Huizinga, *Homo Ludens*

We are treating carnival in Spain as ritual, consisting of a series of performances or routinized events strung together over time. These events include bardic oral performances, burlesques and farces, aggressive but controlled threats, drunken revelry of a predictable kind, licentious and provocative promenading, spontaneous and sometimes quasi-violent street theater, transvestism, and so on. The first question we must contend with in examining all this is: should a secular (and in fact frankly obscene) celebration like carnival, with its irreligious antics, be called a ritual, in the anthropological sense? After all, the word "ritual" is usually used by anthropologists in connection with sacred or solemn rites: worship of deities and observation of life crises. Can the irreverent carnival be seen as belonging to this category of formulaic behavior and studied along with the often dignified observances of preliterate peoples?

Originally, following Emile Durkheim (1915), ritual was defined in cultural anthropology as a repetitive sequence of activity, culturally sanctioned and regularized, but always involving an appeal to the supernatural: spirits, gods, God (Firth 1951; Lewis 1976:129–130). More recently, however, a less restrictive approach has broadened the definition to include all forms of standardized social action with or without a religious element. Jean La Fontaine, for example, following the lead of S. F. Nadel (1954:99), defines ritual as "social action; its performance requires the organized cooperation of individuals, directed by a leader or leaders. There are rules indicating what persons should participate" (1985:11). In the same vein, Billie Isbell describes ritual as "a series of formalized values that are obligatory and standardized" (1985:17). Such actions form a pattern of symbols (Leach 1965:14) that dramatize shared values and beliefs concerning the world in which the people live (Turner 1969: 6). With its set routines and activities, symbolic expressions, and formulaic genres, carnival can be described as a secular ritual.

Since the days of Durkheim, anthropologists have agreed on one basic premise: that ritual, secular or mystical, is not "empty" rote behavior but has important societal effects. Most important, ritual seems to promote social solidarity among its participants. Ritual brings people together physically and expresses in powerful symbolic terms common goals and shared values. All societies (and within societies, most subgroups) have their own self-serving mythologies that explain their origins, justify their ideologies, and legitimize or sanctify their values and norms. Ritual practices are an important means of expressing and propagating these self-serving political myths (Kertzer 1988: 61–62). Ritual also symbolically "creates" an ordered universe of forms. In providing a structured series of prescribed events and associated beliefs, ritual imposes a cognitive map on the world and externalizes the group's collective representations. As Harold Nieberg puts it (1973:30), "Through ritual action, the inner becomes outer, and the subjective world picture becomes a social reality."[1]

Given its role in reaffirming or highlighting norms, ritual has often been regarded as a force for bolstering the status quo. As numerous observers have recently shown, however, ritual can, in certain contexts, be a force for political change — even for revolutionary upheaval (Scott 1985). Kertzer sums it up (1988:2): "Ritual may be vital to reaction, but it is also the life blood of revolution." The complex relation between politics and ritual has been approached in a variety of ways, all of which are useful in grasping the meanings of the Latin carnival. For the sake of simplicity, we can distinguish at least four distinctive though overlapping approaches.

Structural-Functional Approaches

Debate on the sociopolitical implications of carnival ritual continues in anthropology. Most of the work so far adheres to the "safety valve" model, in which the exuberance of carnival is seen as a letting off of steam among the masses — although of course the Marxist class-conflict model also receives its due. Nancie Gonzalez, in her study of Caribbean carnival (1970), one of the first such anthropological studies, argues that the festival reinforces participants' sense of their place in the social hierarchy. Again, a certain ambiguity characterizes this interpretation: carnival emphasizes social distinctions; yet it also brings the different segments of society together in play. The ambivalent interpretation of the "social functions" of carnival is shared by Roger Abrahams and Richard Bauman (1978). They describe carnival and the associated belsnicking (mumming) on the island of St. Vincent as follows:

> Most of the time in the communities we have examined, the forces of order and disorder, respectability and license, do not confront one another. . . . On those occasions when these opposed segments of the community do come together, the result is characteristically confusion or embarrassment. In carnival and belsnicking, however, the two sets of elements, each clearly identifiable, participate together within a unified event productive of enjoyment and a sense of community. The picture is not one of hostility, but of harmony. (1978:207)

Such a view attributing functions of social solidarity to carnival festivities originates with Durkheim and Radcliffe-Brown and the notion of a social organism. From this standpoint, the social animal is seen as in need of continual renewal and rebirth, failing which, like an organic thing, it withers and dies. Durkheim was very concerned with the "problem of order" — indeed, it underlay most of his anthropological work. He believed that society was fragile, always threatened with disintegration. For society to persevere and prosper, individuals need continually to reaffirm the justness and strength of their society and its values and pledge their commitment to it. This need, he felt, was most readily and effectively served by community ritual: "It is by uttering the same cry, pronouncing the same word, or performing the same gesture in regard to some object that they become and feel themselves to be in unison" (1915:230). Thus communal ritual in a society represents the principal force for upholding the social order; it follows from this that despite its levity, carnival, like any other ritual, must have the same effect.

A follower of Durkheim, Alfred Radcliffe-Brown (1952:157), also held that the social structure and the people's commitment to it are what maintains an orderly social life. This indispensable structure is not a given; it can be maintained only if people commune together to express and reinforce common sentiments. Thus, ritual is essentially the people coming together to worship their unity and thereby collectively enhance it. This profoundly conservative viewpoint goes back to Edmund Burke and Thomas Hobbes; it finds many adherents in the British structural school, for example, in a joint work by Meyer Fortes and E. Evans-Pritchard (1940). They argue that ritual functions to elevate the social system "to a mystical place, where it figures as a system for sacred values beyond criticism or revision" (1940:17–18). In other words, what people are celebrating during ritual is the social system itself, a kind of secular deity in need of constant propitiation.

As critics of functionalism pointed out, however, this view of society as essentially static ignores social conflict and discontinuity. The critics asked: If ritual enhances solidarity so effectively, then why is there any conflict at all? Also, most societies, even the simplest and most homogeneous, display some degree of disharmony and tension: "No human society is a completely integrated entity" (Wertheim 1965:26). Gradually, in response to such telling criticisms, structuralists attempted to accommodate conflict. The principal names associated with this refinement are those of Victor Turner and Max Gluckman.

In his work on the Ndembu, Turner (1957, 1969, 1985) argued that all societies have "pressure points" or nodes of stress, where individuals' alienation from their fellows collects. Most important, virtually all social structures impose authority and hierarchy on their members. This regimentation tends to generate psychological tensions, or moments "of affliction," as Turner calls them (1968), which require periodic remedy if the society is to endure. Turner argues that people must somehow reconcile their ego needs with societal demands for restraint and harmony — a synoptic approach to the "problem of order" that blends Durkheim with Freud and Hobbes.

The way this periodic release takes place is through ritual. Through joint ritual action, people are able to create a special *liminal* period when the alienating stresses of normal life are withdrawn. People then jointly discharge their pent-up psychological energy in common action. Ritual activity produces social experiences "of unprecedented potency" (1969:128–129) and galvanizes the participants through shared feelings. Their joint experience, in turn, helps to promote group solidarity by diverting psychic energies into appropriate sublimations.

To simplify somewhat, Turner favors a modified safety valve theory which presents ritual communion as a means of sublimating impulses and thus rescuing society from its own contradictions. For Turner, therefore, rather than reflecting consensus, the existence of ritual in any society points to fissures in the social edifice that cannot easily be repaired by other means. Of Ndembu ritual, he says that the "profusion of types and frequency of performance of ritual in Ndembu society are, in a way, confessions of failure in the power of secular mechanisms to redress and absorb conflicts that arise in and between local and kinship groups" (1957:289).

Turner's thought finds a reflection in the work of the symbolic anthropologist Nancy Munn, among others. For Munn, ritual, by dramatizing and reinforcing collective concepts and values that link the individual and society, mediates between ego and others. In her view, ritual creates a "social control system" that unites "the individual to a community of significant others through the symbolic mobilization of shared life meanings" (1973:605). A similar viewpoint is found in studies of life-crisis rites by, among others, Frank Young (1965) and La Fontaine (1985); and of course it figures implicitly in Jan Van Gennep's classic work on rites of passage (1908). Throughout this oeuvre, the implicit functional thesis is that ritual reconciles individual with collective needs; ritual sublimates raw human energies. A certain hydraulic assumption is also evident: social life builds up pressures that call for appropriate release. This view can be criticized as teleological, or circular, although relations between cause and effect are not always linear in the eyes of the more sophisticated theorists.

Dynamic Equilibrium: The Ritual-of-Rebellion Approach

The safety valve concept seems useful for studying such rituals of rebellion as carnival. First described systematically by Gluckman for Africa (1963), these are rites that seem to challenge or threaten, rather than corroborate, the set order of things. As anthropologists began studying more stratified societies, they encountered many ceremonies that seemed to subvert or question the basic social order. Leaders and ruling groups were often vilified instead of revered, basic values were cheerfully overthrown, and normally forbidden behavior was acted out in disgraceful detail (see Kertzer 1988:54 for a summary).

Gluckman argued that rites of rebellion act like a thermostatic device in African tribal societies, by reestablishing the dynamic equilibrium of a social order threatened by inner tensions. Studying some examples from southern Africa, he found that "rituals of rebellion proceed within an established and sacred traditional system in which there is dispute about particular distributions of power, and not about the structure of the system itself. This allows for institutionalized protest, and in complex ways renews the unity of the system" (1963:112). Like Turner, Gluckman pointed out that the expression of ritual conflict reveals tensions between segments of society: "The acceptance of the established order as right and good, and even sacred, seems to allow unbridled excess, very rituals of rebellion, for the order itself keeps the rebellion within bounds. Hence to act the conflicts, whether directly or by inversion or in other symbolical form, emphasizes the social cohesion within which the conflict exists. Every social system is a field of tension, full of ambivalence, or cooperation and contrasting struggle" (1963:127).

This paradoxical notion finds an echo in the work of other anthropologists (see LeVine 1961; Scheffler 1964; Brandes 1988), and among sociologists like Georg Simmel (1955) and Lewis Coser (1956) who have studied the "latent" functions of social conflict. Their work demonstrates that ritualized aggressions and violent status reversals may have "group-binding" consequences, when they occur within homogeneous societies where the participants share common basic values (for examples drawn from Spain, see Gilmore 1987; Mitchell 1988). The relevance of this idea in complex, class-stratified societies, however, is open to question. Is the model useful where there is basic disagreement about the political order, where class struggle occurs, or where the possibility of real revolution, as opposed to symbolic inversion, exists?

This problem has been broached in some advanced complex societies, especially in Latin America. Eva Hunt, for example, working in modern Mexico, has studied rites among oppressed Indian groups (1977), as have Billie Isbell (1985) and Stanley Brandes (1988). All three seem to agree that the main social effect of such rituals, even the most conflictive or violent, is paradoxically to reaffirm the existing order. Hunt provides the clearest statement of this view. She argues that where social groups are in conflict and where no higher mechanism can provide mediation, "ritualism provides a safe outlet for the expression of potential conflict, as well as a restrictive frame in which the potential anomie or entropy is under control." She thus agrees with Gluckman that even in a complex society, rites of revolt can work as a mechanism for enhancing the "structural status quo" (1977:144). Isbell found that indigenous ritual among peasants in Peru helps to defend the corporate community from exterior threat and that the rites are "essential to cosmic, spatial, and economic and social order" (1985:165).

A similar view has been enunciated for the Spanish carnival, particularly in the southern part of the country (Andalusia). Brandes (1980a, 1980b) has also studied popular celebrations and folklore in an Andalusian agrotown (as such large agrarian communities are called) much like the ones we shall discuss later on, as well as in a similar peasant village in Mexico (Brandes 1988). Brandes writes that in Andalusia, carnival-like celebrations "that ordinarily might be perceived as highlighting social differentiation may be viewed equally well as bringing distinctive and opposing segments of a community together" (1980b:208). Burlesques and satires like those of carnival "reinforce extant social relationships" by "bringing people together in an emotionally charged atmosphere" and demonstrating to the powerless the need for order and predictability in social life. In Brandes's view, the celebration has political significance, but mainly as a latent mechanism for "letting off steam" and stabilizing the status quo. In his book on Mexican celebrations, he again argues that "fiestas are unquestionably agents of social control" (1988:186).

Historians working with European materials have also probed rites of reversal like carnival. The literature is especially rich for early modern France. Emmanuel Le Roy Ladurie has written a whole book describing the violence unleashed by the celebration of carnival in the town of Romans in the sixteenth century, "with greedy nobles on one side and rebellious peasants on the other" (1979:xvi). Natalie Zemon Davis (1973) has also written about the "rites of violence" that occurred on Corpus Christi Day in sixteenth-century France. While these authors do not subscribe to any rigid theoretical position, they seem to suggest that rites of violence did contribute to the cohesiveness *of each antagonistic group;* and by bringing internecine conflict to a head — to the point of suppuration — at a given time, contributed to societal continuity. Both writers, however, acknowledge that these rites of violence may also have intensified internal cleavages and contradictions yet may at the same time have furnished controlled outlets for their expression. Davis (1973) notes that the Corpus Christi celebrations pitting Catholics against Protestants served to "dehumanize" the opposition and encourage religious hatred. This ambiguity does not indicate epistemological confusion; rather it reflects the inherent multivalence of ritual and its variable relation to politics.

The Culture of Resistance: Marxist Approaches

Marxist observers espouse a conflict model rather than a consensus model of class society. For Marxists, then, the "rebellious" rituals of the common folk should be seen as a weapon in the political struggle against class domination, as a symbolic form of struggle. Popular festivities, rather than being a political prop for the status quo or a means of dissipating individual energies and animosities, are a major source of class unity and an ideological defense against dominant groups. Carnival-like events may therefore be seen from this point of view as an exercise in resistance against "hegemony" in Gramscian terms — "counterhegemony," to adopt Hermann Rebel's term (1989:357).[2]

Denied the freedom to organize and protest openly, the poor manipulate cultural symbols of resistance, thus giving voice to their opposition indirectly. The ensuing ritualized activities, such as pre-Lenten carnivals, charivaris, or the King for a Day bacchanalia of medieval Europe, provide not only a conceptual means of resistance but also a device for proletarian unity and for actual challenge to the prevailing system (N. Davis 1973; Babcock 1978).

Some theorists go even further and argue that through such ritual expressions of resistance oppressed peoples create, in symbolic form, a revolutionary model of the world. James Scott (1976, 1985) holds that it is in the realm of imagination that political resistance to oppression is most readily articulated. Thus, rituals of rebellion like carnival become not only *a* means of class struggle, but *the* means of class struggle. It is through expressive ritual that the oppressed imagine a new social order: "The fact that serfs, slaves, or untouchables have no direct knowledge or experience of other social orders is, I believe, no obstacle to their creating what would have to qualify as 'revolutionary' thought. . . . In a great many societies, such a simple feat of the imagination is not just an abstract exercise: It is historically embedded in existing ritual practice" (1985:331). In classic Marxist epistemology (see Kertzer 1988:144), Latin carnival is sublimation of class struggle in its purest form, ritual resistance to elite hegemony.[3] In Abner Cohen's view, for example, carnival is always a "contested event," and class conflict is "the very essence of the celebration" (1993:131, 153). Le Roy Ladurie interprets the violent sixteenth-century Romans carnival to be a "nearly perfect example of class struggle" (1979:290).

Popular rituals, with their historically generated modes of symbolic dissent, their intense heritage of affective fervor, have the power to create momentarily an alternative (popular) social order. In this sense, they are not only symbolic, but actual, acts of revolution. Through the "joyeusetés collectives" of communal ritual, the popular classes establish their own essence and power (Bercé 1976:73). Although there may be some revolutionary wishful-thinking going on here, one can readily agree with Kertzer (1988:149) that emotionally charged popular rituals like carnival may be a powerful tool in class struggle. For Spain, Jerome Mintz (1997), in a masterful study of carnival in Cadiz Province, has recently shown the revolutionary potential of carnival songs as rallying cries for the lower classes up to and through the Franco regime — and after.

Interpretive-Symbolic Approaches

Secular celebrations have been viewed from a semiotic viewpoint. Here ritual is seen as a symbolic text, or "story grammar" (Hanks 1989:97), awaiting interpretation. Primary examples from non-Western societies are Geertz's work on Balinese rites (1980) and Richard Bauman's work on public performance (1975, 1977, 1986). Some useful insights have come from this school. Anthropologist Bauman (1975) and literary critic Kenneth Burke (1969) have independently studied the communicative and rhetorical elements of ritual.[4]

For Bauman, the public performance of ritual provides a means of symbolic communication that unites participants through psychological "release keys" of universal appeal (1975:295). Burke, too, notes the "universal" power of public symbols to create social intimacy. Rhetoric follows certain culturally prescribed forms whose built-in logic makes the course of the expression both predictable and credible, while at the same time drawing in the actors as collaborative witnesses. Burke refers to this ritualized intimacy as the "attitude of collaborative expectancy" (1969:58).

Carnival has also been studied by members of the semiotic school, especially the Russian post-structuralists. Mikhail Bakhtin (1984) has restudied carnival and popular culture through his exegesis of Rabelais and the medieval world. For Bakhtin, the medieval European carnival is the apotheosis of the liberated solidarity of the poor in perennially renewed rebellion against the political and spiritual restrictions of the social order and its prevailing hierarchies. Overthrowing the structures of society, the celebration was marked by "the suspension of all hierarchical precedence" and the "temporary liberation from the prevailing truth" (1984:10). While regarding carnival as moral and social "inversion," Bakhtin's work also places particular stress upon the strikingly *ambivalent* nature of its aggressive mockery: "Folly is, of course, deeply ambivalent. It has the negative element of debasement and destruction . . . and the positive element of renewal and truth. It is the other side, the lower stratum of official laws and conventions derived from them" (1984:260). Recognizing the contradictions and complexities of carnival culture, both historically and contemporaneously, Bakhtin's work is a subtle and insightful document and we will refer to him many times in the following chapters.

Other semioticians have regarded the burlesques of carnival in similar ways. For Umberto Eco (1984:2), carnival can be seen as a ritual means of controlling social tensions while providing an illusory sense of "freedom" for the oppressed. Eco regards the travesties of carnival as providing not real release, but only a simulacrum of freedom: "Carnival can exist only as *authorized* transgression (which in fact represents a blatant case of *contradictio in adjecto* or of happy *double binding.* . . . In this sense comedy and carnival are not instances of real transgressions: on the contrary, they represent paramount examples of law enforcement. They remind us of the existence of the rule" (Eco 1984:6). Writing about the Spanish carnival, Mintz seems to adhere to this cautious mode of reasoning when he points out that "carnival is shadow play . . . only play acting and not open rebellion. . . . Rather than touch off rebellion, carnival has a place in the flow of ritual" (1997:251).

For Ivanov, a follower of Bakhtin, carnival is an attempt of subordinated groups to create an "inversion of polar opposites" by restructuring relations and hierarchies (1984:12). Especially important here is carnival transvestism, or sexual reversal. Ivanov takes carnival transvestism as a primary instance of the ritual merging of opposites in culture: "In contemporary ethnology, transvestism (as other carnival rituals) is considered to be an instance of a ritual neutralization of semiotically significant oppositions, in this case the opposition male/female. The basic tenet of structural anthropology . . . is that there is a constant striving for equilibrium between binary polar oppositions in ritual and myth. This balance may be achieved by mediation between them."

Monica Rector (1984), Roberto DaMatta (1991), and Candace Slater (1982) have analyzed the subliminal messages inherent in the songs and dances of Mardi Gras in South America. For Slater, as for many of the anthropologists discussed above, these popular entertainments serve to reaffirm the identification of individual and group (1982:217). DaMatta takes a more political approach, seeing the Brazilian festival as a way for the poor to assert their "positive" values in an "extraordinary moment characterized by joy" (1991:32).

These approaches are therefore not in basic disagreement with the ethnographic work of Turner, Gluckman, Scott, and Kertzer. But it is clear that most students of European carnival, past and present, have been struck most of all by the *ambivalent* nature of its rituals: these rituals both challenge and support the established order, both subvert and reinforce existing boundaries, hierarchies, and sexual moralities. As DaMatta notes for the famous Brazilian Mardi Gras: "In short, the *communitas* of Carnival is a function of the rigid social position of the participating groups and segments in the everyday world. The universality and homogeneity of Carnival serve precisely to reinforce, and compensate on another plane, the particularism, hierarchy, and inequality of Brazilian everyday life" (1991:43–44).

Wherever it occurs, carnival is therefore nothing if not blatantly contradictory in its "promiscuous mixing" of bodies, statuses, images, egos, and sexes, as Richard Parker (1991:144) puts it, also referring to Brazil. It is the very nature of the celebration to superimpose opposites, and by so doing achieve new and more powerful ways of interpreting the world and its possibilities. Carnival permits "people to destroy and react violently without fully assuming the political consequences and implications of their actions" (DaMatta 1991:59).

To summarize briefly: as a form of ritual play and moral commentary, carnival can subvert the normal order while at the same time reinforcing normalcy. Carnival can create a moral unity through symbolic means among classes and sexes. This unity can extend to the whole society or to conflictive subsets — be they social classes, the oppressed, or women — within the society. Rituals of rebellion, like carnival, can therefore paradoxically enhance the existing social order; or contrariwise, they can subvert the existing order by promoting horizontal solidarity among oppressed groups. What seems to matter is the context in which the inversive ritual takes place.

In a sense, then, carnival seems like a celebration not so much of antiestablishment feeling per se, in some undiluted form, but rather of *ambivalence itself*, of dualism, contradiction, and mixed feelings. As we shall see, the rituals and the oral extrusions of the February frolics in Spain are never monolithic, but promethean effulgences of the divided and the contradictory.

We can now move on to an analysis of copla texts. Our first song specimens concern sex and gender. In the next chapter, we look at a special genre of chirigota satires that denigrate and abuse women, in both a sexual and political sense.

4

Woman Degraded
Chirigota Satires

That's the nature of women . . . not to love them when we love them, and to love when we love them not. — Miguel de Cervantes, *Don Quixote*

It is noon on a cool overcast day in mid-February in Andalusia, the Saturday before Ash Wednesday. Carnival has arrived! Without any recognizable signal, but by common assent, people pour out of their homes into the village streets. Most of them are in colorful masquerade, both men and women. The mascarones, the male clowns, are all in drag, their faces covered. Their women counterparts, the máscaras, or harlequins, appear as exotic maids and princesses, Hollywood movie stars or Russian ballerinas, their faces likewise hidden.

The onlooker, even if motivated to do so, has a hard time distinguishing the masqueraders by sex, for all are completely covered from head to toe. Knowing the sexual confusion they cause, some of the women go out of their way to show you the delicate skin on their wrist to corroborate their femininity. "See, I'm a woman," a fairy princess whispers to bystanders, "Couldn't you tell? No? Why, how stupid you are!" Enormous nervous energy, electricity, is in the air. People mill about excitedly, taking in the scene, exchanging insults and witticisms.

The transvestites move smartly through the streets. They grotesquely mimic women's mannerisms and, in a strange falsetto whine, shout obscenities that

5. Transvestite clowns, 1973.

would make a harlot blush. "Stick it in my arse," they bellow. "Touch my tits!" They push and jostle, they brawl and challenge, picking arguments, accosting passersby. Pulling down their shawls and raising their hems, they show off their padded "breasts," their hairy legs, their lush derrieres. The colorful harlequins, though, parade with a little more dignity. They move at a stately pace, waving grandly, flirting, undulating, making lewd suggestions to passing gentlemen. Everyone — clowns, harlequins, bystanders — is happily involved, elated. Adolescent boys and girls are excitedly waving sticks, poking with mock menace at pedestrians, blowing on pipes, beating spoons on metal pots and pans. Though vaguely threatening, the jostling and ear-splitting cacophony are all good-natured; even the wicked humor is all in good fun — or so they say.

"Eso es el carnaval!" the young boys shout as they careen through the streets, wielding their poles and noisemakers. "El que diga 'no,' vete al diablo!" (This is carnival! Anyone who says No can go to the devil.) On a slightly more ominous note: "Eso es el carnaval! El que diga 'no' se le cortan los cojones!" (This is carnival! Anyone who says No gets his balls cut off!). The belligerent youths' point is that carnival has no room for naysayers, for negativity. During carnival there is no No. It is forbidden to deny. Carnival is Yes. If you want to keep your *cojones* intact, say Yes, and join in!

Suddenly, freezing the chaos in the streets into a blurry montage, a bugle blares off-key, a sour note. The milling crowd is still for a moment, watching expectantly. A band (*murga*) makes its first appearance (Figure 2). The minstrels have come out! Around a corner come twelve men in marching costumes, sparkling white tunics festooned with ribbons. The murga approaches the center of town where the throngs part to let it pass. "¡Viva la murga!" the people shout. The minstrels pause, and the maestro emits two harsh blasts from his trumpet for quiet. His companions rhythmically beat their tambourines. The singers clear their throats; the maestro taps three times with his baton. The songs of carnival are about to begin. Vox populi will now be heard.[1]

According to one Spanish sociologist, carnival in Spain is a time for the administration of "collective justice," when "citizens are publicly censured and their flaws announced, and during which no one is permitted to take offense, and in which the victim must accept the punishment of public shaming and the ridicule of his fellows" (García de Diego 1960:295). The main vehicle of mockery is the murga's piquant song. The poets direct much of their venom at women. Naturally, the victims are those who have transgressed the pueblo's rigid moral code in one way or another during the past year, as often as not, sexually — wayward girls, unfaithful wives, unwed mothers, and so on. But beyond the richly inventive metaphors for women's sexual frailties and peccadilloes that add spice to these attacks, the joke in each case is grounded in serious satire about generic feminine flaws (as men see them), irrespective of sinful acts. The subject is the farce of sex itself — man and woman, repression and desire — and at a higher level the battle of the sexes. The songs are about the primacy of the id, the comical weakness of the poor defenses that civilization erects vainly against the power of nature.

Let us now sample some of the coplas. Our first song, debuted more than forty years ago in the town of La Campana, reflects the tendency to deride women, in the service of male vanity. The song celebrates the comeuppance of a pretentious "woman of high status." This particular lady, supercilious and sexually unattainable, is a universal straw woman for carnival satire: the prude degraded. The lady is typically brought low by a wily workingman, who gets the better of her and tricks her into having sex, which of course she subconsciously wants and enjoys. But she is not brought down because she has sinned. She is victimized only because of her sex, because she is aloof, the unresponsive object of male desire. Her punishment is a collective vindication of male dominance and sexuality; her guilt, also collective, lies in her desirability. An example must be made.

In our first song, note how the barber, the wily, predatory male, is given center stage — as the trickster, a culture hero. The poet makes him the judge of

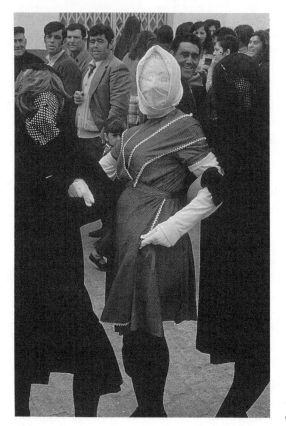

6. Typical faceless transvestite clown, 1973.

the woman, who remains captive in the barber's chair, restrained and passive like a prisoner in the docket, while he "operates" on her. In a reflection of Andalusian sexual attitudes, the man is given the power to initiate the action, to enact the seduction. He has the autonomy, or "agency" in Michael Herzfeld's words (1985a), as indicated through tropes of domination and control:

Una niña de elevada distinción	A girl of high station
Fue a cortarse las melenas	Went to the barber to have her bangs done
A lo garzón.	In the newest Parisian fashion.
El barbero "mu" tunante y diligente	But the crafty barber had other ideas,
Se la puso en postura diferente.	And he got her in a certain position.
Vaya salero:	How clever of him:
La peló y la afeitó con esmero	He gave her such a marvelous haircut
Y la niña de gusto bailaba,	That she started jumping for joy,
Cuando le pasaba	Especially when he used the
La brocha el barbero.[2]	Barber's brush on her.

Obviously, "going to the barber" means having intercourse, and like "skinning the turkey" and a host of other idiosyncratic phrases, this euphemism for sex is employed by cultivated women. But what the song really does is parody bourgeois women's sexual circumlocution in the process of constructing a shared male joke about seduction.

The tonsorial adventure exemplifies what Bakhtin (1984:18–19) has called the grotesque realism of carnivalesque parody, which takes as its essential principle degradation, the lowering of all that is high, spiritual, or abstract: "It is a transfer to the material level, to the sphere of earth and body in their indissoluble unity." In the spirit of the carnivalesque, the versifier attributes concupiscent intent to the "lady," but he confers agency — the power to act or to consummate an intention — on the (lower-ranking) male. Thus what is high is lowered, fastidiousness is circumvented, and the modesty of woman is exposed as fraudulent.

While the minstrels sing, the crowd may also be treated to a pantomime, such as the following one that I witnessed in the town of Fuentes de Andalucía in 1977. As a ribald *murga* performance concluded, one clown leapt into the circle vacated by the departing musicians. He did a lewd female impersonation, complete with bumps and grinds and pelvis thrusting. Then, producing a filthy pair of women's panties from the folds of his costume, he began to twirl them over his head like a bull roarer. Next, the underwear became a bullfighter's cape. Another clown, wearing a set of horns on his head, emerged from the surrounding crowd at a signal. The two began to enact a parody of the *corrida*, lurching about the streets to cries of encouragement from the throng.

Continuing the skit, the transvestite matador led the bull around with the panties, but he was hopelessly outmaneuvered. The bull got the better of him, as both man and animal shrieked obscenities about intercourse. "How hard it is to get it in!" wailed the matador. "Go fuck yourself," shouted the bull, "you're not trying hard enough. Come on, stick it in, you fairy." The two continued in this vein, until the matador finally produced a huge wooden phallus, which the bull rushed in to grab, and with the effigy in hand, did the job himself. The skit then concluded with a crude imitation of bestiality, culminating in the bull's gasps of satisfaction.

The act over, the crowd wandered off to search out other bands or resorted to spontaneous street theater for further entertainment. Other songs and skits followed, one after the other, until the day drew to a close and, exhausted, people wandered home to sleep it off. At twilight, they refreshed themselves by napping, washing, changing costume (or perhaps abandoning the masquerade to become onlookers), and in general prepared for the night's events, which would last until dawn. Sleep is never important. This is carnival! *Eso es el carnaval! No one sleeps for long.*

7. Women masqueraders, 1977.

Let us look at some other examples of carnival verse. The following coplas, all collected between the years 1970 and 1980, come from various towns in Seville Province, including Fuentes de Andalucía, La Campana, Carmona, and a few others.

The following ballad employs another trope often encountered in Andalusian allegory — prurient food metaphors. The poet plays on the pun of *pescado* (fish) and *pecado* (past participle of *pecar,* "to sin"). In Andalusian Spanish, both words are pronounced "peca'o," giving rise to many puns and jokes. The young woman who is made fun of here appears both naive and worldly, sexually repressed and salacious, and again in need of the male instrument to "fulfill" her and resolve her indecision. Her boyfriend needs metaphorically to "fill her" with phallic foods, here a "big fish." This song exemplifies what Louise Vasvari (1991:3) has called the "gastro-genital equivalences" of Spanish carnival verse, which identify sexual with alimentary "hunger," a motif we will return to often.[3]

Una niña muy bonita	A pretty young woman
Que a su madre le decía,	Went to her mother one day
Que le comprara pescado	And asked her to buy some fish
Que en la plaza se vendía.	To satisfy her craving.
La madre por complacerla,	To placate her, the old woman
Compró lo que gustaba;	Brought home some of what the girl wanted,

Y uno de ellos traía	One small fish with the head peeled.
La cabeza desollada.	But her daughter shouted with great
	displeasure, saying
La niña al verlo gritó,	I only like big fish, ones that fill me
	up.
Causa con mucho disgusto:	This one is too little.
A mi me gusta el pescado	Now, my boyfriend has a real big
	skinned fish
Que de grande me de susto.	That just fills you up so much when
	you eat it,
Mi novio tiene un cazón,	And they tell me that this swelling
Se hincha la que lo come,	Is due to all that oily stuff
Y dicen que es da la grasa	That comes out of skinned fishheads.
De los peces cabezones.[4]	

The joke is pretty obvious if one remembers that Andalusian men are uncircumcised. When the fish is "peeled" or skinned, the "head" emerges from the foreskin. The swelling can refer to pregnancy in the one who swallows the juice or, alternatively, to the tumescence of erection. The girl wants "a big fish," the kind that is itself swollen and that swells her up, fills her up.

The following copla, from the town of Carmona, uses the same gastrosexual imagery. It combines the "hunger" of repressed female desire with a favorite automotive trope for sexual intercourse in which the bumpy motorcycle ride serves as an easily identifiable allegory for copulation.

Venimos contentos	We were minding our own business
Del Jueves Lardero	One Shrove Tuesday
Y hemos presenciado,	When we ran into a guy on a Vespa,
Por casualidad,	Carrying a picnic basket
Un niño en su Vespa	With his girlfriend on the back.
Llevaba una cesta,	Then, going downhill rapidly,
Una gran merienda,	The girl shouts out,
Y la novia detrás	Slow down, watch out where you're
	going,
Por la cuesta abajo.	For God's sake, Juan José,
Gritó la chiquilla:	And try to avoid all this
¡Vete pa la senda,	Shaking and bumping,
Por Dios, Juan José,	Because the eggs are going to break!
Y evita, si puedes,	Well, from all that
Esos traqueones!	Jerking and bouncing about of the
	Vespa
Mira que los huevos	The driver's sausage flew out of his
	basket.
Se van a romper.	And the girl exclaimed,

Y el conductor,
De tanto saltar la Vespa,
Se le salió el chorizo
De la cesta, y ella exclamó:
Malo se presenta el plan,
Con los huevos rotos,
Sin el chorizo, ¿que vamos a
    merendar?[5]

Hey, this is ruining our picnic plans.
With the eggs broken and without
Any sausage, how can we
Have a proper picnic?

The "eggs and sausage," of course, come in for a good deal of shaking and vibrating during foreplay (women often decorously use the word *huevos* in place of *cojones*, for balls), and the girl worries that the fun will be spoiled unless her lover slows his motor down. The song portrays the woman as "hungry" (for sex) but unsure of her impulses and hypocritically mixing metaphors to avoid appearing avid: a common representation of female self-deception throughout carnival versification.

The song's deeper structure suggests the romantic complicity of women and their supposedly insatiable appetite for amorous nourishment provided by the male. But the point of the song, my sources say, is to make fun of women's tendency to beat around the bush. In fact, the song does something else. It symbolically inverts male-female dependencies. This reversal banishes the actual male need for women and replaces it with food. Again, the grotesque realism of carnival metaphors works to transform the male into the possessor of the sexual energy (or sustenance) that animates the object-subject relation and the sensual gratification. His motorcycle gives his girlfriend "the ride," and it is his organ that provides the erotic nourishment. The woman is passive and receiving, the male robust and provisioning. He provides the "food of love" that makes the picnic possible. This phallocentric vision reverses the normal oral dependency relations in Andalusia that bind men, in childlike fashion, to wives and mothers as the purveyors of cooked food, since men never do kitchen work. But during carnival they do have eggs and sausages.[6]

The following copla uses an inversive alimentary trope for the helpless hunger of desire and reversing relations of oral dependency.[7] It plays on the same theme of women's conflicted impulses and the virile response of the male, both peremptory and minatory. The poet equates semen and "milk."

Y una moza de servicio
Que iba dándose cartel,
Por leche una mañana
Para tomar el café.
Como iba tan "deprisa"
La muchacha preguntó
Y como no estaba el cabrero

One morning a servant girl
Went out in a great hurry to
Buy some milk for coffee.
Being very distracted,
She asked for the goatherd
But since he did not answer,
She started milking by herself.

Ella misma ordeñó.	But she grabbed the wrong thing
Estando ordeñando	And the young man [the goatherd] said:
Le dijo el muchacho;	Careful now, girl,
Cuidado chiquilla,	
Que ordeñas el macho.[8]	Because you'll milk my manhood.

The song makes a wordplay on the polysemous verb *ordeña,* which technically means to milk a cow or other animal. But it can also mean to rub or manipulate an object in the manner of milking a cow, that is, masturbation. Using the same verb, Andalusians joke about "milking" the branches of an olive tree during the harvest in order to collect the fruit or "seed."

Drenched in the sexual symbolism of male fantasy, the scene is a pastiche of mixed bodily metaphors. What is less apparent is the moral message to the effect that the serving girl, going about her business blindly (but unconsciously willing), stimulates the "macho" man. Accidentally on purpose, she initiates his threatening response, expressed as a warning. The serving maid is portrayed as sexually provocative, but the male retains a privileged position of both genital domination and moral authority.

The following song, from Fuentes de Andalucía, dates from the late 1940s. Like the picnic ditty above, it employs the metaphor of the bumpy conveyance to relay a similar message. Here the vehicle is the ubiquitous bicycle, which was the poor man's "horse" during the lean postwar years. To explain the omnipresent transportation imagery, people say that riding front-to-back is very much like sex, because a man and woman are "bouncing" in unison with the man in control (or "driving"). The newly popular bicycle provided the perfect metaphor for sex, or at least the androcentric vision of it, before the widespread availability of cars and motorcycles (Gilmore 1983). The woman is again portrayed as secretly seeking copulation and achieving it in a literally roundabout way.

Se ha puesto muy popular	Bicycles have become
La bicicleta,	Extremely popular,
Ya las mocitas de Fuentes	And all the gals of Fuentes
Están muy contentas.	Are very happy about it.
Cuando salen de paseo	Whenever they go for a walk
Suelen decir:	They say: I'm going to find my boyfriend,
Voy en busca de mi novio	He just bought a new bike
Que ha comprado una	And I'm going to get on with him.
Y me va a subir.	Well, this couple we know
Salieron una buena tarde	Went out one fine evening
A echar un paseo,	To take a ride on the bike,

Hacia el "Barrancón."	Out to the "Ravine."
Tuvieron una avería	But they hit a bump
Y al suelo cayeron	And fell down on the ground,
Rodando los dos.	Rolling on top of each other.
Préstame por Dios auxilio	For God's sake, Nicholas, help me, she says.
Y muévete, Nicolás,	And move over a little, please,
No sea que pase alguno	Someone might come by
Y vea que tengo la bomba "clavá."⁹	And see me impaled on the bicycle pump.

Resorting to obvious "downfall" imagery (which may be read as both willing capitulation and disgrace), these bicycle songs warn women that forwardness with certain objects will lead to serious consequences. But it is an ambivalent warning, the implication being one of women's complicity: the songs simultaneously express a warning about female receptiveness and the wish for it. And, of course, the usual claim is made that pleasure in sex provided by the virile "driver." But the male fantasy of the willing sex object remains the central motif.

The following song similarly makes fun of women's sexual confusion and "weakness," through a host of animal, in this case veterinary, images. These also occur commonly in Andalusian coplas. In Andalusian sexual slang, "rabbit" means vagina and "gruel" (or serum) stands for semen. Like many other bawdy songs, this brief lyric makes the oft-repeated point that female sexuality, while vital and "hot" (to use the favored term), is so repressed by convention that it is deformed into neurotic symptoms (the rabbit's illness) requiring the attentions of a man to return to health and well-being. Thus, the singer attributes to men not just the agency and primacy in sex, but also wisdom and restorative skills. The woman is reduced to object, needful of male genital attention, as in a doctor-patient relationship.

Common to much of this magical imagery, the rhetoric of active and passive reminds one of the seed and soil imagery that Delaney (1991) reports in rural Turkey. There the plow symbolizes the male principle, and the fertile but inchoate earth, the female. This subject-object metaphor is common in the masculine appropriation of the active role in sex, as in knowledge and other forms of power.

Mariquilla tenía un conejo,	Little Mary had a bunny rabbit,
La mas de gracioso que lo he visto.	The sweetest little thing I ever saw.
Yo, asombrao, me dije ¡vaya!	I was surprised at how skinny it was,
La hambre que tenía que pasar	And I said to myself, Gosh, what hunger

Yo no he visto en otro animal.	This poor thing must have suffered!
Yo le pongo de pronto una inyección,	So I gave it an injection of the
Sí, es de suero bastante mejor.	Very best serum just as fast as I could.
Con la inyección que le hemos puesto	And wouldn't you know it?
Ya está el conejo repuesto.[10]	With that injection I gave it,
	That little rabbit revived in a wink.

Bad Girls

We now move to songs that carnivalize sex and gender from other angles, and seemingly show us the obverse of the earlier picture. The first specimen exemplifies a moralistic genre that criticizes women not for prudery but for promiscuity. The following copla, from the mid-1970s, takes "modern" girls to task for their provocative miniskirts and go-go fashions. Written and sung by conservative older men, the lyrics attack the immodesty of young girls in a period of social change, with the message that such behavior will drive suitors away rather than attract them. Again, women are given implicitly to understand that serious judgments (marriage being the most serious in life) are made by men; here, though, the demand is for prudence rather than promiscuity.

Este año las mocitas	This year, this year,
Este año las mocitas	All the girls,
Ya han dado por llevar	All the girls are wearing
Colgada una cadenita	Hippy beads and
Y unas medias muy calá.	See-through blouses.
Por las calles ellas	They sashay through the
Van diciendo, vida mía	Streets exclaiming
Quiero ser ye-yé,	Oh, la la, how I want
Llevando una minifalda	To be a go-go girl.
Llevando una minifalda	Wearing miniskirts, miniskirts,
Que el obligo se levé,	That barely cover their navel,
Parece el mono en un circo	They look just like circus monkeys
Cuando charlando se ven.	Chattering through the streets.
Cualquiera llega	Who is going to ask you for a date
A pedirle un paseíto	With that face you put on?
Con la cara que suelen poner.	Hussy, you're like a left-over [rotten] olive
Si es que eres un rebuscao	After the last gleaning,
Pues no llegues	No man will choose you.
Y quedarás mejor.	With all that paint
Lastima pintura	You shamelessly slap on your face,
Que te pones	You don't know how ugly you look.
Y no sabes lo fea que está.[11]	

8. Transvestites, 1977.

Next, a typical example of comic verse satirizing "modern" widows along the same lines:

Viudas a lo loco	All these crazy old widows, absolutely mad,
Nos presentamos,	They've got their own "Maestra"
Todos con la Maestra	And their own wild gangs.
Y organizados.	Their behavior and their nutty fashions
Su tipo y su hechura	Are truly something to behold,
Es lo que tienen que ver,	They are dressed to kill;
Cuando se queden mirando	You must get a load of these gals:
De la cabeza a los pies.	Dressed to the nines,
Viste a la moda	All in the latest fashion, too,
Como ninguna;	Makeup smeared all over
Con el vestido corto	With tiny little skirts and

Y la pintura.	The sportiest threads in town.
Las alpagatas blancas	They go traipsing through the streets
Y las medidas de "sport"	Saying to themselves:
Van por las calles diciendo:	Now, what poor guy am I
¿Con que me casaré yo?[12]	Going to catch and marry?

It seems that women are damned if they do and damned if they don't.

We now turn to more recent examples of moralistic misogyny. The following song, from the early 1980s, a period of sexual freedom and experimentation in Spain, again attacks "liberated" women as shameless and sexually provocative. The message once again places the onus on the woman for the behavior of the predatory male aroused by her immodesty. The lyrics use the favorite vehicular metaphor for sexual seduction, with the man as usual in the driver's seat; in fact, the man's "hard object" becomes the driveshaft. Little has changed since the 1950s.

Una noche que llovía	One rainy night
Un murguista se encontró	One of our troubadours here
Una pareja de novios	Saw a couple that
Que le llamo la atención.	Caught his attention.
Ella buscaba las bragas	She was looking for her panties
Debajo de un automóvil,	Underneath a car,
Y le hecho mano al embrague	And she grabs the clutch by mistake
Y dijo usted me perdone	And the driver inside says,
El chofer que estaba dentro.	Hey, pardon me, lady.
La cogió por la cintura	He grabs her by the waist
Y se la sentó en la falda;	And sits her down on his lap,
Le cogió una cosa dura.	And the next thing you know
Y cuando salen del baile	She's grabbing something hard.
Vienen jarta de cubatas,	When these modern girls leave
No saben las infelices	Their midnight parties, liquored up
Que pueden meter la pata.	They don't know what trouble
Deben de tener un castigo	They can get themselves into.
El que da esa libertad.	It's because of all this new liberty.
Así no habría en el mundo	There should be a severe punishment
Mujeres tan desgraciá.[13]	Meted out to whoever gives these women such license.
	In the whole world there are no women
	More disreputable than in this town.

While the song mentions no one specifically, it is clear that those responsible for the young women's "disgrace" are their lenient fathers and brothers who "permit" them this scandalous freedom. More masculine control is needed, the poet pleads, because a wayward young woman is fair game. The lyrics convey the panoply of Andalusian sexual double standards. Touch the gear-shift, the message warns, and you start the engine; the blame is yours. The woman who "starts the car" is always to blame in the case of an accident, or overheating, as the case may be.

Battle-Axes

Let us examine a contrasting genre that deplores the duplicity of wives and mothers-in-law. These songs are not so much about sex as about the other male needs met by women, such as for food and cosseting. Addressed specifically to women in the audience, often in scolding tones, these coplas starkly convey the image of women as withholding and niggardly. In this type of misogynous verse, the wife, in contrast to the selfless mother (a romanticized image that we will explore in the next chapter) is characterized with ironic disillusionment as selfish, rejecting, and judgmental. Frustrating, demanding, and depleting, the wife and mother-in-law are like Harpies.

One such song bemoans the conditional nature of uxorial affection. Here the singer again portrays the wife as the antithesis of the selflessly loving mother. The wife is not only critically evaluative but also greedy, loving only a man with money. Her love is qualified, conditional. To meet her harsh demands, the husband must uproot himself and travel to alien places. There, miserable and bereft, he toils to win his miserly wife's affection. The final five stanzas go like this:

Ni que te vaya a Alemania	Even if you emigrate to Germany,
Ni a Suiza ni a Belén,	To Switzerland, or to the Coast,
La mujer no quiere a nadie;	A wife only loves a man who
No quiere mas que'r parnel.	Comes back loaded with dough.
Eso le pasa a la tuya,	This happens with your wife,
A la mía, y a las demás.	With mine, and everyone's.
En viendo billetes verdes,	If she sees those greenbacks,
Mira que amoroso están.	Look how amorous she becomes.
Teniendo billetes verdes	Man, if you have those greenbacks,
Está visto y aprobao;	You're approved and accepted;
Eres bonito y gracioso,	You're handsome and charming,
Sabes mas que un abogao.	You're cleverer than a lawyer.
El hombre que sea muy feo	A guy who's really ugly
Y no se encuentre casamiento,	And can't find a girl to marry him,
Teniendo billetes verdes,	If he's got greenbacks,

Pierden el conocimiento.	He's suddenly a handsome swain.
Aquí termina la copla:	Here ends our ditty:
Esta es la realidad.	It's the absolute truth.
Mira como "toas" se rien,	Look how everyone is laughing,
Pa'que saben que es la verdad![14]	Because you all know how true it is!

Our next song decries the most fearsome problem in a man's life: the united front of wife and hostile mother-in-law. The two hard-hearted women mount an aggressive exploitative conspiracy. Again, the man is bled dry and thrown out. Though he gives and gives, it is never enough. They are insatiable.

Trabajando, trabajando,	Working, working,
Trabajando noche y dia,	Working night and day,
Pa'que cuando estoy parao,	For if I am unemployed,
Aumentan las penas mías.	All my worries grow.
Pa'que cuando estoy parao	When I am unemployed
Y ni ganando ni una perra,	And not earning a red cent,
Cualquiera aguanta en mi casa	No one in my house
A mi mujer y a mi suegra.	Can control my wife and mother-in-law.
Como esta de moda, ayer les	As is the custom, yesterday
Compré una lavadora,	I bought them a washing machine
Y una olla exprés,	And a pressure cooker,
Y hasta un molinillo pa' moler café.	And even a little mill to grind their coffee.
Y no puedo volver a mi casa,	I can't go home any more,
Yo no puedo, no puedo, no puedo.	Oh, no, I just can't go home,
Y si vuelvo me encuentro en la puerta	Because whenever I go home,
Casi siempre sentao el ditero.	I always see the bill collector waiting for me.
Mire usted si estaré cabreao,	Look for yourself if they're not cuckolding me,
Que me tienen pela'a las pestañas,	They have the shirt right off my back.
Y este año estoy apuntao,	And this year, my name is down as the first
Y me voy er primero a Alemania.	Poor guy to leave for Germany.
Es la forma que me han recetao	It's the only way they say I can earn
Pa' pagar lo que debo en España [reprise]![15]	Back what I owe in Spain! [reprise]

Finally, of course, a host of songs—understandable given the anxieties about wives and the domestic dungeon—are sung warning men against the trap of marriage. These misogamous songs are funny to the audience because they invoke the always hilarious domestic comedy with its stereotypes: the put-upon henpecked husband, the shrewish, grasping wife who keeps a sloppy house, the brutal mother-in-law. The following song reviles women for ignoring their obligations, for being poor housekeepers, for bossing their husbands, and for not properly attending to their husbands' personal needs.

Me ofrecen una novia con salero	I was offered a beautiful fiancée
Pero yo no la quiero porque te voy a decir.	But I turned her down for reasons I'll now relate.
Mientras me encuentre yo soltero	While I remain a bachelor,
Hago lo que quiero y nadie manda en mi.	I do what I want and no one orders me about.
De primera parece una cosa	At first glance a woman seems like a blessing,
Buena moza como tu la ves,	Lovely to look at, good and sweet,
Y se casan y nunca se lavan,	But after they get married they never clean house,
Y salen diciendo pues yo ya pasé.	Saying, I'm above all that now.
Si eso fuera una sandía que se pudiera calar	If only a woman were like a watermelon
Antes de casarse niña enseñate tu a lavar,	That you could tap to test its flavor.
Que es una vergüenza niña [bis]	Before you marry, girl, learn to wash,
Como tu marido va.	And care for your husband;
Por eso darse cuenta muchachas	It's a damned shame how you neglect him [bis].
Ya sabeis lo que pasa si se quereis casar;	So take care girls, if you want to marry
Algunas teneis la ajuar comprada	You must learn what marriage is all about.
	Some of you have your trousseau made up,
Y no os sirve de nada	But it's all to no avail,
Por no saber lavar.	Unless you learn housekeeping.
Aplicarse la que quisiera casarse,	Apply yourself, girls, if you want a husband,
Pa' que pueda su casa llevar	Learn to clean house,
Que parece mentira chiquilla	You're deceiving yourself
Que valla [sic] el marido como algunos van.	If you think you'll keep a man If you neglect your duties.
El otro día vimos a uno	Why, the other day, we saw one poor guy
Que estaba recién casado,	Recently married, he was,

Y llevaba la chaqueta	And instead of a coat, he was wearing
Que era un papel de pescado.	A smelly old fish wrapper:
El se fué buscando lana [bis]	He went looking for fleece in marriage [bis]
Pero salió trasquilao.[16]	But instead came away shorn!

The next song also scolds women but takes a slightly different slant. Written in the 1960s during the high point of the labor emigration to northern Europe, it chastises wives for exploiting their husbands economically, forcing them into labor abroad, ignoring men's needs, and caring only for money. The theme is foreign emigration, which working-class men were forced to undertake at that time to make ends meet. Naturally, most men hated and feared leaving home, but they felt that they were required as breadwinners to make this "sacrifice" for their family. John Davis (1973:94–95) reported that Italian men in the town of Pisticci would say of their work, "If it were not for my family, I'd not be wearing myself out [sacrificing myself]" (*non mi sacrifico*). In Spain, men also protest that they must "sacrifice" in order to satisfy their wife's insatiable desire for consumer goods. Here the man is portrayed as victim of female perfidy, driven from his natal village into a hard life of thankless toil in foreign lands.

Esto de los emigrantes	This labor emigration stuff has become
Se ha puesto mu popular	Very popular these days;
Todo el que va a Alemania	Everyone's going to Germany
Una casa quié comprar.	To make enough dough to buy a new house.
Otros se van a Suiza	Others are going to Switzerland
Por ver lo que pasa allí,	To see what's available there,
Que quiere comprar una vaca	Some to buy a milk cow
La vaca la dejo aquí.	To leave behind here in Spain.
La vaca que tu has dejao	That cow you bought, says the wife,
todo el día dando suspiros	Sits around doing nothing, moaning
No me importa que tu vengas	Just like you do all the time.
Pero mándame los giros.	I don't care if you never come home,
Si no me mandas los giros	Just send me those remittances.
No me tengas que escribir	If you don't send me money
Cojo la ropa y me marcho	Don't bother writing;
A Barcelona a servir.[17]	I'll just go to Barcelona and Get a job myself.

The Female in Comic Frames of Freedom

Performed during a liminal period of ritual liberation, these doggerel verses and skits enact a masculine usurpation of the critical voice of judgment, appropriating the role of initiator and master — as well as the active voice — through the pyrotechnics of verbal artistry. Women are downgraded, ridiculed, put in "their place."

The carnival wits of Andalusia find fault with women for a welter of sins, both sexual and ethical. As self-appointed judges, the men retain the authority to "imagize," or frame, the sexual other as an object both of desire and of derision. This is of course a form of symbolic control. Both the songs and the skits put the woman in a position at the same time inferior and superior to the man's, but it is always a position inviting aggressive response.

Anthropologists Bauman and Briggs (1990:76) say that the performance of verbal art "is a mode of social production," closely allied to the political economy of power and communal authority. Disguised by comic imagery, sweetened by laughter, the carnival coplas, full of whimsical tropes and ribald characterizations, make possible a monopoly over what might be called the means of seduction, the power of sex. The composers imagine a masculine genital hegemony and a moral authority, neither of which exists in reality, and thereby invent a satisfying female passivity and receptivity. Thus, the singer derives both the power and the opportunity to write the script of sexuality and solidify claims to sovereignty as poet and man.

Yet carnival protocols write a gender script that is just as ambivalent as it is compensatory and interlocutory. As Heath argues in her analysis of women's dance in urban Senegal, such thematic ambiguity reflects and publicizes "a central contradiction in gender relations" (1994:95). In Andalusia this central contradiction is twofold: it is the antithesis between phallic assertion and the need to shelter kinswomen from male predators, as well as the ambivalence about untrammeled female sexuality, expressed here as the libidinized image of woman bursting the bounds of convention. Balanced tenuously between power and weakness, masculine carnival discourse spawns an affective bivalence that furnishes the underlying motif and chaotic reversals of carnival burlesque. "Scatology and obscenity reaffirm the vital body" in the crazy music of February (Hutcheon 1985:71), while at the same time imploring women to satisfy man's contradictory desires.

Because it is irresoluble in emotional life, this conflict between fleshly desire and denial finds an outlet in carnival laughter. Specifically, it finds expression in sexual travesty, where inner contradictions pleasurably conflate phallocentric fantasies and bizarre corporeal associations. In this topsy-turvy world,

9. Male masqueraders, showing mix of colcha and witch costumes, 1995.

food and carnal desire are equated through the gastro-genital symbolism be-loved of the Andalusian poet. "Hunger" has many meanings (Vasvari 1991).

   This erotic inventiveness is not simply the negation of the normal order but the creative enlivening of "the other side," of that which is denied. This defor-mation is accomplished by the means of florid metaphors, or what Bakhtin (1984:410) has called the grotesque realism of carnivalesque literature. In this idiom, the carnival poets stand firmly within the classical tradition of the master of Castilian storytelling, Cervantes. According to Bakhtin, it is just this carnivalesque spirit that makes the imagery of *Don Quixote* so powerful: "The fundamental trend of Cervantes' parodies is a 'coming down to earth,' a contact with the reproductive and generating power of the earth and of the body" (22). Indeed, as Bakhtin points out, Sancho's "fat belly (*panza*) and thirst still convey a powerful carnivalesque spirit." And Cervantes' whimsical use of everyday objects like the barber's basin, windmills, and so on, as fantasy props in the adventures of the Knight of the Sad Countenance, also fall into this tradition of Spanish surreal lyricism: "All these images form a typical grotesque carnival, which turns a kitchen and banquet into battle, kitchen utensils and shaving tools into arms and helmets, and wine into blood. Such is the first, carnival aspect of the material bodily images of *Don Quixote*. But it is precisely this aspect which creates the grand style of Cervantes' realism, his universal nature, and his deep popular utopianism" (Bakhtin 1984:23).

Similarly, the carnival poets employ the language of grotesque realism to bring the female principle down to earth. But in presenting discordant and negative messages about woman's "nature," the texts also represent the woman as a riddle or enigma, and in so doing promote masculine control and appropriation. The mixed messages in carnival rhetoric echo the Freudian notion of female sexuality as a psychological dark continent. That is, the poets publicly promote an image of the female body as mysterious, one that invites men to explore and conquer it.

Both body and text are carnivalized in the linguistic juxtaposition of the contradictions of gender, in the mastery over the sexual opposite, the woman as other, as an act of the erotic imagination. This juxtaposition of affective opposites, of desire and repulsion, neediness and autonomy, constitutes what Roland Barthes has called *figuration*: "Figuration is the way in which the erotic body appears . . . in the profile of the text" in protean forms (1976:55). Figuration relaxes the barrier between the represented object and the audience, creating a polymorphous unity of bodies that transforms the relations between subject, object, and symbol. In the texts the poets strip the female object of creative potential, in addition to stripping her naked. The parodist conceives the sexual other, the woman, as the recipient rather than merely the represented object of his judgmental narrative.

The lyricist, the maestro of Andalusian carnival, speaks the Bakhtinian "double-voiced" word. His discourse has a dual textual and semantic orientation that reinvents the masculine order as it invites woman — the sexual object — to participate in a ludic dialogue that ensures "natural" compliance with male dominance. The maestro is the master over woman and over reproduction. He has overthrown the sovereignty of the object; he has made woman, as much as his audience, his prisoner by wrapping her in a rich web of masculine oratory. Carnival poetry thus may be seen as the ultimate rhetorical weapon in the war of the sexes.[18]

But as in all other things, carnival verse also conveys a dual and contradictory message. The poems are also a kind of oratorical white flag signaling male supplication and surrender. As we shall see in the next chapter, another tradition stands in opposition to the chirigota burlesques. In their serious guise, as estudiantiles, the virtuosos sing of forgiveness and love, of female perfection, motherhood, and male dependency and inadequacy. In the spirit of carnival, the female, brought impossibly low by the comedians, is raised impossibly high by their counterparts.

Woman Redeemed
Estudiantil Laments

Negation in popular-festive imagery has never an abstract logical character. It is always something obvious, tangible. That which stands behind negation is by no means nothingness but the "other side" of that which is denied, the carnivalesque upside down. — Mikhail Bakhtin, *Rabelais and His World*

In the carnival coplas, the poets deconstruct the image of woman, which they then demonize, degrade, "carnivalize," and symbolically reconstruct in a form that is more to their liking. The poets break down woman's presumed haughtiness with the rhetorical solvent of "spicy" eroticism. Their songs are degrading in Bakhtin's sense of the term: bringing what is "upright down to earth," portraying woman in the scatological imagery of "the lower stratum of the body" (1984:21). In the carnivalesque inversion of woman, her indignity at the hands of the jesters is only partial; for the very same poets, in a quicksilver transformation typical of carnival, turn the defiled image right side up and put woman on a lofty pedestal. Woman is thereby redeemed, her purity restored. This topsy-turviness is related to the split image of woman and to inherent and unmodulated contrasts in Andalusian sexual culture.

In the Mediterranean countries where the cult of the Virgin Mary is most conspicuously observed (Carroll 1986), the critical symbol "woman" often takes on an essential dualism or affective bipolarity in the male consciousness and in male folklore. This means that in public discourse a split image of women, and an ambivalent attitude toward them, emerges that must be dealt with in carnival lore and custom. Carnival, being not one thing or the other but everything all at once, superimposes dual images without softening inherent ragged antitheses. As in the development of a photograph, in which negative and positive sequences take form in their respective chemical baths, in the song lyrics women emerge as starkly negative *and* positive.

A tendency to split woman symbolically in two, into good and bad, is probably a universal male tendency, at least in Western culture. Reflecting on male sexuality, Freud expressed this view on numerous occasions in his writings. Nancy Chodorow (1994:22) summarizes Freud's attitude as follows:

> Freud discusses women as sex objects to men in "A Special Type of Choice of Object Made by Men" and "On the Universal Tendency to Debasement in the Sphere of Love" (in which his developmental account implies that this "universal" tendency is found exclusively in the male). Men, he suggests, split women symbolically and erotically into mothers, or mothers and sisters, on the one hand, and prostitutes on the other. The former cannot be sexually desired, though they are supposed to be the kind of woman a man should marry; the latter, though they are maritally and socially forbidden, can be sexually desired. . . . Freud here gives us the psychodynamics of a split long present in Western culture, literature, and social organization.

Though ubiquitous, this symbolic splitting of the feminine in male thinking achieves its fullest expression in Mediterranean Catholicism, where the image of woman is on the one hand idealized as the sacred Madonna and on the other repudiated as the shameless whore (Giovannini 1981). In a cognitive juxtaposition of icons, the image of woman is at once high and low, pure and defiled. Nowhere in the Western world, except perhaps southern Italy, does the veneration of the Holy Mother achieve such emotive power as in Spain. "Not even in Italy, with some exceptions, did the cult of the Virgin attain such intensity and fervor. The defeat of the Spanish thesis on the Immaculate Conception at Trent proves this point" (Bennassar 1979:77). In southern Spain, and in Andalusia in particular, Marian worship reaches its pinnacle.

The maestros celebrate both sides of womanhood through the twistings and turnings of their carnival verse. Looking now at the "other side" of woman, we find the martyred mother, the self-sacrificing nurturer, the saintly caretaker, the chaste homemaker. The poets lovingly portray her as a sympathetic figure. She is rendered in the estudiantil carnival texts as the object of both veneration and identification.

Matriolatry

We begin with some typical verses from the carnivals of various towns in Seville Province. The first two songs presented below, dating from the middle of the Franco period, are basically idolatrous laments full of maudlin morality. Both songs are maternal elegies. They mourn the irreparable loss of the mother, whose virtue, the singer realizes, is fully appreciated only after her death and burial. The experience of parental loss is an emotional trauma that is portrayed as diminishing the singer, reducing and impoverishing him. The eternal light of the maternal tomb, the immortal love of mother and son, and the morbid veneration of the mother and her sacred memory are treated with considerable sentimentality. Both songs express deep regret and the singer's yearning for reunion with the image. The first song informs the audience about the unique value of the mother. She alone shows unconditional devotion to her son:

Recordemos todo ser humano	Remember that all human beings
Que estamos en el mundo por una mujer,	Come into the world through a woman.
Y que hablamos sin tener conciencia	We often speak thoughtlessly
De aquella mas buena	Of that best one of all [our mother]
Sin saber un porque.	Without really understanding what she means to us.
Nadie escoge madre	No one chooses the mother
Pa' vivir con ella.	Who bore him.
To'a su grandeza	But all of his glory and accomplishments
Se lo debe a ella.	are owing to her.
"Si una vez en la vida	"If once in his life
Cometió un delito	My son committed a sin,
Yo no veo culpa,	I see no blame, nor do I ever
Ni niego ese hijo.	Disown a wayward son.
Una venda tenemos en la frente	We [mothers] wear a blindfold
Que cubre la vista para nunca ver	That hides from our sight
Esa falta que todos tenemos.	Those faults which everyone has.
El bueno y el malo nadie se lo ve."	The good and bad: it's all the same to us."
[Spoken:]	[Spoken]:
¡La conciencia limpia es una fortuna!	A clear conscience is a blessing!
No hable de tu madre	Do not speak lightly of your mother,
Que no hay mas que una.	For you have but one.
Yo perdí a la mía,	I lost my own:
Tan pura y tan buena.	She was so pure and good.
¡En las ocasiones	How often I think of her!
Que me acuerdo de ella![1]	

The poem stresses the uniqueness of unconditional maternal love, a common theme in Andalusian folklore both within and outside carnival. The words convey the conviction that the mother alone offers nonjudgmental loyalty to her son. She is blind to his faults; she never makes a negative judgment; she accepts all. Her loss, therefore, should not be taken lightly. When she disappears, so does the sense that the world itself is a benevolent place. Recapturing that belief in a sympathetic, forgiving universe, the singer ends on a profoundly grieving note and invites the audience to share his adulation for the mother. The mother, in a sense, therefore represents the world as seen through a benevolent lens: she *is* the world.

As such riveting poems of mourning are sung, the mood of the audience changes dramatically. The hilarity ceases, and people adopt serious looks. Men listen attentively, respectfully. When the morbid words of the poet end and the last horn notes die away, the women in the crowd nod in agreement with the sentiments expressed, thinking of their own mothers and of their own children, perhaps. But the men in the crowd are louder in their response. They shout their feelings: "How true, maestro, you have spoken to my soul!" "How deeply you have touched me, maestro." "There is nothing so perfect as a mother's love." Some men may cry silently. The men are quietly composed for a few moments as they appreciatively offer drinks to the murga band.

In the next sample, the linked themes of maternal longing, personal diminishment, and symbolic restoration take on a more poignant aspect. Here, in a lament composed in the late 1950s, the singer dwells on early memories of a nurturing mother. The song emphasizes tactile images of warmth, softness, and sweet embracing fragrance. Such nostalgia for the mother conjures up dreamlike sensations of an enveloping, enchanted mutual bliss that contrast sharply with the harsh image of the sepulchre, death, and loss.

Si supiera lo buena es una madre	If only you knew how good a mother is,
¡Y la falta que te hace en toda la ocasión!	And the need you have of her always.
Yo quisiera tener la mía:	I wish I had mine back:
Soy desgraciado desde que faltó.	I am disconsolate since she passed away.
Ella me llevó en su seno,	She carried me in her womb
Y al mundo me trajo un dia;	And brought me into the world,
Y en una cuna de flores	And in a little cradle of flowers
Con esmero me mecía.	She rocked me lovingly.
Ella que en mi se esmeraba,	She cared for me so devotedly
Pa' que no me hiciera daño,	And protected me so carefully that

Hasta el viento que corría	Even when the wind blew gently,
Me tapaba con su manto.	She covered me with her shawl.
Hoy descansa en una tomba sagrada,	But today she rests in a sacred tomb,
La que nunca olvidaré.	She whom I will never forget.
Como madre, dentro de mi pecho,	Dear Mother, always within my breast
Como un recuerdo yo te llevaré.²	Will I carry your memory.

Another lament for the lost nurturer, this song repeats the gloomy sentiments of the first song, but it adds an interesting theme. Emphasis is placed on the physical intimacy between mother and son. The song conveys a poignant nostalgia for that childhood closeness, which is literal, tactile. It is brought out in the images and tropes of an almost somatic symphysis, symbolized by metaphors of engulfment: the womb, the cradle, and the mother's blanketing shawl. All these images conjure up a picture of the child, secure and satisfied at the mother's breast. Later the maternal "enwrapment" is reciprocated by the son, who carries a changeless representation of the mother eternally in his breast (*pecho*). The mutual incorporation enacts a restorative symmetry through which the mother's sacred memory is internalized organically, after her death, within the body of the adoring son, who carries and nourishes her as lovingly as she once carried him. This image of mutuality corresponds to what Chodorow (1994:25) calls "the mother who signifies the limitless narcissism of childhood, symbolized by her breast and her sometimes perfect love." Expressing that perfect symmetry, the poet, literally wrapped in his mother's bedclothes for carnival, sings of his own mother, held closely in his heart—literally, *pecho*, male breast.

Many men who have committed these songs to memory will repeat the words outside carnival for reassurance in times of stress. Thus recited in times of difficulty, the mother-songs bring great consolation in recitation. Such sentimental verses are said to illustrate the poet's ability to "reach down" (*profundizar*) into the depths of the human soul and unite all listeners in *sentimiento profundo* (deep emotion). When they recited such paeans to motherhood to me, which they always did with much feeling, the men would inevitably ask about my own mother: was she alive, they would inquire politely, and, if so, how was her health, and did I not miss her greatly? Many of these men seemed to believe that the loss of the mother is the single greatest tragedy that can befall a man. No one, certainly not a wife, can harbor such selfless "perfect" feelings toward another, and the inevitability of the mother's death made them sympathetic toward all life's unfortunates. It was for them the universal human tragedy, comparable to original sin.

In estudiantil verse, then, the internalization of this miraculous lost object triumphs over both death and the physical separation from the departed. The elegy itself, through memory, traces an almost Proustian act of recapturing the past, represents a magical reversal in which the son declares himself the nurturer of his mother's image. Such obsessive feelings are well known in psychological literature. Freud described a similar response in his discussion of melancholia (excessive mourning) as the restoration of the love object through incorporation and identification (1917:249). Freud argued that the introjection of the idealized deceased into the self is a refusal to "let go," an attempt to defeat death by denying the separateness of egos (1917:249–250). The grieving singer, metaphorically becoming *both* the suckled child and the nurturing mother, thereby magically regresses to what Robert Stoller, in his work on male gender identity, calls "the blissful, frustrationless, traumaless experiences in the symbiosis with mother" (1976:184). Stoller believes such regressive longings to be a universal affect in all males.

Naturally, motherhood is sacral, in accordance with the ecstatic fantasies of childhood. The beatified image presented is clearly also an appeal to the supposedly instinctual maternal tenderness of women. Another song concludes with almost exactly the same sentiment of tender nostalgia and ardent attachment:

Como una madre, no hay na',	There is nothing like a mother,
Aunque este en la sepultura.	Even if she lies in her tomb.
Ningún hijo pasa pena	No son can experience pain
Mientras su madre le dura.[3]	While she remains with him.

Many similar songs convey this feeling of longing for the mother. They also poetically enact a renewed symbiosis after death. Most are even more mawkish and clichéd than those just cited and do not bear repeating here. All the carnival verses about the "good mother" strongly emphasize her unqualified benevolence and protectiveness, but they also get across the message about how different she is from the selfish, unfeeling woman of the "other" variety. Without the mother, danger and emptiness threaten. And all the songs express a similar narcissistic longing for the passive nurturing experienced in childhood, suggesting either a return to the womb or the bliss of nursing. Such sentiments of dependency, vulnerability, and pathos, of course, are never publicly articulated by men on other occasions. Carnival permits the feeling open expression; carnival songs, once memorized, become oral talismans warding off danger.

We move on to another kind of serious copla. Our next song turns the mother-son unity around through a second inversion. Through the common vehicle of mother-worship, it communicates a didactic message about the anguish of elderly widows and urges filial piety. That is, it instructs the man on his duty to the mother who has suffered for him. What is most interesting in the lyrics is the contrast between the sentimental lament, with its invitation to pity, and the bitter, mocking tone that characterizes songs about old women from the comic genre. The chirigota poets depict widows, and old crones generally, if not as "crazy" or "wanton," as in the songs in the previous chapter, then as "dragons," "tomcats," "lizards," witches, and the like. The serious songs, by contrast, replete as they are with images of feminine sacrifice, celebrate feminine purity as embodied in the mother's self-abnegation. The figure of the old hag undergoes a spectacular metamorphosis.

Vi que lloraba una anciana	Once I saw an old woman weeping,
Con sentimientos profundos.	Racked with the deepest despair,
Es que no tiene familia	All because she had no family
O está sola en este mundo.	And was plunged into black loneliness.
Siete hijos yo he criado	Seven children have I raised, she cried,
Honrada, pura, y decente,	I am honorable, pure, and decent,
Y ahora mis hijos no quieren	But now my children ignore me,
Que se lo cuente a la gente	Ungrateful, indifferent, and heartless.
Por una mujer cualquiera	As if I were just any woman
Que se la encontró en la calle,	Passing on the street,
Ahora paso y no me mira,	They ignore me, yet they know
Sabiendo que soy su madre.	I am still and always will be their mother.
Pa' una madre no hay hijo malo,	But for a mother there is no bad child,
Te perdona tus motivos,	And so I forgive you all your cruelty,
Pero cuando nos casamos,	But you must remember that when you leave home,
Pa su madre no es el mismo.	Your old mother pines away for loneliness.
Ese egoismo embustero	This heartless egoism of the soul
Separa nuestro cariño.	Eats away at our natural sentiments,
Yo siempre seré tu madre,	But I will always be your mother
[. . . . . lines lost . . . .]	
A veces de ella murmura;	My children, you may speak ill of your mother,
Se viste de luto negro	Yet you will dress in blackest mourning
Cuando está en la sepultura.	When she lies cold in her grave.
¡Que rostro lleva de pena!	Yes, when I'm gone, you will

Que el mundo va demonstrando	Put on a face of inconsolable grief,
Como una madre no hay na'	But however you fool others,
Aunque esté en la sepultura.	You are only deceiving yourselves.
Ningún hijo pasa pena	In this world there is no love like a mother's;
Mientras su madre le dura.[4]	Although she may lie dead in her tomb,
	No child will suffer,
	So long as he remembers her love.

No child can suffer while his mother lives. The mother is a martyr, a figure of compassion. No wonder the cult of the Madonna reigns supreme! The next text, like the narrative above, discourses on the selfless purity of maternal love. But here it is celebrated in an outpouring of grief over the tragic death of a son. The event in question happened sometime in the 1940s. The young man died of a gunshot wound while away from town, under mysterious circumstances. He was thought to have committed suicide, very unusual in Andalusia. The case was never solved. Some hint, though, at a violent love triangle, others at an obscure political assassination. No matter—the point the poet makes is that the moral beauty of the mother's undying adoration of her child is the most perfect human emotion and one familiar to all mothers and all sons. The child's death signals the mother's death also, a kind of emotional death in life, because the extinguishment of the "maternal ray of light" marks the end of her reason for living.

Triste y fatal noticia	The saddest and most terrible news
Para una anciana,	That an old woman can hear
Leyendo muy de prisa	Came suddenly one morning
Correspondencia de la mañana.	In a missive from afar.
Desesperada gritó	Distraught, she cried out:
¡Que la Virgen te perdone,	Oh my son, may the blessed Virgin
Hijo de mi corazón	Absolve you, may God protect you,
Y fruto de mis amores!	Son of my heart,
El sentimiento me "ajogá":	Fruit of my love!
Mi muerte será	Grief overwhelms me:
Al fallarme la aureola;	Your bloody signature
Rayo de luz maternal	Signs my death warrant too;
Descansa, hijo del alma,	It signals the quenching
Que nunca te olvidaré,	Of the torch of my maternal love.
Y hasta mi tumba sagrada	Rest peacefully, oh son of my soul,
Tu retrato llevaré.	I will never forget you,
Perdonemos nuestros enemigos;	And until I too rest in my sacred tomb,

Me despide hasta la eternidad	I will carry your blessed portrait on my breast.
La conciencia que dicte justicia	Forgive us all, friends and enemies,
Para que procese	For I hasten to meet my son in eternity,
La acción criminal.[5]	And to seek vengeance for this criminal act.

The Theme of the Fallen Woman

Turning from the sentimental matriolatry above, we look now at the theme of the dishonored woman in carnival coplas. In this estudiantil genre, which is often tragic or elegiac in tone, a sympathetic identification with the persecuted woman emerges. The poet's empathy with the lowly woman crosses the boundary of sex and all the barriers of moral probity that separate the upright from the fallen. The effect is the exact opposite of that produced by the malicious condemnation and satire of the chirigotas. The following songs touch on the subject of the deceived virgin, always a compelling theme in Andalusian carnival verse. The first song, which asks for Christian forgiveness, urges listeners to put themselves in the place of the ruined family and not to shun the unhappy girl. Thus in this poem empathy becomes a device to teach a moral lesson, in contrast to chirigota satires that encourage the venting of harmful feelings against the wanton woman. Timothy Mitchell (1988:94) speaks of the "persecutory mythopoetics" of the deviant or sexual transgressor in Spain. In this case, instead of blaming the deflowered girl, the poet places the full burden of guilt upon the seducer. Defying public opinion, the poet takes the side of the fallen woman. He feels for her and with her.

Vestida de velo blanco	Dressed in white linen,
Y un ramo de azahar en la mano,	An orange blossom in her hand,
A la iglesia se dirije	At the church she waited,
Como todo fiel cristiano,	A devout Catholic soul.
Granaba como una rosa,	Shimmering like a rose,
Toda llena de ilusión,	Full of innocent illusions,
A echarse las bendiciones	Eager to make her vows,
Ante un altar le juro.	She awaits the benediction.
El hombre que ella elegía	But, alas, the man to whom she gave herself
Nunca se llego a pensar	Has abandoned her, has cruelly spurned her,
Que cuando fruto tuviera	Never even caring that
El la iba a abandonar.	She carried his child in her womb.

No abandones lo que es tuyo,	Men, do not abandon what is yours,
Que nadie te ha de alabar	For we all know truly
Que el que malamente anda	That he who acts badly toward others
Malamente ha de acabar.	Will end up badly himself.
No te rías sin conciencia,	Do not laugh at her, do not
Después si no te agredaba	Mock her misfortune, you who have seduced her,
Hombre no a verla engañao,	For you have deceived only yourself.
No le llamas prostituta	The rest of you, do not call this woman a prostitute,
Aunque la veas en ese sino,	Although you see her dishonored,
Que fue un hombre sin conciencia	For remember that it was an immoral man
Que la puso en el camino.	Who deceived her, who drove her to ruin.
Todo aquel que tenga hermana,	All you men who have a sister,
Que puede ser que la tenga,	Or whoever might have a sister some day
No se puede vengar mañana	Remember, before you yourself suffer this fate:
Si a ti te duele tu hermana,	Whatever befalls my own sister today
A mi me duele la mía.	May befall your sister tomorrow.
Y ahora no podrías	So act honorably toward my sister,
De la deuda que debías.[6]	As I do toward yours.

The song invites identification. Every man has a sister, or a mother, so every man must acknowledge his own solidarity with the plight of women. The next song, from La Campana, also deals sentimentally with the loss of women's innocence. Its subject is the delicacy of young girls and the fleeting beauty of romantic love. Dating from the 1940s, the "time of hunger" after the Civil War, the lyrics attack the selling of girls for money, which apparently occurred at this time among the desperate.

Un severo castigo	Our laws decree severe penalties
Las leyes imponen	Against the corruption of minors,
Con la trata de blancas	And we must guard against
Y la corrupción de menores.	Such treatment of young girls.
Es preciso que vigilen,	We must pay attention,
Deber de la autoridad,	We must respect the authorities
A esas 'matronas' que viven	When it comes to these procuresses
De ese comercio inmoral	And their vile commerce.
Aproven la ignorancia:	They take advantage of ignorance;

El lujo y la plata	They use promises of luxury and money,
Sirven de cadena,	They use tricks and evil stratagems
Para poder deshojar	To lure these innocent lilies from their homes.
Aquella blanca azucena.	The poor girls are dishonored, disgraced,
Luego se van despreciadas	Dragged off to a brothel
Y arrojan al lupanar	After they've been violated
Porque ha sido violada	And lost their beautiful virginity.
La hermosa virginidad.	They will never know the flower of real passion,
No conocen la flor de pasión,	The font of all virtue;
La semilla de toda virtud;	But they will forever keep
Pero queda en su corazón,	Within their hearts
Grabado a puñales	Engraved with bitter gall,
Con la ingratitud.[7]	The memory of their downfall and disgrace.

In another specimen, from the mid-1950s in Fuentes de Andalucía, the poet also commiserates with fallen women. His song, too, condemns gossip and elicits empathy for the sinner as a potential mother, sister, or daughter. The lyrics specifically preach against spiteful laughter at disgraced women. Again, although he does not speak in her voice as in the songs above, the poet gives the impression of powerful identification with the disgraced woman, who is depicted as the hapless victim of an impersonal "fate," so that individual blame is minimized and dissipated. Using floral imagery, the poet likens women to fragrant and regenerative beings, to purity and goodness.

Mujeres puras y decentes	Women, so pure and decent,
Grana como una ampola	Are the apple of their father's eye,
Su padre lleno de orgullo	He is full of pride to see his daughter
Al verla pura, pura y frondosa.	So pure and so radiantly growing.
Aquella que por desgracia	Yes, sometimes a woman may stray
Se aparten del buen camino,	From the righteous path,
Pues no le llamemos mala,	But do not call her wicked,
Porque ese será su sino.	Because the fault lies with her fate, not with her.
La desgracia ella la mete en su casa	She has been disgraced, yes;
Al pecar por edad,	Her family distraught and ruined,
Y su padre la está mirando	Her father now feels only pain
Siempre con pena por ser desgraciada	When he remembers her disgrace.
Muchos seres de este mundo	Many people in this cruel world

Que les gustan murmurar:	Enjoy snickering at misfortune;
Se ríen de las mujeres	They gossip about and they laugh at
Cuando se ven desgraciada.	A poor unfortunate woman.
Date cuenta y no te ría	But remember this, and cease your mockery,
Que tu madre pa' ti es buena	Your own mother who is so good to you
Y tambien puede ser un hombre	May have strayed from the straight and narrow
Se hubiera reído de ella.	And some man may be laughing at her too.
Tiene hermana, a ti no te da la gana	You have a sister; remember her
De tenerla murmurada.	Before you gossip about others.
Que no toque, que como toque;	What befalls others may just as easily
Quiera o no quiera, te ha de conformar.[8]	Happen to you, for we are all only too human.

Empathy for the Woman

The "serious" carnival poems I have presented are by no means literary gems. Riddled with malapropisms, stilted metaphors, platitudes, and raw sentimentality, these estudiantil ditties often border on doggerel. Other interpretations than those given here are doubtless possible. Perhaps, too, a different sampling of poems might produce different interpretive results. To the possible charge of overinterpretation of the sentiments expressed in the maternal elegies, however, I would like to point out that the emotional involvement of the audience, though intense, cannot easily be communicated without long descriptive digressions. Still, the poems are interesting and useful if considered in the light of the poet's relationship with his audience.

The relationship between singers and audience reveals several distinct meanings. As Lila Abu-Lughod (1985:258) suggests in her analysis of Egyptian Bedouin genres, the alternative discourse of poetry provides a means of personal expression through which "discrepant" sentiments reaffirm central cultural values in settings like Egypt or Spain where stoicism is required of men. In the Andalusian case, men's feelings of helplessness, loss, and dependency, which on the surface are at odds with the masculine code of autonomy, are communicated through the poet's "deep" voice as appeals to a virtuous motherhood. The poetry reconciles sets of "contradictory sentiments." It also strengthens primordial values and political relations by illustrating and condemning the forces endangering them.

What the estudiantil poet does, then, is to express, legitimize, and publicize masculine fantasies and anxieties by overcoming the distance between the sexes, a distance which is exaggerated and defended by the jokesters. This contradiction can occur only during carnival, when all barriers are at once magnified and smashed. A successful poetic performance is one of moral transformation in which the inexpressible desires of men also become the wishes of women. In this way, the songs represent the dialectic of an "emergent" culture (see Williams 1973:11). That is, they are improvisations that both interpret and corroborate shared longings and ideals (matriolatry and its obverse) and turn these feelings to political use to put woman in her place and to establish masculine hegemony. But since the songs are both admonitory and empathetic, both "serious" and "comic," they also break down this very same structure that distances the sexes, by merging the egos of the son and the mother, by putting the male listener in the woman's "place," and by inviting him to share the pathos of the woman's persecution.

The immense popularity of the "serious" carnival songs and their universality also have meaning. In his work on male psychology in Andalusia, Stanley Brandes (1979, 1980b) has shown how Andalusian men, disunited politically in so many ways, achieve solidarity and moral unity through the shared enjoyment of public folklore, art, and poetry. The shared quality helps create the contours of both the physical and the moral community (Brandes 1980b: 12–13). As a genre of collective representation, these songs tell us much about how Spanish men conceptualize the social world through the prism of childhood experiences retained and a collective dream of maternal devotion. The mother is always with the singer; he carries forever within his heart a female representation — his female side, his savior, his alter ego.

Splitting and Psychic Symbolization

Of course, the lyrics also have a psychological function. Psychocultural and psychoanalytic explanations have been proposed for the cognitive polarization that drives the Spanish poets' work, as well as for the more universal play of regressive costuming, which is, after all, an alternative form of self-expression for the tongue-tied. Anne Parsons (1969) sees male ambivalence in southern Europe from a Freudian perspective, as resulting from unresolved oedipal wishes. She postulates that these are attributable to prolonged mother-son intimacy. In southern Italy the mother-son bond, augmented by an absentee father, intensifies erotic ties to the mother, which later inhibit libidinal attachments to other women. This drawback is later resolved by psychologically splitting the feminine love object into the virginal Madonna and the wanton temptress (Giovannini 1981).

In a review article, George Saunders (1981) widens the discussion about the mother-son relationship and its vicissitudes. Instead of stressing oedipal conflicts (though he does not discount them), he emphasizes the role of pre-oedipal attachment to the mother, especially via oral gratification. In his opinion, the moral conflict is generated by an "intense, indulgent, smotheringly affectionate but simultaneously aggressive style of mothering" (1981:457). This kind of mothering, he believes, satisfies infantile dependency wishes only too well and prolongs them by discouraging separation or individuation. Thus, later attempts to assert masculine independence are "correspondingly frustrated" (1981:457). In order to separate from the engulfing, binding mother, the boy "splits" the image of the nurturing mother from that of the "hostile, devouring, grasping mother."

This splitting is reflected as ambivalence in public culture. Similar arguments have been made recently for Hispanic culture by Marcelo Suarez-Orozco and Alan Dundes (1984), among others, who also regard Hispanic machismo as the resolution of a conflicted and insecure male identity. Both arguments are potentially useful. They fit the Freudian notion that the pattern of the boy's libidinal tie to his mother provides a psychic model for his adult heterosexual attachments.

Although this psychic splitting is probably universal, the southern European countries stand out in this regard. As Michael Carroll (1986:10) puts it in his survey of Marian worship: "Mediterranean scholars . . . have always noted that the Mary cult seems to be a distinctive feature of the Latin Catholic countries, primarily Italy and Spain, that border the northern edge of the Mediterranean." This is because of the well-known social respect paid to legitimate motherhood in Latin Catholicism, and to a degree in the Orthodox traditions of the eastern Mediterranean (Dubisch 1993). In Spain (as in southern Italy and Portugal), local cults have long centered on Marian worship, the various local Virgins; in parts of Greece, the "most venerated holy figure" is female (Dubisch 1993:281). Indeed the Virgin, as a moral model of the "good mother," is a central cultural icon, exceeding in importance the entire pantheon of male deities, saints, and lords throughout southern Europe (Carroll 1986) — but again, especially in Spain and southern Italy. In local worship, motherhood is venerated with an almost religious intensity, and the good mother remains the personification of life-giving cultural values.

Such veneration for a specifically feminine ideal puts men at a disadvantage in daily life. While it is impossible for males to identify fully with either God or Christ, or to achieve a sanctified status, every woman can emulate Mary through legitimate, sacrificial motherhood. In addition, in contrast to many parts of the world (Shapiro and Linke 1996), in southern Europe, few ideas about women as agents of pollution or the dangers inherent in sexual contact receive cultural endorsement. All the taboos about childbirth, including the postpartum period of quarantine and various prophylactics against the evil eye, are in fact intended to protect the mother-child dyad from the potential dangers of the exterior world, men among them.

Silent Splitting: Cross-Dressing

So the male singer identifies with the sexual "other," with woman, both as the life-giving mother and as the innocent victim of society. Both are tragic and noble figures entirely at odds with the cruel chirigota caricatures, which defame women and demand punishment and persecution. The powerful, and positive, transsexual identification is reflected as much in the silent rituals of carnival transvestism as it is in the affective and moral dualism of the texts.

One area where this ambivalence toward women is dramatically manifested is in the cross-dressing styles of the men. As we have seen, carnival clowns generally take on two female roles. Many of the transvestites, usually men in their thirties or forties or even in late middle age, are "traditional" colcha-dressers. They appropriate the pure white linen colcha from their old mother's bedroom, usually during a rapid "raid," which the old woman manages to avoid noticing. Thus armed, they then meet privately in pairs or small groups in order to enact the "enwrapping" ritual in which they wind the linen many times around their bodies, now "feminized" by the addition of the appropriate maternal padding. Adding a white sheet, towel, or other blank material over the face to ensure absolute disguise, and throwing on outer layers of scarves, mantillas, aprons, or other female outer garments (Figures 3, 5, 6, 9), they saunter out into the streets to promenade regally for hours, often instigating little sexual minidramas such as those described above.

Although the colcha-clowns perform a parody of womanhood and although they make fun of femininity, their behavior is never truly misogynist. They parade calmly and majestically through the streets, occasionally lifting skirts or pushing out their "breasts" for the admiration of bystanders, but they do not attack others with violence, and they do not engage in lewd or offensive behavior. Feminized and motherly, they thus stand in contrast to the more ferocious parodies of the "witches" and female demons who also pour out into the carnival streets to attack bystanders and each other.

Garbed in horrid rags and sinister masks, the carnival witches and demons are usually younger men in drag. The witches project a more malevolent image of femininity than the colcha-clowns, one that is truly frightening (Figures 9, 10). Their bodies are hideously misshapen, thanks to liberal padding. The

deformed creatures hobble menacingly through the streets, flailing and shout-
ing at bystanders. In keeping with the spirit of grotesquerie, the witches renounce the staid colchas, instead throwing on mismatched rags and all manner of loose or discarded female clothing to create a purposely ugly costume,
identifiable only as monstrously female. Their method is bricolage — collecting
stray items wherever they find them, stitching together clashing elements to
create a thing of shreds and patches. Their masks are not blank sheets like
those of the colcha queens but rather hideous witches' or blood-soaked demons' faces — Halloween or bizarre graveyard images. The men either construct the masks out of materials at hand or, failing that, buy them from
costume stores in the city and add such details as bloodstains and scars.

Like the more stately colcha-clowns, the ugly witches also parade boldly
through the streets. But they are wilder, less controlled, and their cavorting
more aggressive. They corner passersby and flaunt their grotesque sexuality,
provokingly, tauntingly. The witches surround people and scratch like tomcats. Venomous and loathsome, they are both ugly and threatening.

Some Closing Thoughts

The transvestite clowns exemplify two images of women. One is softly
maternal, the other hideously destructive. These two reflect the affective dualism that we found in the songs of the two murga genres, the chirigotas and the
estudiantiles. The carnival poets alternately present woman as mother and as
whore-witch, the former sweet, gentle, asexual; the latter violent, grotesque,
hypersexed. But of course both cultural images are acted out by male transvestites and represent male fantasies.

At one level, we might opine, along with many of the men who participate in
the carnival cross-dressing, that the colcha-clowns are "like" the mother and
the witches "like" the mother-in-law, the latter being a ferocious scourge that
all men fear; and that the masqueraders thus represent the two halves of
woman. At a higher level, in Spain the male theme of magical enwrapment
within the maternal colcha corresponds to the overvaluation of the mother-
son dyad and of "sacrificial" mothering in Latin Catholicism (Carroll 1986).

The aim of carnival mimicry is therefore not simply, as it is in many other
transvestite rituals, the denigration or "humiliation" of women in any unequivocal sense (Shapiro and Linke 1992). Rather, the objective is the splitting
of womanhood into good and bad halves. The estudiantil poets seek to restore
the child's ties to the good, split-off mother, just as the chirigota poets seek to
distance and blame the other half, the frustrating, icy-hearted she-demon. The
serious poets take the route of regressive denial of time to triumph over sepa-

ration trauma (as well as to deny the split-off bad mother, who is often represented by the mother's alter ego, the mother-in-law, a stock villain in Andalusian folklore). I think this interpretation goes a long way toward explaining the intense feelings of excitement and childlike enchantment that so many men experience during the colcha ritual. At carnival-time, men are able to experience both aspects of womanhood simultaneously, to become fully disinhibited and to engage their complex feminine side.

The ambiguities of the female object as represented in the Spanish minstrels' words are exactly the qualities that, as Bakhtin notes (1984), characterize all Latin carnivals. The images are both positive and negative, simultaneously gratifying and denying, so that the woman's body furnishes both the arena and the materials for symbolic deformations. Bakhtin writes: "The popular tradition is in no way hostile to woman and does not approach her negatively. In this tradition woman is essentially related to the material bodily lower stratum; she is the incarnation of this stratum that degrades and regenerates simultaneously. She is ambivalent. She debases, brings down to earth, lends a bodily substance to things, and destroys; but, first of all, she is the principle that gives birth. She is the womb. Such is woman's image in popular comic traditions" (1984:240). Both the songs and the costumes of Spanish carnival portray the men's ambivalent feelings about women and about the femininity lurking within their own psychological makeup.

But of course the men find no resolution, because both good and bad sides of woman are simultaneously frustrating and gratifying. Even the contradictions contain contradictions. The good mother offers food, love, and care, but she also dominates; the whore offers sex but coldly exacts payment, depleting the man. The dialectic is interminable because the antitheses renew themselves at (and on) every stage of life.

6

Macho Man and Matriarch

Disguise our bondage as we will,
'Tis woman, woman, rules us still. — Thomas Moore, "Sovereign Woman"

We saw previously that the carnival vocabulary and its rituals together provide a key to Andalusian men's ambivalent relationship to women — most important, to the mother. The carnival message was shown to be not only misogynist but also, paradoxically, reverent toward woman. The serious estudiantil genre provides men with a regressive experience and yearns nostalgically toward the lost child-mother symbiosis and an idealization of womanhood.

Perhaps understandably, most studies of Mediterranean codes of masculinity ignore all evidence of pre-oedipal fixations in men and take the grown man and his adult heterosexuality as the starting point (see, for example, Chodorow 1994). Regardless of the geographical area under study, many anthropologists who have broached this subject, in fact, continue to look at the adult man's relationship to his wife and potential lovers as the key to the meaning of male sexuality. In other words, anthropologists, like most other observers of men and women, remain fixated on the "normal" and the culturally manifest — on conventional heterosexuality.

But as the poet said, the boy is father to the man. When it comes to understanding masculine self-image in places like Spain, the father is perhaps con-

10. Witch clown, 1991 (note padding).

sidered as an influence on the boy (Murphy 1983b), but the mother is often left out. Here we will ask, What about the mother's role in male development? After all, given the division by sex of labor in southern Spain, where the mother is so utterly housebound and devoted to childcare, it is the mother, not the father, who is the educator of the young son and thus by far the greater influence on the boy in his formative years.

The mother must therefore contribute somehow to the creation of the masculine codes and mentality that we looked at earlier. But how does she influence the boy's psychic development? And how does she affect his fledgling masculine identity in childhood? Because of the central importance of this question to carnival ritual and, as we have seen, to the genre of mother-oriented "serious" poetry, we must digress here to consider the mother's role in the creation of a particularly Spanish manhood. For reasons that will become clear, coming to grips with this issue helps understand both carnival as a commentary on the masculine-feminine dichotomy and the enveloping culture that nurtures carnival.

Masculinity and the Anthropologists

One unintended side benefit of feminist revisionism in cultural anthropology since the 1970s has been the reinvigoration of cross-cultural study of male gender identity and of masculinity cults (Herdt 1982; Chodorow 1994; Vale de Almeida 1996). For Hispanicists this study inevitably invites informed investigation of that good gray concept machismo, which is so often equated with Hispanic notions of manhood (Paredes 1971; Gutmann 1996). While "machismo" is a word rarely heard in everyday speech in Spain, except among educated elites, ethnographers frequently use the term, usually with little rigor, to describe a supposedly "hegemonic" complex (Gutmann 1996:19; Vale de Almeida 1996) emphasizing male dominance, sexual assertion, and hyper-virile display in Latin America and Iberia.

Despite surface differences, causal models of this hegemonic (or dominant) masculinity seem to converge on one point. The consensus is that such a hypermale code, despite thematic variations, is at least partly attributable to endopsychic compromise-formations. These involve compensatory efforts to shore up a fragile male identity or to defend against intolerable residues of feminine identification or psychic attachments (Ingham 1986; Chodorow 1994). In all this, the concept of gender identity is crucial as a heuristic tool in broaching masculine self-image; but the concept is rarely examined or justified either by Hispanicist anthropologists or by social psychologists. What exactly is gender identity, and how does it differ from sexual orientation? How does gender identity figure in the developmental processes of psychic and social maturation? It is clear from an observation of the transvestism and the pseudohomosexual hilarity of carnival that this gender identity, whatever that really is, represents a critical issue for the Andalusian men who wait excitedly to metamorphose into one or another variant of "woman" for the February follies. Why is female impersonation a matter of such intense interest? Here we must look at the mother's role, for the mother is the first and possibly most important of the young man's cross-sexual relationships and influences.

Male Gender Identity

Already with Freud, there is a certain ambiguity in the concept of gender identity and its forerunner, the undifferentiated concept of ego identification itself. In a late work on the ego (1922:61) Freud notes that "identification, in fact, is ambivalent from the very first; it can turn into an expression of tenderness as easily as into a wish for someone's removal." Later attempts to codify Freud's use of the concept of identification have failed, largely because the idea is scattered throughout his works, without any single unifying definition. Moreover, he often uses "the same terms to refer to what are basically quite different concepts" (Bronfenbrenner 1960:14–15) in discussing the matter. One basic theme, however, is the continuing emphasis on ambivalent or conflicted affect in relation to the cathected object (that is, one in which the subject is emotionally invested). Identification of the child with the parent involves, on one hand, love and the wish to incorporate and merge; on the other, love and the wish to remove the parental object. This theme had its inception in Freud's discussion of primary narcissism and other *anlagen*, or precursors to ego development, the former often described as the primitive psychic dissolution of ego boundaries between mother and nursing child (Greenson 1968:370).

Later theorists have tried to substantiate the concept of ego identification (see Chodorow 1994 for a review). Their attempts have led to some basic conceptual distinctions between sexual orientation and gender role, from which has developed the separate notion of a gender identity. This is distinguished from both sexual orientation and a more broadly defined ego identification, although it forms an organic component of both. John Money and Anka Ehrhardt (1972), for example, employ a tripartite definition of gender identity, which includes (1) an early private sense of gender, or *core* gender identity, (2) the gender *role* of publicly appropriate gender-specific behaviors, and (3) a sexual orientation appropriate to items 1 and 2. Stoller (1968, 1976) actually leaves primary sexual characteristics out of the picture entirely, distinguishing clearly between gender *identity* and gender *role*. Gender identity, he states (1968:10), "starts with the knowledge and awareness, either conscious or unconscious, that one belongs to one sex and not the other." Gender role comprises expected behavior and is entirely different from, sometimes incompatible with, gender identity — as in transsexuals (1976). The uniform assumption of cognitive polarization in the formation of gender identity unites these and other definitions. Usually the child has an awareness, conscious or not, of being either male like the father or female like the mother but not both. This awareness is a gradual and often problematic process of epigenetic progression.

It appears then that whatever minimal agreement exists about the definition occurs with regard to a dichotomous "core" gender self-awareness. One chooses to be either male or female, but not both simultaneously. There exist an internalized self-identification, either conscious or unconscious, and a distinguishable public persona that conforms to accepted cultural norms: a core identity and a public "periphery" (Stoller 1976:184–185). Both individuals and societies impose an either/or choice between male and female, for both endopsychic and social reasons. These, of course, may be contradictory or ambiguous (Gilmore 1990a), but that is a separate issue, involving notions of deviance. What matters is the universal need for relatively unequivocal self-assignment during maturation and a consistency, or "gender constancy"

(Maccoby 1979:197), as the basis for further consolidation of a necessary ego identity and social role. There are also, it seems, various organically connected or sequential stages in the growth and crystallization of gender identity (Stoller 1976). Additionally, certain internal contradictions and hurdles must be resolved or reconciled through what Willard Gaylin (1992:xxvi) refers to as the initiating pathways to adulthood. What are these pathways, and where do they lead?

Already with Freud we see a uniform basic approach. He and his followers see the onset of the identification process as more or less diphasic, much as they interpret genital sexuality as diphasic development. The first, or "preliminary," stage of identification occurs during the period of symbiotic dependency between child and mother from birth to the earliest stirrings of individuation in the child (Greenson 1968:372; Mahler et al. 1975). At this time, ego and object are as yet indistinguishable for the child, and no *gender* identification exists as such. Mother and child are fused in a single undifferentiated pattern that Freud calls primary narcissism (1914). Later, during the period of separation and individuation, the child begins to make distinctions between the self and external objects, discovering anatomical gender-specific differences. This embryonic ego differentiation is the basis for the cross-sexual gender identification process that is both the consequence and the resolution of subsequent oedipal traumas. During this period the child forms a heterosexual object-choice that complements the formation of a nascent gender identity. Also, the child has a sense of the self as being anatomically and morally like the mother or father (Freud 1925).

Most early psychoanalysts apparently believed that a solid, differentiated gender identity developed more or less simultaneously with sexual object-choice during the oedipal phase, not before (Bronfenbrenner 1960:25). But later authors have argued that gender identity formation actually *precedes* the oedipal period and is fully under way during the period of maternal intimacy in which the child is psychically not yet fully differentiated from the mother. The work of many clinical psychologists posits a very early pre-oedipal gender identity *before* sexual orientation, between approximately eighteen and thirty-six months (Luria 1979:173). If that is the case, then the inescapable consequence is that boys as well as girls form an infantile and therefore inextinguishable "protofeminine" identification with the mother (Stoller 1976:184). For boys in patriarchal societies, it includes the components of what will later be experienced as an antithetical and ego-dystonic femininity; that is, a feminine identification unacceptable to the ego ideal (see Chodorow 1978:174). It follows from this argument that the primary female identification necessitates for boys a complementary developmental process of disidentification from the mother and counteridentification with the father or another appropriate male figure (Greenson 1968:370). As Stoller puts it: "There are special problems in a boy developing his masculinity that are not present in the development of femininity in little girls. In contrast to Freud's position that masculinity is the natural state and femininity at best a successful modification of it, Greenson and I . . . feel that the infant boy's relationship to his mother makes the development of feminine qualities more likely. . . . The boy . . . must manage to break free from the pull of his mother's . . . femaleness and femininity" (1968:263).

The theory gaining credence in psychoanalytic circles (see Gaylin 1992) is that masculine gender identity is problematic and "elusive" (Chodorow 1974: 50). This idea of masculinity as the "unending quest, unattainable goal" (Levant 1995:134), is the basis for the interpretation of macho codes as reaction formations against gender identity conflict. The sociological or contextual component has to do with aspects of socialization as well as with domestic and community organization. The concept of a primary or protofeminine identification and psychic merging with the mother is rather hypothetical and calls for amplification. It is insufficient to say that the boy identifies with the mother "symbiotically"; the form of this symbiosis and its endopsychic repercussions have to be clarified before the concept can become an explanatory model in culture study that can be built upon.

In this context Freud's discussion of primary narcissism and its correlate, anaclitic object-choice (1914), is of some utility. Freud refers to the early symbiosis of mother and child as frequently producing an anaclitic form of attachment; he means "leaning" or "reclining upon," that is, indicative of a reciprocal dependency. Freud says that this dependency is more characteristic of males (1914:88), but he does not elaborate. "Anaclitic" refers to the choice of an object of libidinal attachment on the basis of resemblance or concordance, rather than difference or complementarity (see Chodorow 1994:26 ff. for a useful critique of Freud). A later psychoanalyst, Orval Mowrer (1950), uses the terms "developmental" or "defensive identification" to describe the infant's wishes for somatic unity. Of course, it is exactly this wish for ego unity that is most strikingly expressed in the sentimental carnival poetry about the lost mother.

Let us take the idea one step further. This identification between the boy and the mother seems biologically grounded in a narrowing of libido to autoerotic satisfactions in which the "ego-instincts of self-preservation" are the motivating constitutional factor (Freud 1914:87). According to Freud, anaclitic identification differs functionally from later postoedipal associations because it is based on prephallic nutritional instincts. It derives specifically from fear of *object loss* rather than from fear of loss of the object's love or from fear of

punishment by vengeful parental figures. The immature ego attempts to neutralize the danger of object loss by fantasizing a psychic unity, incorporating
the object, and failing to recognize ego boundaries between self and caretaker.

Consequently, although Freud does not make an explicit connection between anaclitic object-choice and feminine gender identification, he does suggest that this ego unity of mother and child is basically a feminine *form* of
identification because it is passive and promotes an oral-incorporative mode of
reality testing rather than an active and phallic one (1933:121). He intimates
that unless transcended in later development, the ego unity can lead to sexual
inversion in men. The implicit connection proposed between oral dependency
wishes and the blurring of ego boundaries of mother and infant is important.
The boy, passing through anaclitic merging that involves a reduction of erotic
object-choice to nutritional instincts, perceives a conceptual equivalence (or
rather fails to differentiate) between *feelings of dependency and a culturally
intolerable femininity.* That is, he comes to think — whether consciously or
unconsciously — of passivity or receptivity or "need for another" as female.
They represent a reduced ego autonomy that threatens the phallic "wholeness"
of masculinity (see Chodorow 1974:51). The boy must, therefore, repudiate
such dependency wishes in order both to confirm and to protect a later masculine identification. The resultant hypermasculine displays of machismo may
be regarded in this light as "masculine protest" — in Adler's terms — against
inherent feminine wishes and identification retained from infancy.

The Mother's Role

In much of the literature on Spanish masculine codes, the mother is
simply taken for granted; her active involvement in socialization and her own
needs and fantasies are rarely probed. By looking at the mother's role in depth,
however, it is possible to explore the cultural premises about the sexes from a
different perspective.

As is true in most of the European Mediterranean (Saunders 1981), the
ethnography of Andalusia is replete with descriptions of rigid sexual segregation confining women to the sequestered household and men to the "social
world" of the public domain (we take up the question of sexual segregation in
Chapter 9). In Andalusia, as elsewhere in southern Europe, men avoid spending too much time in *la casa* (the home) because to do so provokes damaging
questions about their masculinity (Brandes 1980b; Driessen 1983). Hence, a
father's participation in childrearing, especially with young dependents, who
are confined to the "private" domain and whose care is considered "women's

business," is likely to be minimal, even today (Uhl 1991). Although exceptions of course exist, the pressures on men to conform remain strong.

To illustrate, let me recount the case of Juan, a "progressive" worker. He was a prominent member of the local Socialist Party (Partido Socialista Obrero Español, or PSOE). The party has made women's rights an important issue in its program since political parties were legalized in 1977. A loyal militant, Juan goes along with this in principle and publicly voices his support, theoretically, for women's issues. But one day, his indignant wife collared me in front of her house and launched into a long, rambling tirade accusing her husband of a primitive male chauvinism. "That so-called progressive," she sneered, "won't even move his pinky to help me in the house. He won't clean a dish, he won't touch a bedsheet. He has one foot in the workers' paradise and one foot in the Middle Ages."

Juan, just leaving for work, paused to explain, "What would my pals say? A man does not do women's things." End of argument. So men still refuse to do "women's work," for the sake of appearances.

Our knowledge of sexual norms and of household dynamics in Andalusia is still ethnographically *shallow,* mainly because of a lack of feminist work in the area. Information about family dynamics is largely derived from secondhand sources outside the home rather than empirical evidence. What is the mother-son relationship like in the early stages?

The first and most important fact is that in rural Andalusia, the mother-child bond not only is a pivotal one in the household but also, and correlatively, is a defining criterion for *female* adult identity and social status. The birth of a first child has a critical effect on both the gender *and* the social identity of a woman. This parallel process of biological and social "creation" enhances understanding of the intensity and duration of the mother-child bond. The sociopsychological connection between the mother and her expected devotion to childrearing cannot be overestimated.

Before the birth of the first child, a household in Andalusia is said to be preliminary or incomplete; implicitly, so is the wife's status. She is not a true woman as yet. For newlyweds, individual return visits to their separate family homes are frequent. The childless marriage or newlywed couple is said to be "not yet cooking," not yet a true conjugal pair. They are in a transitional state between marriage and family, and the new home has a surprisingly meager larder. Furthermore, in-laws visit the household infrequently and mostly by formal invitation, usually to celebrate some special event — a new refrigerator, a Saint's Day. The childless household is not yet "real," only embryonic, and the young wife's status is likewise uncertain.

The birth of the first child changes everything. This event is a centripetal social event that certifies the new social entity. Now the marriage is "cooking." The visiting pattern changes, as the in-laws now come to cook, clean, and keep company while the newly confined mother assumes her responsibilities of caring for the baby and the household. She is now complete: an adult, a woman and a mother, a social persona, the beaming sun of the familial solar system.

For the first few years of the child's life, mother and child are rarely apart, in home or in public. She carries the baby everywhere. The father's participation is variable, though (ideally) it is expected to be minimal, since men are awkward around babies. The sudden "activation" of the new household culminates in a joyous baptismal party, celebrating both the birth itself and the establishment of a new family. Through her child, the woman, as mother, creates herself and her milieu.

The reciprocally "procreative" mother-child bond is powerful but cannot be treated generically. According to my Spanish friends, the sex of the child makes a substantial difference in degree of generational continuity. Boys are considered obstreperous, needing greater supervision. Their orbit around the mother is eccentric, erratic. Struggles for control play out daily, as "incorrigible" boy toddlers are chased down, held firmly by the arm, and, often in tears, frog-marched along within a manageable radius from the mother. In slightly older boys, expressions of defiance against maternal authority manifest themselves in other ways. The mother often then becomes more attentively watchful and mindful of her son's movements than those of her often more compliant daughter. Whether the boy's defiance is genetically or culturally caused is not at issue here; the relational consequences of the gender-based difference, however, are critical.

One little boy in the town of Montemayor (Cordoba Province),[1] for example, wandered into the street as a car approached. His mother alerted him about the danger, but he paid no attention. She grabbed him and roughly dragged him to safety. He stood there trembling in fury, stamping his feet, and finally sticking out his tongue at his mother, who laughed at the provocation. His sister remained nervously in the doorway during the entire time. His mother then spent the next two hours following the boy around, hovering over his every move, but not interfering. In another case, a young boy, angry with his playmate, picked up a large toy truck and walloped his friend over the head. His mother, always vigilant, told him to stop. He looked at her directly and continued his attack. She took the truck away and shrewdly shifted his attention to a small passing group of older children. As the boy's attention wandered and he resumed his aggressive behavior, the mother maintained constant vigilance to the exclusion of her daughter, who was busily engaged in doll play. While such sex-based differences in toddlers are probably universal, in Spain they have achieved the status of recognized folklore.

Mothers state that their girls rarely engage in the violent and aggressive behavior that is "natural" to boys. "Girls don't get 'ideas,'" they say, meaning get into mischief. Boys are different from girls, "hard to control." This attests to a cultural stereotype that is both the cause and the effect of differential treatment of girls and boys. For whatever cause, it is firmly believed in Andalusia that little boys are aggressive, little girls passive. Thus mothers put more effort into "controlling" boys, and that control leads to inevitable conflicts over independence and autonomy.

Both at home and in public, such scenes happen much less frequently between mothers and daughters. Women claim that their daughters are more tractable than their sons. Parents unanimously exclaim that girls are "easy to manage," require less supervision, less effort, less investment of the mother's energies. The boy, as in many other places, requires constant minding, which in turn provokes further aggression, testing, and exploration of boundaries. While this cycle may occur elsewhere, it is intensified in Spain by the absence of the father from the home and by the unusually dominant role of mothers in childcare.

Thus, much of a mother's time with her young son is spent watching him, hovering, sometimes admonishing him, in order to protect him and to maintain her control (Figure 11). Conscientious vigilance is a permanent aspect of mother-son relations. The mother-daughter relationship unfolds quite differently, as a matter of principle. Little girls are encouraged to emulate their mother in taking care of household tasks. Admired and treasured toys, miniature replicas of women's mops, brooms, pails, and so forth, are widely available in shops. Little girls, brandishing their implements, are seen trailing after their mothers, sweeping and mopping in imitation. Food preparation and cooking are another shared sphere. Girls receive sets of plastic dishware, pots, pans, and little recipe books, which they play with while the mother cooks. Sewing and knitting kits are also prized gifts. The female child's efforts to imitate her mother are greeted with affectionate and proud amusement by both men and women. Girls are more eager to win parental approval than boys, people argue. Many adult activities are replicated in structured activities that girls share, which is not the case for little boys. The daughter is bound to her mother by approved socialization techniques and clear-cut developmental stages, rather than by repressive apron strings.

The mother's and daughter's lives are routinized, changing little over time. The girl at age seven or eight is expected to be helpful in the house. And even

11. Housebound mother
with son in tow, 1980.

after marriage, as we have seen, mothers and daughters carry on together as before — cleaning, cooking, raising children in tandem, keeping company. The mother's relationship with her son is both more amorphous and more complicated because the relationship is based on patterns of the mother's working, cajoling, and giving (especially food), and the son's receiving.

The important but subtle difference, therefore, between boys and girls lies in maternal constancy, dependence, and expectations. Both sexes grow up with almost exclusively female parenting. As others have noted, both boys and girls suffer a relatively traumatic weaning from the previous paradisiacal indulgence when siblings are born (see Suarez-Orozco and Dundes 1984:123). But boys suffer a deeper separation trauma — partly, of course, of their own making. Though displaced by siblings, they remain more physically dependent on their mother before puberty than girls, for, as "men," they are totally unable or unwilling to care for themselves, unlike their sisters, who have mastered rudimentary domestic skills. But later, when the boys enter the homosocial world of men, they must abruptly renounce maternal support and resignedly seek it elsewhere. In contrast, girls are not only instructed early to be self-reliant but are also permitted to remain virtually forever in the embrace of maternal love.

Like peasant mothers everywhere, the older women attempt to overcome the threatened loss of their boys by tying invisible apron strings and adopting a "smothering" style of mothering (Saunders 1981). As their sons often mildly complain, mothers do not like to let go. They demand frequent visits, express a sometimes overbearing curiosity, and constantly attempt to exert control and authority through gifts of "filling" food and assistance. A good son stoically accepts these intrusions, shares his problems and experiences, and submits dutifully to advice and counsel. For her part, the mother continues her gratifying role of buffering and consoling. But eventually her son must leave the maternal hearth. In competition later with her daughter-in-law, a mother may take on a more aggressive, though disguised, role in her son's life; especially if she feels that he is not achieving his (that is to say, her) potential or that she is losing control or that her son's behavior is reflecting badly on her "mothering" — her primary means of achieving public recognition.

Of great importance in Andalusia is the texture of mothers' emotional investment in their sons. In the literature on masculinity, the primary identification of mother and son is viewed almost entirely as a one-way street; that is, it is discussed from the boy's point of view, which is surprising because the main feature of the identification is its symbiotic nature — its dualism and reciprocal dynamics (see, for example, Mahler et al. 1975). As the son develops an unbreakable attachment to the mother, so the mother identifies with the son. Later, he serves as her male representative, permitting her surrogate entry into the impenetrable world of men and public life. Mothers' ego investment in their sons is a well-known theme in literature (take D. H. Lawrence's novels, for example) and in history, but has been given short shrift in ethnography and psychology. As psychoanalyst Gregory Rochlin puts it: "The role of her child's sex in fulfilling herself as woman, although well known in history and scarcely less familiar to us in literature, has nevertheless had scant attention" (1980:30).

Only Helene Deutsch, one of Freud's earliest women followers, has explored this subject in any depth (1945, vol. 2). Both she and Gregory Rochlin (1980) see the primary psychic merging of child and mother as a two-way process of "filling up": the boundaries of ego identity are blurred and indistinct for both (Rochlin 1980:29–30; see also Chodorow 1978, 1994). Thus, in cultures where masculinity is highly overvalued and where women are secluded, the male child may fulfill the woman's egoistic "masculine" needs vicariously. Deutsch (1945, vol. 2; 297 ff.) points out that in androcentric cultures where women experience feelings of inadequacy about being female, they often seek to compensate through a male child who becomes their masculine alter ego or surrogate; they then become "complete."

In patriarchal cultures there is a powerful incentive for mothers to establish and perpetuate a strong bond of identification between sons and themselves and to prolong the psychic merging or "filling up," which the boy semiconsciously experiences as both gratifying and threatening. In this way, the mother achieves a kind of representative masculinity that is otherwise proscribed by the culture. Or as Freud (1925) would probably have put it, the son becomes a libidinal object: the mother's missing phallus. Although we need not go so far as to conjure up a "phallic mother" (Chodorow 1994:23), there is no doubt that for Andalusian mothers the boy child represents the part of her that is permitted entry into masculine affairs outside the house, that fulfills an aggressive, phallic destiny — her masculine surrogate. In their mutuality, son and mother enact a reciprocal inversion of mutual fulfillment.[2] In his book on Marian worship in Latin Catholicism, Michael Carroll (1986:73) expresses this phenomenon succinctly: "There are solid psychoanalytic arguments and ethnographic case studies which suggest that this exclusion [from public life] leads mothers to develop an especially close and indulgent relationship with their sons, since it is only through their sons that they can achieve success — albeit vicariously — in the outside world."

Let me provide an illustration of this mutualism through identification from fieldwork. A young man from Fuentes plaintively complained about interference from his domineering mother. He was an ordinary man, unprepossessing, unadventurous, with a decidedly passive character. Such flaws were a constant bane to his ambitious mother who hoped for great things from her eldest son. He also had an unusual physiognomy, for he was the resigned owner of a tiny, flattish nose, which had never fulfilled its hoped-for destiny of postadolescent enlargement and noble appearance (flat noses are associated with lower-class peasants).

During his late teens, some of his peers christened him sotto voce with a novel nickname, paying homage to the failed development of his proboscis. They called him El Chato (Snubnose). He sheepishly reported this insult to his family. His new moniker affected his parents differently; it was a matter of no consequence to his distant father, but a spark that ignited uncontrolled rage in his mother. Indignant and shaken, she issued stern orders that her son forbid the use of this derogatory label, by force if required. Her anger was unfathomable to the young man, as he recalled it to me. Unable to combat this onomastic disgrace publicly, El Chato fought it out instead in domestic skirmishes with his mother, who remained, despite all entreaties, adamant that he "do something." As he told me, "She feels that I'm being ridiculed and made a laughingstock, and that it's a slur on my manhood." (Consider the sexual symbolism of the nose.)

While El Chato was discomforted and embarrassed by his ugly nickname, his mother was the one who mounted the aggressive defense of his manliness.

It was she, apparently, who felt her own aspirations under attack. In sexually segregated Andalusian towns, women like "Mama Snubnose" live to a large extent through their men. The son was, after all, once a part of the mother's body, an organic extension of her self and her ego.

Once the oedipal stage is reached, the highly charged bond between mother and son has other implications for the growing boy. It is a commonplace assumption in psychological literature that an already problematical cross-sexual identification is made more difficult for boys who form close libidinal relationships with dominant or seductive mothers. It is probably true, as Henry Biller argues (1971:91), that the boy's inability to cope with later oedipal feelings toward his emotionally intimate or intrusive mother (in addition to any obstacles due to primary associations) "may lead to a defensive feminine identification," as Freud argued in his study of Leonardo.

Although this hypothesis certainly has never been proven, it is apparent that Andalusian boys face powerful situational factors encouraging prolonged intimacy and identification with mothers and, therefore, with a set of feminine cultural norms. As we have noted, these factors encourage an unconscious association of regressive dependency wishes — to be "filled up" — with an ego-syntonic femininity and, according to our argument, a reaction formation against the dependency wishes that takes the form of identification with the aggressor. This would indeed explain the sexually aggressive or phallic stance of Andalusian machismo, given that cultural norms against violence prohibit other forms of masculine physical assertion. This phallic stance may be viewed as a residual but powerful defense against the unconscious masculine anxieties about passivity or receptivity — of being dominated, penetrated, victimized. Machismo plays an active role in restoring the boundaries of the male ego, in surmounting threats of feminization from both within and without, and in repairing injuries to masculine narcissism (see Rochlin 1980:169). Further ethnographic evidence for this supposition comes from recent studies of the masculine self-image in Andalusia, especially in the pathfinding work of anthropologists Stanley Brandes (1980a, 1980b, 1981) and Michael Murphy (1983a, 1983b, 1983c).

Both Brandes and Murphy have convincingly shown that a primary focus of sexual anxiety for men in Andalusia is the fantasy of being placed in the passive, receptive position of a woman. It is not homosexuality itself that men abhor, but the prospect of being forced into a receptive role in sexual encounters. In Monteros (Jaén Province), for instance, as Brandes (1980b:25) shows, men place a fundamental emphasis on personal autonomy in all social and economic affairs, which is reflected in an aggressive stance in erotic life. To be passive or "acted upon" socially, sexually, or in symbolic relations with others is to be feminized and emasculated and therefore subject to homosexual attack and penetration. The husband of the adulterous wife, for example, is said not only to be socially disgraced but, much worse, to be "transformed symbolically into a woman" (Brandes 1981:229). A man who is dominated or cheated economically is equally victimized and feminized by a more powerful male figure who, as Brandes's interlocutors put it, "screws" him and puts it "up his ass" (1980b:95). Such apprehensions are naturally reducible to an overwhelming fear of anal attack and insertion. Brandes (1980b:95) writes: "If masculine behavior, for the people of Monteros, has its conceptual locus in the male genital region, then feminine behavior is concentrated linguistically on the anus. Men show themselves to be constantly aware that the anus can be used in homosexual encounters, in which case the passive partner is perceived as playing the feminine role and indeed of being converted symbolically into a woman. It is this sexual transformation that men fear."

In my opinion, men fear this sexual transformation not simply because it represents a repudiated wish for homosexual contact (although that may play a part), but rather because they fear sexual reversal which stimulates repressed wishes for the restitution of the psychic symbiosis with the mother. Such wishes can be acknowledged openly only during the madness of carnival. The regressive wishes are specifically for the passive, receptive, anaclitic dependency that corresponds to the merging with the mother, which we saw so clearly expressed in the "serious" coplas. These wishes are a menace to both masculine somatic integrity and the boundaries of ego. It is not the fantasy of the homosexual act itself that produces the horror; it is the image of assuming the passive woman's role, of helpless dissolution of ego boundaries. The same desires that lead during carnival to pleasurable reveries based on the coplas frighten men outside of the carnival context.

Further evidence for this hypothesis is presented quite starkly in Murphy's (1983c) innovative work on selective homophobia in Seville City. He found that men there classify homosexuals in two ways. First are the flamboyant transvestites who have "come out of the closet" since Franco's death; they assume the female role in courtship and intercourse. Second are the "masculine" homosexuals who seduce unwary young men into playing the passive role. Those who assume the role of aggressor — and thereby maintain their masculinity — are most feared and despised, because of the danger of gender reversal and inversion of the active versus passive role that they represent to their partners. The flamboyant "hyperfeminine" homosexuals are merely tolerated and ridiculed, not hated or feared as dangerous.

Murphy chooses a sociological explanation, arguing along the lines of Robert Levy's functionalist interpretation (1971) of the Tahitian *mahu* (transsexual). As formulated by Levy, the argument runs that the obviously feminized homosexual is socially tolerated because he provides an institutionalized alternative and negative example for conventional masculinity (Murphy 1983c:7). But one could also argue that he is tolerated because he assumes the female role in sexual relations and therefore poses no threat to the masculine self-identity of his partner.

We can now return to another question regarding the development of male gender identity in Andalusia: What other situational factors, aside from the father's absence, the mother's overwhelming presence, and sociopolitical vulnerability, contribute to ambivalence over masculine identity in southern Spain? So far, the argument stressing the father's absence, familism, and mother-son intimacy seems relevant and useful for Andalusia. But these conditions could also be said to characterize many other androcentric, matrifocal societies where children are sequestered with strong mothers.

Since van Gennep's day, it has been an anthropological axiom that all societies must provide some sort of institutional framework for the transition from childhood to adulthood (see Erikson 1950). Frequently, this change of generational status coincides with the formal bestowal of the status of man or woman, that is, of gender role and public sex identity (Young 1965). Comparative evidence suggests that when boys in ideologically patriarchal societies are confined exclusively to the female (domestic) realm until relatively late in life, male status is conferred only grudgingly, through rituals of testing that are analogous to hazing (Whiting et al. 1958; Burton and Whiting 1961; see also Parker et al. 1975). Such strenuous rites of passage subject boys to stressful, bloody, painful ordeals in which they consolidate claims to manhood at the same time as they renounce childhood associations with their mothers (see Herdt 1982:xv).

Perhaps most striking about the Spanish ethnography in this regard is the contradictory nature of the masculine transition. While strong emphasis is placed on the elusive goal of masculinity, virtually no formalized rituals facilitate the achievement and public recognition of this masculinity. Murphy (1983a) has accurately depicted the maturational process of Andalusian boys as an amorphous "riteless passage to manhood." Apart from being drafted into the army at age twenty, Andalusian boys find themselves in a kind of institutional limbo between puberty and adulthood, in which freedom from social obligations and unstructured autonomy are the main themes (Press 1979; Aguilera 1990). In essence, no public ceremonies or group rituals, no consensual cultural markers or guideposts acknowledge male biological maturation (conferred indisputably by menarche on girls). No formal tests and few opportunities exist for self-assertion or manly achievement in a world dominated by older, more powerful men. As Murphy remarks (1983b) also, this feckless transition is often impeded or overtly challenged by nonsupportive, distant, or even hostile fathers. This is true of all social classes and in both rural and urban contexts (Press 1979).

Puberty itself is recognized in only the most tacit fashion in Andalusia, and virtually no strenuous demands are made on boys that might serve as symbolic stepping-stones to the desired manhood. Under such conditions, it is left up to each individual to attain and demonstrate an exemplary masculinity in his own way (see Parker et al. 1975). Since an abiding manhood is neither culturally conferred nor confirmed, the man's personal effort must be unequivocal and unrelenting. Vigilance is necessary because manhood is undermined perpetually by outsiders' incredulity. It is only during the latitude of carnival that such conflicts may be consciously addressed and experienced, and of course in ritualized forms.[3]

I believe this is one of the reasons for both the intensity and the inverted quality of carnival sexuality in this part of Spain. Burdened with the gender identity conflicts outlined earlier, and given little other opportunity for release, Andalusian men seize on carnival as an outlet and a script. In the transvestite lunacy of carnival they may act out their feminine side in act, dress, and song; in fact they are able literally to become their own mothers for three or four days, wrapped in her bedding and clothing. As the mother in childhood is a violently split image, on the one hand controlling, repressive, and frustrating and on the other hand nurturing, indulgent, and loving, so the carnival imagery is violently split in two and each half given life in powerful imagery.

By contrast, women and girls experience less conflict. They therefore do not need such an outlet as carnival provides, or such a ritualized resolution. Furthermore, because they have their own sons to act out the masculine side of their personalities, women can seek to overcome inner tensions through surrogacy and sublimation. Hence the drag-queen dramas of carnival and the maintenance of poetry as an exclusively male preserve are not merely historical survivals or empty custom. They can be seen as resulting from the structural and psychic constraints of Andalusian rural culture, family organization, and gender scripts.

7

Who Wears the Pants?

Suegra y yerno: antesala de infierno (Mother-in-law and son-in-law: gateway to hell) —
Spanish proverb

Carnival exalts the poor man, glorifies the child hidden within the adult,
rescues the henpecked husband, uplifts the downtrodden and the oppressed.
Carnival degrades women, as we saw in the first chapter, although the coplas
also, and with great ambivalence, express veneration of the split-off "good
woman," personified by the sacrificing mother and the martyred innocent girl.
This good side of woman, with its own internal contradictions, thus isolated
from the bad, can then be appropriated, or at least controlled, through men's
psychic identification with women in carnival lyrics. The "lowering" or debas-
ing of the negative female image as an exemplar of the inversive power of
carnival has become almost a cliché: the condemnation of the bad woman —
personified by the vamp, the judgmental wife, the ferocious mother-in-law,
the betrayer, the termagant — constitutes a tearing down of the allegedly high
and mighty.

Degradation of the powerful, debasement of the master (whether a female
or a male oppressor), lies, according to Bakhtin (1984), at the root of the
carnivalesque. For Bakhtin, as for others, inversion of hierarchy expresses the
essence of the festival wherever carnival happens. But why must "woman," or

at least a part of her, be cast down and subdued in this manner? Just how high and mighty are women in Spain, that men regard them as so overweening and ripe for a fall? And how powerless are the men, that they must invert their position relative to that of the all-powerful women in carnival ritual every year? What happened to the famously patriarchal Spanish peasant? Where is the stereotype of the venerable macho who dominates women and lords it over his family, the tyrant whose word is law?

In fact, the so-called patriarchal peasant family is one of the most tenacious ethnic clichés in Anglophone social anthropology, especially in Mediterranean studies. Women in southern Europe are supposedly retiring, mute, passive, and for all practical purposes "invisible" in decision making (Herzfeld 1991). Men are the oppressors of women, the dominant, "active" sex. So, conventional wisdom has it: "male" reads as "powerful, vocal, aggressive"; "female" means subjugated, mute, passive.

Recently, however, this model of gender has been challenged, mainly by a new generation of iconoclastic feminists working in southern Europe. What they have to say is important here, because the southern European model seems an extreme example of a supposed gender universal: male dominance in peasant societies, and to a lesser degree in all societies. So we are dealing with one end of a continuum rather than with discrete typologies, and whatever we may say about southern Europe may have relevance in differing degrees elsewhere.

The feminists, or at least some of them, argue that male dominance is carefully orchestrated pretense, even "a myth" (Rogers 1975) — for a number of reasons. First, women wield the real power in villages in southern Europe because they hold the family purse strings, in societies where most people are poor and economically dominated by distant elites. Second, women rule because men voluntarily relinquish domestic control to women to avoid association with "femininity." Thus, for example, it has been argued that women's control of food preparation, which men avoid as feminine, creates an "oral dependency" that makes men, as well as children, "subordinate" (Counihan 1987). And finally, women wield power because by holding sway in the private or domestic realm, they acquire de facto control of the socialization of children and of religious and cultural indoctrination; and, to invoke an old adage, the hand that rocks the cradle rules the world, at least in remote peasant villages. We have seen that women exercise undisputed authority over the lives of children, especially young boys, in Andalusia. The feminist critics speak of "domestic power" (Dubisch 1986:16), which they say is often feminized. But they rarely explain how this might differ from "political power" or "economic power" or any other form of power in human relations.

But before we can address the question of who has familial power in southern Spain, we have to decide what power is in this context. Then we can go on to define "domestic power." Neither of these terms, power or domestic power, has been clearly explained in the literature; nor has power been distinguished from related concepts such as authority, influence, and legitimacy. Before looking at power in the Andalusian family, therefore, I want to formulate a tentative definition of domestic power.

Domestic Power

In a classic treatise, sociologist Max Weber (1946:152) defines power (*Macht*) as the ability of one actor in a relationship to carry out his own will, despite opposition and regardless of the basis on which that capability rests. For Weber, then, "power" means the capacity to enforce one's will by any means available, without reference to moral considerations. Power is dominance over others, without a basis in "right." Indeed, one of the basic tenets of Weber's approach is that the ability to dominate exists independently of authority, which is dependent on the consent of those at the receiving end of the power.

To summarize: "power" implies institutionalized command emanating from established relations of dominance or deference, rather than from competition or conflict over resources in which neither actor has established control. Ultimately, power in this sense derives from coercion and is independent of moral justification. In the most extreme instance, power stems from a monopoly over the application of force or violence or over the threat of force. Power rests on the ability to compel fear and thus compliance.

Power has also received some attention in cultural anthropology, although less than in its sister discipline, sociology. Like Weber, and in an equally classic formulation, the British anthropologist S. F. Nadel distinguishes between power and authority. Nadel says that power can be taken to refer to "unexpected" command over the actions of others — not ethical command but rather de facto control over resources. For Nadel, though, authority is always "expected" and de jure, that is, "ethical" according to local criteria (1954:169).

Thus, to summarize the social science literature: *power* is generally the de facto ability to prevail in decision-making processes within any relationship, formal or informal. *Authority* is power accepted by those on the receiving end.

When it comes to political affairs — dominance over persons — the question of coercion becomes important. Power is the ultimate guarantor of control over political processes, but we have to remember that there are many types of force other than physical violence — for example, psychological manipulation or the withholding of love or other desired assets. The aspect of coercion is a complicated issue, especially at the ethnographic or microsociological level. We must guard against the Western tendency to associate "force" with physical violence. Affective sanctions may be of equal or greater effect than physical enforcements.

That men are usually bigger and stronger than women, for example, does not necessarily imply that they have the unrestrained ability to enforce their will. Other means of control may be equally effective, such as the withholding of monetary or sexual rewards, shaming, gossip, cultural proscriptions against wife beating, and other moral constraints. In most social contexts, power is almost never wielded, at least in the long run, without some degree of legitimacy.

With a working definition of power in hand, let us consider what "domestic power" is. We can define domestic power in Ernestine Friedl's terms, as the capacity to impose one's will in decisions "concerning sex relations, marriage, residence, divorce, and the lives of children" (1975:7). Domestic power is the ability of the husband or wife to get his or her way in family decisions, regardless of what is morally or ethically "right."

So Who Has It? Decision Making

Before describing power in marriage, let me give an example of the way in which important decisions are made earlier on, between fiancés. It will set the stage for later battles. In Andalusia, the engagement is usually a long-drawn-out process, sometimes lasting years. Consequently, decision-making patterns during that period can serve to predict the future direction of the marital relations. The following incident involves a young couple from Fuentes who must make the most important decision: when to marry.

The main characters in our story are Eulogio Valdes, a man of about thirty, and his girlfriend, Carmen Velázquez, twenty-eight, both of Fuentes de Andalucía (the names are made up). In early 1972, the two had been engaged for four years, a relatively long period, but not unusual by any means. Finally, Carmen got impatient and decided it was time to wed. She had collected enough of a trousseau, and her parents had rebuilt and furnished an upstairs apartment in their home for the newlyweds. In the face of mounting pressure, Eulogio, however, resisted setting a date. Consequently, the wedding was becoming a sore point.

Eulogio was a trucker with a growing business in transporting comestibles to the local market, and he felt he needed more time to amass assets before marriage. As he explained to his friends, a man wants to gain financial independence before, not after, marriage — a common and approved sentiment among young men. So a disagreement erupted, setting the stage for a battle of wills.

The unfolding of the rather stormy nuptial story is revealing for two reasons. The first reason is the personal characteristics of Eulogio, and the second is that among his circle of bachelor friends, the fiancé was considered an exemplary *hombre fuerte* (strong or stalwart man) whose relations with his fiancée were observed closely and hopefully for evidence of male domestic prerogative. He was somewhat of a test case for patriarchal forcefulness and served as a model for other unmarried men in his group. Whether or not he would prevail would be an augury; as elsewhere in Spain, men pay lip service to an ideology of patriarchal privilege — at least, before actually being married.

Tall, athletic, and gregarious, Eulogio was a successful risk-taker in business, a good earner. He was stentorian and somewhat boastful in conversation, but generous and "correct" in his dealings with men. He certainly appeared dominant during the courtship to Carmen (that is, he appeared to be in charge, at least in public). He was considered a leader: during his teens, he had been a leader of his *pandilla* (boys' gang); later he became a noncommissioned officer in the army. Independent and self-assured, he was respected by both men and women in Fuentes. Carmen, by contrast, was small, demure, a physically ordinary woman, who gave no indication, at least to the men, of possessing any outstanding characteristics.

In late 1972, Eulogio told his friends that his wedding would be postponed for another year because, as he explained, *he dicho* (I have spoken). The consensus among the men was therefore that Carmen would simply have to wait. Yet within a month, Eulogio astonished his friends by sheepishly confiding that the wedding date had been set; Carmen would have her way for an early marriage and that there was, as he put it meekly, "no remedy." What happened?

Attempting to understand the debacle, a number of friends and I sat around in a bar one evening, animatedly debating Eulogio's defeat and commiserating. One bachelor, Geraldo, expressed shock over his friend's capitulation. How was it possible, he asked, that a big, strong man like Eulogio could relent so easily, put up so ineffectual a struggle, and be dominated by a woman so small and demure? "Who rules," Geraldo plaintively asked, "the man or the woman?" The verb he used was *mandar* (to command or dictate), a word commonly used in discussions about Spanish politics. Significantly, the traditional term for the elite powerholders (the "señoritos") in Andalusia was *los que mandan* — "those who rule."

As George Collier (1987) pointed out in a brilliant account of the class struggle in a nearby town, this concept of *manda* (rule) has historically played an important role in masculine self-image in Andalusia. To maintain their honor, men must rule themselves, be their own master; that is what defines them as manly. To be ruled means to be controlled by or dependent on others, to be dominated. The one who is ruled is *manso* (tame), the same term used on the farm for a steer (castrated bull). "Rule" is a polysemous concept that finds symbolic expression in all areas of life — political, sexual, and interpersonal. To use expressions of domination like *mandar* is important in contexts where male self-image is involved. Geraldo's question, therefore, had resonance beyond the simple call to colors in the battle of the sexes. It brought a reflective response from Carlos, an older, married man.

Experienced in the ways of women, Carlos was well acquainted with the engaged couple and their battles. As men often do in Andalusian bars, Carlos gave a short speech, with standard preludial pontification: "Look man, what happens is the following" (*Mira, hombre, lo que paza e' lo ziguiente*). The other men found his subsequent comments both amusing and truthful. His remarks are worth repeating for the light they shed on both male behavior and male attitudes.

Carlos spoke candidly about the balance of power between the sexes. He allowed that the man rules in Spain, except, he ironically added, "when he doesn't." And he doesn't in most matters that are important to the woman, because he is preoccupied with other matters and cannot concentrate his full attention on the details to which his fiancée or wife devotes her energies. The final say in such matters, according to Carlos, is held not by the man or the woman but by the interested kin from whom they muster support. The woman will prevail in domestic matters because she has the unfailing support of her mother, whose self-assigned role is to protect her daughter and advance her interests; whereas the man, to be a "real man," must stand alone. The women in tandem can almost always "wear the man down."

Carlos had introduced two important principles: (1) the inherent power of women in conjugal matters, owing to their deeper commitment, and (2) the considerable role played by the infamous bête noire of Andalusian husbands, the *suegra* (mother-in-law). In the first case, men are weakened on the domestic front because their attention is divided; they must concentrate on work and spend time with one another. In the second case, the *suegra* simply terrorizes her son-in-law. The mention of the mother-in-law drew sighs of comprehension and self-pity from most of the men present.

He added that personality is, of course, very important in this situation. To prevail against his suegra and wife, the man must be unusually fuerte. Even if he is fuerte, and his wife is *floja* (submissive), his suegra is always strong. "It is the nature of suegras," Carlos asserted, "to be small but fierce" (*feroz*).[1] The alliance of women, fierce or otherwise, is too formidable to resist without an intolerable expenditure of male energy. Equally decisive are the husband's frequent absences from the home, during which the field is left open to usurpation by his wife and suegra.

The "power" in this case was clearly wielded by a woman, or by women in domestic alliance. Their ability to prevail in an important decision was unexpected, unequivocal, and unaffected by what was "right." Although my sources would be surprised to hear the word "power" used in this trivial context, they would nevertheless agree that the important decisions affecting a man's life often lie beyond his control and completely within the grip of manipulative women.

As Carlos finished his peroration about the power of the *novia* and the dreaded mother-in-law, a popular local poet and carnival comedian entered the bar. He is known to all by his nickname, Juanito "El Chocho." Overhearing our conversation, Juanito joined in by doing a credible imitation of his "pugnacious" suegra, a pantomime replete with right hooks and uppercuts. His contortions ended in a crescendo of obscene gestures suggestive of a man's submissive sexual posture. Finally, before wandering off to the bar to reward his own performance with a drink, Juanito sang a copla from one of his carnival epics, "La Vida del Hombre" (Man's life). Such performances are a typical way of concluding philosophical discussions. After catching on to the lyrics, the other men joined in. This is the verse:

Yo peleé con mi novia	I had a fight with my fiancée,
Y mi suegra se enteró;	And my mother-in-law [to be] found out;
Me pegó con una caña	She pounced upon me with a club
Y encima me la cascó![2]	And gave me a thorough drubbing!

Again, I want to emphasize the importance of the phraseology. The Spanish word *encima* literally means "above" or "on top of," in physical sense. But unlike other terms for "higher than" — *arriba* (high up) or *sobre* (above), for example — "encima" carries an implication of domination and subjugation that has powerful political (and sexual) overtones. It implies social ascendancy and dominion, as in the widely heard expression "Los ricos nos están encima" (The rich are on top of us). To stand "encima" another person is tantamount to oppression. The word has a powerful psychological resonance.

Conjugal Politics

After the long courtship and engagement, the Andalusian couple finally marries, as did Eulogio and Carmen, and begins to establish a home. At last, the two are one. Now they face three immediate decisions, which will have a permanent impact on their future relations. First, where will they live? Second, how will they manage household finances — for example, how will they allocate their previous savings to create a comfortable home? Third, when will they have children, and how many? Naturally, other questions arise, depending upon the particular circumstances of each couple, but these are generally the seminal or "organic" decisions that shape the future.

Postmarital residence in Fuentes shows a very strong neolocal but matrivicinal tendency; that is, newlyweds tend to choose a home that is near the wife's family. "Near" usually means within five minutes' walking distance. Minuscule degrees of distance are a major issue. I have heard both men and women seriously state that a house two blocks away was *lejos* (distant). People describe a house on the other side of town (about ten minutes' walking distance) as *muy lejos* (very far away) — a cognitive distortion noted by other Hispanicist ethnographers. In addition, when the newlyweds must live in one of the parental homes because of financial constraints (a new location is preferred), there is a marked uxorilocal tendency (that is, a tendency to live near the wife's family). In Fuentes, of the 416 extended families for which I found information (26 percent of all households), 295, or 71 percent, showed a matrilateral extension.

As a result, many Andalusian towns display a female-oriented residence pattern that creates female-centered neighborhoods, as is true of some southern Italian and Greek areas (Davis 1973; Casselberry and Valavanes 1976). These data seem to fly in the face of conventional wisdom about the patriarchal, patrilocal Mediterranean peasantry. As Davis reports for the town of Pisticci in southern Italy, the pattern of residential preference creates a female neighborhood infrastructure, or matri-core. Women's ties dominate neighborhood relations because married women, more often and longer than men, maintain close associations with longtime neighbors, kinswomen, and parents (remain co-residential). According to villagers' perception of spatial-social distance, the husband is most often the "stranger" in his home or neighborhood, residing "very far" from his parents (who may be located more than two blocks away). In an observation that applies to Andalusia, Davis writes: "The neighborhood is a community of women: women bring their husbands to live there; women have their close kin there; daughters will continue to live there when parents are dead" (1973:71–72). As Davis astutely notes, this matri-core continuity is a woman's "chief source of power," for it provides allies, sources of information and gossip, and a reliable basis of kinship support (22).

Equally prevalent in western Andalusia as in southern Italy, pseudomatrifocality raises two epistemological questions with regard to domestic power.

The first is, To what degree is the matrilocal or matrivicinal pattern consonant with the assumed male domestic prerogative? The second, What is the effect of such a residence pattern on conjugal decision making? Despite some variation from case to case, certain patterns emerge.

When I first noticed the matrilocal tendency in postmarital residence, I queried the men about it, because such behavior seemed at variance with the androcentric, patriarchal emphasis in Andalusia. Most of the men I spoke to said that they acquiesced to the wife's request to "live near Mama," for several reasons.

Where to live, the men admitted, was one of those issues that meant a great deal to the wife and less to the husband, as he was by nature more independent of parental ties. The new bride needed the support of her mother to establish a new home. So why break up this proven domestic team? Basically, the men felt that any attempt on their part to "come between" wife and mother-in-law would backfire and lead to a passive-aggressive campaign by both to undermine the husband's comfort and peace of mind for the rest of his life. Therefore, the battle for the upper hand in the matter was just not worth the price in aggravation.

To be sure, part of the answer reflects self-interest rather than mere passivity, because the men want their homes to be run efficiently. They believe that since women are in charge of domestic operations, they must be allowed full control over such issues; otherwise, the man will suffer from a chaotic household. As one man put it: wife and mother are a "clique" that works well only when the two women remain in physical proximity. In other words, the intrusive mother-in-law is a necessary nuisance. The most common response to questions about uxorial dominance in the choice of a residence was a resigned acceptance of proven practice. *No hay remedio* (there is no remedy for it) is a rhetorical device that features in many male pronouncements concerning wives, mothers-in-law, and women's ability in general to get their own way — as it did in Eulogio's admission of defeat. Although the deprecating response reflects, in part, the customary male indifference to "feminine" preoccupations, it also indicates a degree of surrender, or face-saving, which sometimes leads to much dissatisfaction later. In this sense, we can characterize male abstention from involvement in domestic matters as de facto recognition of uncontested female supremacy in domestic decision-making processes.

Battle-Axes Again

The most important consequence of this ambiguous acquiescence is that the suegra, often intruding into domestic arrangements and arguments, maintains a high profile in the man's life. This female scourge is an overbearing presence among urbanites, also, in western Andalusia (Press 1979), a testimony to how deeply rooted the regional stereotype is in male consciousness. In his delightful book on family life in Seville, Irwin Press (1979) has some fairly impressive photographs of determined-looking Andalusian suegras, burly and square-rigged in their black sacks. I can assure you, these are not damsels to be taken lightly.

Most bilateral societies, including our own, have their own folklore about the horrors of this stock villain in domestic comedies. Yet, because of the preponderance of the domestic matri-core, the Andalusian husband often finds himself outmatched when this fierce harridan throws herself into the fray in support of her daughter. His laments often offer a revealing image of masculine powerlessness before a female dyad elevated to domestic hegemony — there is no escape, given the unbreakable nature of the mother-daughter bond. The suegra's power is enhanced by sheer residential proximity, but more telling psychologically is the fact that she and her daughter represent a sentimental unity that the husband cannot match. Although he may have many friends, his male friendships are founded on competition as much as on cooperation, and he cannot plead for help from his own mother in domestic skirmishes without endangering his reputation as an "hombre fuerte."

His own mother may intercede, of course, but no man wants his mother to fight his battles. So he assents, thereby maintaining a respectable facade of "indifference" before his peers. The husband knows all too well that *jaleo* (trouble) with the suegra leads to marital discord, unless the wife is "strong" and prefers to mollify her husband while alienating her own mother (this is exceedingly rare according to male observers).

Carnival and the Conjugal Dilemma

Bottled up for most of the year, Andalusians' feelings about all this are expressed in February coplas. Indeed, the alliance of wife and suegra, with the latter assuming a mythopoetic role as masculine nemesis, has achieved a kind of apotheosis in chirigota poetry. What is most interesting about these comic verses is the formidable physical power ascribed metaphorically to the suegra through virile animal and military imagery, a tradition in which "marital" becomes "martial" and the male appears victimized and indecisive. As an illustration: during the Fuentes Carnival of 1970, one famous comic poet sang the following coplas and received accolades from the cheering men. This is the song:

Todas las suegras del mundo	The mothers-in-law in the world
Son igual de condiciones.	Are all of a kind.

Yo peleo con la mia —	I fight with mine, too,
Hay que ver como se pone	So listen how it goes.
Me echa fuera de su casa	She kicks me out of her house
Cuarenta veces al dia.	Forty times a day.
La buena por la mas mala,	Good, bad, indifferent,
Son todas de caballería.[3]	They all belong in the cavalry.

Another poet in the same village sang in 1973 about the brutality of the mother-in-law:

Señores, todo el que tenga suegra	All you men with a mother-in-law,
Haber que hace con ella	I'm asking you honestly
Le vamos a preguntar,	About how you deal with her,
A muchos de los que están presentes	And many of you present who are valiant
Que sea mas valiente nos puede contestar.	Can tell us the truth about her.
Nos parece que nadie contesta	Well, it seems no one is answering,
Por si algunos la tienen detrás,	Perhaps because she is standing near,
No sea que por lo diga	You're afraid she's ready to pounce
La suegra esté encima y le vaya a pegar.[4]	And give you a good beating.

Yet another maestro describes his suegra as a *bicho fiero* (fierce beast), which he hopes to *desbravacer* (tame, or, more colorfully, geld) someday, as though she were a wild stallion. Listening to these verses, one man in street clothes told me that his suegra was a "dragon" who expelled him from "her house" (his too) whenever he disagreed with her. Other men described their suegra as a "brave bull," a "tomcat," an "armor-plated lizard," or other such scaly or bellicose creatures.

These hyperbolic, pseudojocular laments about fierce beasts intimate sex-role reversal and power inversion with unconscious implications of sublimated male insecurities about masculinity. Also revealing is the sense of powerlessness due to ambiguous integration into the domestic setting, the result of the man's partial structural connection to the home. This residence is, after all, "haunted" by his mother-in-law, as they say. Sometimes she owns it outright. Even if the man lives in a separate home with his wife, the suegra's intrusion into his home is so all-encompassing that the man feels like a stranger in his own house and is correspondingly insecure. As we have seen, his domestic weakness is partly attributable to male abdication of domestic responsibilities in exchange for a full larder and efficient housekeeping. Acceptance of this domestic "service" does not quell the unending panegyric about his lost powers.

Faced with the powerful matri-core, the working-class husband finds some of the simplest decisions in his life taken over unilaterally by in-laws. Many men, for example, complain that although they hate to emigrate for work, they are forced into it: the decision by wife and mother-in-law is a fait accompli. A peasant farmer in the town of La Campana echoed a recurrent complaint; he confided that when he went to Madrid for work, his wife decided that they must have a new refrigerator — an item bought by many women for "show" rather than need (since women go shopping for food daily, the empty refrigerator often stands in disused splendor in the kitchen). Most men, of course, want to provide well for their families, but often decisions about consumption, and therefore about income, are made jointly by kinswomen, with the suegra playing a fiendish role in the process. Remember the popular carnival copla "Working, working, working night and day" (Chapter 4), which shows how little say the men have in purchasing decisions, and how they experience a feeling of helplessness before the power of the "uncontrollable" matri-core.[5] The man naturally feels that he is a passive victim. Occasionally, a husband expresses the opinion that his wife cares more about her mother than about him, a complaint conveying his sense both of injustice and of exclusion. Adolfo, for example, whose wife continually forgot to make his lunch (the main meal of the day), was told by his spouse that her mother was ill and needed attention.

One day I accompanied Adolfo home directly from the bar where we often enjoyed preprandial beers. He invited me to join him for the midday meal, after which I could interview him. But when we arrived, Adolfo was chagrined to find that no lunch had been prepared, and the cupboard was bare, except for a small sausage. A note taped to the wall announced that his wife had gone to visit her mother. Although embarrassed and disappointed, Adolfo confided with equanimity, "that's how women are." A man is a fifth wheel in his own house, he noted, adding peevishly that at least he had the consolation of knowing that the "old dragon" would not be bossing him around that day. It is obvious that many men feel marginalized in their own homes.

In addition to controlling the economic planning (with her mother's active participation), the Andalusian wife, especially among the working classes of Fuentes and La Campana, usually acts as the unofficial domestic bursar. The husband may surrender his entire day's wages to his wife each night. In return, he expects the house to be run properly and reserves a small "allowance" for bar expenses and his nightly card game. Many lower-class men refer to their wives (again, in a semicomic vein) as the *ama* (boss) or *jefa* (chief) of the house — words usually reserved, in their masculine form, for authority figures (employers, political leaders).

One man in Fuentes spoke seriously of his wife as the "administrator" of household finances and added that he did not care what she did with the money he earned, so long as he had enough to buy refreshments at the neighborhood tavern. I remember one worker getting up from an exciting card game to run home to wheedle more money out of his wife. His friends remarked that his wife was a "peseta pincher," but they agreed that her attempts to control his gambling were probably a good thing, given that he lost most of the time. Most men present admitted that their wives held the family purse strings, and that this was appropriate.

They said that a man works ("sacrifices") to give money to his wife and family. A man who withheld his wages from his wife was a skinflint and a reprobate. As before, such male acquiescence can be seen as morally ambivalent. Men evade onerous domestic responsibilities by giving the wife final authority, but they retain lingering self-doubts about their actions. Self-deprecating humor expresses their ambivalence.

The tendency to let the wife and her mother run the family's finances correlates with lower class or status. Among the better-off peasants, most husbands retain rights in the domestic economy and play a more decisive role in managing the family's money. Among the gentry in Andalusia, most husbands (with exceptions of course) take a more active financial role: they may even control the family purse strings through bank accounts and investments of which the wife knows nothing.

In some landowning families, a husband may simply provide his wife with a monthly allowance, which she distributes to various domestic employees with instructions about purchases. So a rich man has more power in the house than a poor one, but few in these towns are rich.

In the populous working classes, where surplus cash is scarce and the domestic economy is often managed on a credit or deficit basis (because of the uncertainties of agrarian employment), the wife "rules" the household economy, and the husband accepts the arrangement. Hence the many Spanish proverbs attesting to degrees of matriarchy among the poor:

> *En casa del mezquino, más manda la mujer que el marido* (Among the poor, the woman is more often the boss than the man.)
> *En casa del ruin, la mujer es alguacil*[6] (In the poor man's house, the wife is the constable.)

The remoteness of the working-class male is a trade-off, as we have seen: the impecunious husbands sacrifice some personal control for a modicum of domestic comfort. Conversely, among the propertied classes, comfort is assured by servants; additionally, the rich tend to live either patrilocally or patrivicinally after marriage. The suegra is not "needed."

Finally, let us consider the power exercised by wives through their ability to withhold sex. Generally, it is assumed among men in Andalusia that women are highly sexed, or *caliente* (hot), as the men like to say, although it is the man who awakens female sexuality and directs this amorphous heat. Yet it is also understood by both sexes that in marital relations, it is the woman who "uses" the strategy of withholding sex, as a means to control or persuade. Some men are naturally *flojo* (weak or impotent) sexually, and their wives may be frustrated. But observers, both male and female, agree that a husband never withholds sex on purpose to control or punish his wife. "He could not do that if he were a man," one man asserted firmly, adding that this maneuver is an exclusively female weapon, which carries more than just psychological weight. While talking with us, for example, a recently married couple spontaneously asked my wife (a medical doctor, as they knew) and me the best way to conceive a child. They had heard rumors that impregnation could be assured, and the sex of the child predetermined, by particular lovemaking positions. Although we could not advise them about this, the conversation soon turned to other subjects, such as the importance of having a first child exactly nine months after the wedding. The Andalusian husband and wife agreed that having a child as soon as possible is necessary to quell gossip about the man's potency. If conceiving a first child is delayed, they added, people assume that the husband has sexual problems, and they gossip about his manhood. They also implied that since this is so, some brides are able to "lead the groom about by the nose" by threatening to withhold sex. The man must placate her so that she quickly becomes pregnant (another example of female power wielded without respect to "right").

Though Little, She Is Fierce

While it would be unwise to generalize after conducting a few interviews, listening to carnival verses, and observing seemingly trivial marital squabbles, certain patterns become apparent.

The issue of domestic power seems less trivial when the available alternative sources of power are considered in rural communities. It is clear that many Andalusian women dominate their husbands in domestic matters, partly but not entirely as a result of discontinuities in life course patterns of men and women. If power is defined as personal autonomy and the ability to impose one's will, regardless of the source of that ability, then one must conclude that men have less power within the home than their wives — at least among the lower classes in Andalusian communities.

Reality must be distinguished from appearance, and we must be very careful to qualify men's assumptions about their importance with data from daily life — a caution that I will characterize as a kind of gender-sensitive empirical skepticism. Although these men claim that this imbalance occurs by design and that it "frees" them to concentrate on more important matters, I am inclined to regard this assertion as face-saving. Beyond the domestic realm, power is a scarce commodity denied to most men. This was particularly true during the Franco years (1936–1975), but the lingering sense of male vulnerability explains much of the political cynicism of working men in southern Spain today. They neither have political power nor exert power in relations with their peers, all of whom start from the same point in their egalitarian relationships. They may influence their cronies, but few men can be said to have power, whatever its provenance — except perhaps over their sons, but even that is equivocal. Men rarely abuse or beat their wives, because Andalusians abhor physical violence, and wife-beaters in particular are scorned. Since working-class men have virtually no alternative sources of power over their peers, we can conclude that they are relatively powerless compared with women, whose domestic power is real and unqualified. Male dominance is indeed mythical.

I do not see female superordination as uniquely, or even characteristically, Andalusian — or Spanish or southern European.[7] It reminds me of the famous joke about American husbands and wives. In a cartoon in the *New Yorker* some years back, a typical middle-class couple is asked who wears the pants.

The wife answers, "Oh, my husband, of course. He decides all the big issues, like what to do about the Russians and the space program. I decide all the little issues, like where to go on vacation and which house to buy."

Andalusia thus represents one point on a complicated sliding scale of gender and power.[8] Still, one very important observation should be made about relations of domination and subordination in the context of class-stratified marginal communities like those in rural Andalusia. Any approach to the dimension of power that uses only gender as a criterion is bound to be epistemologically invalid. Where power is concerned, there are men and then there are men, and there are women and women. As Davis (1977) has pointed out, what matters is not only sex, but class position and relative access to resources. So the conceptual category "men," in a relatively homogeneous place like Andalusia, loses its heuristic validity.

We cannot speak of "men" as a category opposed to another category "women"; to do so would be an oversimplification that in Herzfeld's (1986: 215) perceptive phrase "sacrifices complementarity to opposition" and conflates rhetorically subtle symbols. For such conflated oppositions we must substitute more precise formulations such as "married men of the agrarian working class," or "bachelors of the landowning class," or "women of leisure." If there is anything to be learned from European ethnography, it is the pervasiveness of social class and its power to determine the infrastructure of gender relations and the principles of group formation.

Gender is one additional dimension of the social organization of production, which, like social class, is not an arbitrary symbolic schema imposed independently of historical context. Moreover, as Ortner and Whitehead (1981a) have argued in a more general sense, one can never speak of genderized power, domestic or otherwise, without first considering the contours of dominance, prestige, and status "among men" in the wider society.

We can see from this discussion that many Andalusian working-class men do indeed at some level regard women as their masters and see themselves as the helpless thralls of powerful women, whether wives, mothers-in-law, or a combination of harridans. Hence the piquancy and the quicksilver mood shifts in the carnival verses about women. With their contradictory messages and styles, the earthy lyrics represent an acting out of all the conflicts about women in all her guises. But the carnival poetry, the transvestism, and the longings for and surrounding women can of course never find resolution. So carnival acts as a perennial stage, a theater for the domestic comedy, as well as for the human tragedy (often the same thing), in a paradox that never ends.

8

Up and Down
The Geometry of Sex

> It is significant that we say that something is "high" or "superior" — or conversely "base" or "inferior" — without considering why what we most praise (goodness, strength, and so on) must be located high. — Carlo Ginzburg, "High and Low"

Reversing the positions of man and woman, carnival plays with stature, bringing down the high and mighty and raising up the lowly. But what do "high" and "low" really mean in this context? Aside from the obvious allusion to bodies and altitude in space, what does it mean to say that some people are "higher up" than others, or "lower down"? Why do people phrase ideas about better and worse, which are after all moral or conceptual values, in what amounts to a *spatial* language of up and down, higher and lower? This geometric phraseology or analogue is of course a common metaphorical device in all languages, one that we rarely stop to think about, but it has great salience in Spain, where people often speak of "uppers" and "lowers" with regard to social status, morals, and, as we have seen, sex. Since carnival is at least in part about reversals and inversions of such comparative schemes, it is essential that we elucidate local concepts of high and low in all their symbolic richness and emotive power. The everyday metaphor of up and down in Andalusia unites many things: sex, power, and status, as well as values, in ways that lead directly to carnival inversion and its grotesque deformations of sex, space, and place.

Recently, anthropologists, not just in Spain but throughout the Mediterranean area, have begun to examine the ways in which cultural distinctions between men and women are linked with differences in power or dominance in the organization of community life. The view of sex and gender as part of the local system of hierarchization has been refined, again, as a direct result of feminist studies. One thinks of the work of Jill Dubisch (1986) and Michael Herzfeld (1991) on Greece and Jan Brøgger (1991), Caroline Brettell (1990), and Sally Cole (1991) on Portugal, among others. Most of this work owes an unspoken debt to the pioneering work of Susan Rogers (1975) on the "myth" of patriarchy mentioned in the preceding chapter. This work has shown that stereotyped dualisms like public versus private, active versus passive, and dominant versus submissive that supposedly circumscribe sex roles are more porous in the Mediterranean area than previously assumed. On certain occasions — during festivals and funerals, for example — Greek women gain a voice and, in doing so, speak for themselves (Herzfeld 1991, 1993).

Another aspect of command over public discourse is the spatial relationship of men and women (Sciama 1981). The public-private split, or "interiority/ exteriority," as Renée Hirschon (1981a:72) calls it, defines sexual segregation in the second dimension: horizontal space. Women are said to be silenced, in the realms both of speech, where the "poetics of womanhood" (Herzfeld 1991) demands silence and submission, and of geography, where norms of modesty restrict women to the indoors and interiority, ensuring their invisibility. The literal "ground rules" (Ardener 1981) for such two-dimensional alignments have been explored at length, especially in recent work in the Mediterranean on the physical boundaries of sex segregation. We will explore the purely geographical, or flat, aspect of sexual segregation in the next chapter. Spatial constructs are important, as important as any other structure that influences social life. As Dubisch (1993:275) astutely notes, the boundary lines of sexual segregation "begin with dimensions of physical space." Physical space becomes *content* rather than *context,* to echo Lévi-Strauss's dictum (1962:256) about human cultural diversity being most accessible to the anthropologist not in time but in space.

Like physical space, social space — the way people relate with regard to their physical positioning — has three dimensions. Besides here and there, there is also up and down — the realm of verticality, or, put another way, of height. Correspondingly, in male-female relations, there exists a third dimension, albeit a purely conceptual one, that encompasses norms about status and place, sexuality, moral values, and the associated comparative semantics of "aboveness" and "belowness," for lack of better terms. Although rarely acknowledged in current epistemologies of gender where space is taken as "natural" (Lock

1993:135), the intangible third dimension is important in the formation of normative hierarchies, because it anchors the physiological and the moral to create formal gender archetypes. This approach, by collapsing physical and cognitive domains, seeks a stereoscopic image, or holograph, of social relations.

If we move from Spain in particular to the Western world in general, we see that throughout history, social distinctions and moral judgments have been represented by stratigraphic and topographical tropes. These have always had sexual and gender referents. When it comes to gender in patriarchal contexts, to what Bem (1983) has called gender schemata, males are almost always "on top." In sociospatial terms, men are therefore physically superior, on the visible surface of things; women are "below," hidden from sight, corresponding to a lower status in the natural order and suppressed by a superior male overlay. But that this common epigenetic metaphor has other epistemological and psychosexual implications is only beginning to be explored in the study of gender in Mediterranean societies (Brandes 1992).

Throughout Western cultural history, as Natalie Zemon Davis (1978) has amply demonstrated, topographical metaphors have been used both to justify and to challenge social hierarchy, especially in relation to gender. The psychological power of tiered models derives from the justification of male claims to superiority by reference to linear scales of value. On such scales, women can be said to be lower, or ruled by "lower" instincts, than men: for example in medieval and early modern European thinking, "the lower ruled the higher within the woman" (Davis 1978:148). Since women's bodies and natures are ruled from "down below," their moral position could be equated with the lower life forms on the "Great Chain of Being" (Lovejoy 1960) that structured Western cosmology as a vertical concatenation leading upward to the angels and God.[1] Bakhtin (1984:401) has summarized the vertical orientation as follows:

> In the medieval picture of the world, the top and bottom, the higher and the lower, have an absolute meaning both in the sense of space and of values. . . . Every important movement was seen and interpreted only as upward and downward, along a vertical line. All metaphors of movement in medieval thought and art have this sharply defined, surprisingly consistent vertical character. All that was best was highest, all that was worst was lowest. . . . The concrete, visible model of the earth on which medieval thought was based was essentially vertical.

Such essentially vertical frameworks find expression daily in common non-sexist colloquialisms such as "above it all," "beneath contempt," "high and mighty," "lofty ideals," "the lower orders," and so on. Like medieval people and many other cultures, both familiar and exotic to us moderns, we tend to orient moral and social criteria — sexual and otherwise — on a perpendicular axis. George Lakoff and Mark Johnson (1980:14) call these the "orientational metaphors of up-down" that "we live by."

In scholarship, too, tiered schemes serve as a convenient mode of conceptualizing organic relations among component parts of systems. Classic examples are Max Weber's (1946) use of social "strata" for status groups, nineteenth-century anthropologists' use of "periods" and "levels" of sociocultural development to construct vertical taxonomies of evolution (see, for example, the work of Henry Lewis Morgan and E. B. Tylor) and Erik Erikson's (1950) theory of epigenetic "stages" or layers of psychosexual development — metaphors taken directly from geology. Another example is Freud's original topographic theory of the mental apparatus, in which the id is located "lower down" than the ego or the conscience; the depth idiom expresses evolutionary priority as well as a repressed status (Arlow and Brenner 1963). Similarly, many cultures associate the head with more refined capacities, by contrast with the baser "lower" body functions. Drawn from an immediate bodily analogy obvious to any observer, the principle of "higher" has come to symbolize whatever in human existence is purer, more spiritual, more evolved. Conversely lower (as in the "nether regions") conveys what is primitive, corporeal, carnal, inferior: formless matter. In evolutionary studies, we still tend to use a topographical metaphor to order levels of social complexity, technological advancement, or chronological sequences. Hence, "earlier" and "lower" become identified as coaxial along the temporal continuum, in what Johannes Fabian (1983) has called chronocentrism. Such paradigms justify higher strata's "giving form" or "lifting up" lower ones. "High status is up; low status is down. Good is up; bad is down. Virtue is up; depravity is down. Rational is up; emotional is down" (Lakoff and Johnson 1980:14–17).

High and Low in Andalusia

This said, let us return to Spain. As in other socially stratified contexts, in many parts of Spain a stratigraphic metaphor is used whenever people make value judgments or comparisons. Rich people are described as *mas alta* or *mas elevada* (higher up) than poor; the rich form a *clase alta* (high class), the poor a *clase baja* (low class). Following James Fernandez (1986:44), we will refer to this as the topographical model of human experience. It is, of course, not unique to Spain, nor are the following lexical usages.

Poor, but heir to a radical class awareness, the workers and peasants of Andalusia speak of their social universe as being sharply divided into discrete, superimposed strata. The operative concept here, as we saw earlier, is the "encima" concept—that is, the quality of being physically on top. "The rich are encima," they say, or the rich have *un pie encima,* a "foot on top of us." To be encima, or its converse, to be *pa' bajo,* or beneath, thus serves as the reigning metaphor for social distinctions based on myriad metaphorical invocations. While most stratified social systems employ such vertical schemata as a social metaphor, in Andalusia the starkly stratigraphic image conveys some powerful moral and sexual meanings in addition to the geometric imagery.

At the low end of the scale, being "above" clearly conveys superiority, political dominance, and exclusivity. But even more, in rural Andalusia, as implied by the metaphor of adjacent layers of earth, the terminology connotes the gravitational force of the overlay, a sense of those above resting oppressively on and crushing those beneath as if they were layers of sediment and rock— concepts appreciated by the plow farmers and agricultural workers of the region. In the class-conscious Andalusian context, this topographical trope conveys an inherent sense not only of superiority but also of violation or abuse of the lower levels underfoot; it is consequently a term heavily laden with affective symbolism. This geological metaphor finds expression also in terms used for the poor for their plight such as "the rich are treading (or trampling or standing) upon us," or "we are crushed down (or mashed) by the rich."

Perhaps not so oddly, one also finds the geological perception in the strongly defined southern regional consciousness of Andalusia. Occupying the southernmost and most backward part of the country, the Andalusians often denounce the Castilians and other northerners for "sitting on top of us," as the map of Spain does indeed indicate. The northerners are "on top, weighing us down" or "on top, screwing us"—locutions commonly employed for denouncing regional exploitation. And people from central or northern Spain will say smugly that they are from "higher up" (*más arriba*) than Andalusia, thereby communicating implicit claims to a "more European" and elevated status. Similar sensibilities ignite Spanish nationalism in general vis-à-vis northern Europeans, who are not only taller, richer, and from more powerful countries but also who come from "above." Since the geographical terms favored here also imply an oppression or domination if only because of the irresistible weight of the "higher" stratum or object, the encima concept is also replete with sexual connotations, suggested by the phrase above about regional rape, as we shall also see later in other expressions of popular culture.

In speaking of higher and lower, we should consider the settlement pattern of the pueblos, as well, a pattern that repeats itself virtually everywhere in lowland Andalusia. The geographical center of the towns, which is always considered the most prestigious and most desirable area, where church and town hall are located, is also higher in physical space. Town centers are always built on a hill or rise, with the outlying settlement "falling away" down the slopes. Within the urban center, architecture is dominated by the taller houses of wealthier citizens. These palatial palaces tower above those of the lower classes, by two or three stories; and consequently, in both a literal and figurative sense, to be located centrally is to be "above" one's fellow townsmen. The loftier mansions of the elite are often crowned with a looming watchtower, providing a dominant vantage point for peering down into the backyard patios and inner recesses of poorer and "lower" neighbors (Figure 12). House height is, therefore, a most compelling marker of social status. The correlation has been noted before by Spanish ethnologists (Moreno Navarro 1972; Rodríguez Becerra 1973).

Accordingly, when townspeople say that the rich "look down" on their inferiors, they mean it in a literal sense. The rich, in their high aeries, are indeed physically above them. The rich people's attaining a concrete manifestation of their claims to moral superiority is a great irritant to the poor. Lamenting their low position, working-class people ironically note that the mud running down to their streets is the only gift they get from the high and mighty, from *los del centro,* the center-dwellers. One often sees false upper decks added to the renovated houses of nouveau riche peasants and emigrants, complete with decorative balconies and miniature watchtowers, in vulgar imitation of the houses of the gentry. Here, keeping up with the Joneses literally means keeping "up."

The battle for height carries over into intervillage rivalries. Neighbors fight over which town is geologically "higher." I have heard residents of many villages engaged in extended debates, marshaling facts and figures to prove a case of altitudinal superiority. Aware of their "low" valley position, which is true of all the settlements in lowland Andalusia, the people of Fuentes de Andalucía, nevertheless, claim to be "higher up" than those in nearby La Campana because of the towering reach of their impressive church steeple. They insist that the bell tower gives their pueblo a few meters advantage in height over other towns in the vicinity. People from La Campana, scoffing at their effrontery, claim a six-meter height advantage based on elevation maps, which they proudly display. The people of nearby Carmona judge themselves "superior" to the inhabitants of all other villagers on the Andalusian plain because their town is built on the highest escarpment in the area, a bluff towering a full hundred feet above the valley floor (Figure 13). Everyone in the area ridicules the inhabitants of Ecija, a big town located in a minor depression, infamous as *el sarten de Andalucía* (the frying-pan of Andalusia), partly because of its vexatious summer heat, but also because of its concave topogra-

12. Elite home with typical tower, 1980.

phy. I found it noteworthy that a few feet of altitude should be invested with so much symbolic power.

Not just towns, but people, too, compete for height advantage. Wealthier citizens tend to be taller, probably because of a more nutritious diet; and physical stature, especially for a man, is equated with high-class status in Andalusia, as is an "elegant" elongated morphology. Body size is almost always an advantage for men, regardless of cultural context, but the height index is particularly important in Spain, where shortness is often associated with peasant status. Classic images of a towering Don Quixote alongside the squat Sancho Panza perfectly illustrate this attitude. All Andalusian mothers want their son to be the tallest in his cohort, and I have heard girls argue passionately about whose boyfriend was taller. I overheard one schoolboy boast at a public gathering that he was the tallest in his class, only to be challenged by other boys who stood within earshot. An impromptu measuring

13. View of Andalusian plain from Carmona escarpment, 1995.

contest ensued. The men I surveyed expressed considerable envy for their taller peers. "If you're tall, you can look down on the rest," they say. The anthropologist Anton Blok wrote a paper (1981) specifically about the admiration for tall and big men in the Mediterranean region. What he says about the charisma of big men certainly holds true for Spain; one very wealthy but physically puny señorito was dismissed by workers as being *rico pero bajo* (rich but short). And to Franco's rabid supporters, his major (and only) failing was his diminutive stature: the Generalissimo, chief of state, and Supreme Ruler for Life was barely five feet tall.

One finds a symbolic confirmation of Andalusian heightism in the construction of the municipal cemetery. Located at the edge of the urban nucleus, the burial ground in Spain, as elsewhere, is regarded as the village of the dead and mirrors distinctions among the living (Douglass 1969:74). In western Andalusia, people favor niche burials, in which the corpses are stacked above ground in crevices in the whitewashed necropolis walls rather than interred in the ground. The walls have six vertical rows of niches for coffins. The spaces, whose prices are based on desirability, are sold to individual families by the municipality. The more desirable higher niches sell for a higher price; the highest rows, of course, are taken by the wealthier citizens. When I asked why height of burial matters so much, I was told that it was the same as among the living: to be "higher up" was to be superior. In addition, local folklore holds that the body fat, or *graso* (grease) of corpses seeps downward, despoiling the bodies below, an idea without any scientific validity. So again, conceptually, being higher implies a certain purity and distance from base contaminants. Once more, the sense is that those above are invading, oppressing, violating, corrupting those below.

A Topography of Sex

Among other writers on Andalusia, Pitt-Rivers (1977) and Brandes (1980a, 1980b) show how concepts of subordination and domination, superiority and inferiority have both political and sexual meaning. Brandes writes (1980b:206): "The prevalence of dominance and submission as a theme in male folklore in part merely reflects the severely unequal distribution of power among the opposing sex and status groups in society as a whole." Accordingly, anxieties among working-class men about political powerlessness and suppression are often expressed in sexual metaphors.

Starting with the workplace, we note some of these metaphors during the sexually charged olive harvest. This harvest occurring in the winter months is a period of special excitement because it is one of the few times when men and women are recruited together in mixed teams (*cuadrillas*). Olives are harvested in different ways throughout Andalusia, some areas using the *palo* (long stave), by which workers on foot bat down the fruit (Martinez-Alier 1971; Brandes 1980b); others employing ladders and more delicate gathering methods that require workers to climb into the branches for hand harvesting. In some parts of Spain the choice of method depends upon whether the olives are destined for table use or for milling into oil, since in the latter case, less care is deemed necessary to avoid bruising the fruit. The farmers of western Andalusia, however, prefer hand gathering even for mill olives rather than the beating method, which they believe damages the trees and lowers future yields. Consequently, some of the workers must ascend into the trees to collect the olives by hand. Strung between the legs of two portable ladders are large tarpaulins, into which the harvesters pitch the fruit. Its accumulated weight creates a natural depression, or "basket" in the tarp for the collection of the crop. No other tools are used, and harvesters never don gloves despite the bitter cold, because gloves hamper dexterity and the harvest would be decreased.

The olive harvest in this region, then, is somewhat unusual because it requires a two-tiered work team. The "lower" cuadrilla works at ground level, harvesting the fallen ripe fruit and the olives tossed down that either bounce off or miss the tarpaulins. The "upper" team harvests the fruit that is still attached by a special method called "milking" — the hand is lightly passed over the branches in a gentle gliding motion that detaches the olives but avoids damaging the tiny leaves and twigs. The skill supposedly requires years of meticulous training. According to observers, for efficiency's sake, those above never perform the "lower" function and vice versa. "The rhythm is everything," people declare. The ladder skills and the ground-level skills are said to be quite different.

Brandes (1980b:147) shows that the olive harvest in Monteros (eastern Andalusia) is a liminal period, a moral "time-out" during which sexual mores are relaxed. The reason is partly that working-class men and women, casually thrown together in a rare instance of sexual desegregation, can banter sexually, joke, and engage in other suggestive behaviors that are normally forbidden. The same is true in Fuentes and La Campana, where the sexes also make lewd comments to one another. In both places, however, there is one important exception to the general disinhibition: the vertical split in labor functions. Throughout Andalusia, people observe a strict sexual division of labor: the men always perform the upper-level work, the women the lower-level. "Whether standing on the ground or sitting on the branch of an olive tree, men are invariably situated at a markedly higher level than the women, who during most of the harvest remain crouched below" (Brandes 1980b:144). "Men above, women below," is also a common statement in Fuentes and La Campana. When asked why this should be so, workers (and overseers) provide several explanations.

First, they say, men are taller; they can reach higher in the trees. Second, men are stronger and more dexterous and can "milk" the trees more efficiently. Men, not women, learn the skill of manual harvesting, which is passed from father to son. These are some of the practical reasons given, which may or may not be true. Reasons of modesty also find expression. If the situation were reversed, the women in their skirts, above, might inadvertently expose themselves to the men below. "Men could look up their legs," some of the men say, pointing out that men will always take the opportunity to catch a glimpse of thigh. But this explanation is specious, as the men themselves know, because the women always wear long pants underneath their skirts during the harvest and are fully covered from head to toe. The men even sometimes comment on the strangely androgynous uniform of the women. "They want to show they are still women," the men remark about the superfluous skirts. So modesty is not served by men being on top.

Finally, and somewhat more plaintively, the men resort to an erotic justification. They say that the olive harvest, with its higher and lower organization in which the men "throw down seeds" onto the women below, between the legs of the ladder, resembles the sexual act itself. At this point in verbalizing male prerogative, a masculine discourse of joking, pantomime, and swagger is inevitably invoked, in which the sexual division of labor serves to buttress male dominance and allay fears of feminine usurpation. "Men should always be on top," as on the bed, men laugh and gesture, because otherwise women will take charge, just as in sexual intercourse. Women, they argue, always want to be on top, but if they got their way, the man would become the passive partner, like a woman, "working underneath," controlled by the active partner on top. Brandes (1980b:144) found much the same thing in Monteros: "My informant points to the fact that the harvesting activity is a metaphor for sexual intercourse."

As Fernandez (1986) has argued about the mission of tropes generally in culture, the conceptual liking of discrete domains is governed by "the law of parallel alignment." Sexuality and spatial orientation become fused within the pyramidal hierarchy of objects in Andalusia and in unison govern the relations both between and among objects. Space itself enters a relativistic modality linked to the shifting geometry of moral discourse.

A similar metaphoric transferral of sex relations into three-dimensional space is evident when men and women cooperate in another tiered labor activity: house construction. As in the harvesting of olives, women and men — in this case, usually wife and husband — work together renovating their houses, which is a simple operation, given that the walls are made of plastered-over hollow bricks that are easily movable. The men invariably climb ladders to do the higher work, the women remain below, mixing plaster and manipulating makeshift pulleys to raise materials to the men. The women wear their usual work costume skirts over long pants. This operation differs from the olive harvest in that the women are essentially stuck with the more arduous tasks: lifting, mixing, moving bricks; whereas the men, perched on rickety wooden ladders, lay bricks and plaster above. So no practical excuses based on anatomical differences can be made to justify the superior male position. Instead, the men rely on the sexual metaphor of place, insisting that "men should be on top." This is especially true, they say, when it is a matter of husband and wife, because the work scene replicates marital relations and thus domestic authority.

To what extent are the men serious about the intense emphasis on being on top? And why do they react so strongly to such trivial examples of subversion? In Brandes's work (1980b:145–147) on sexuality and politics in southern Spain, he writes that the inferior political position carries with it a connotation of sexual disgrace, which, of course, is never trivial. When a man is placed "below" in conceptual terms — that is, in a subservient or subordinate position

—he loses his bodily integrity in a sense and is emasculated; his manhood is compromised, and he becomes a woman (the penetrated partner), the one "done to" by the physically and socially superior agent. We can see how this interchange takes on particular poignancy from the stratigraphic metaphor in which "higher" implies a pressing down or crushing of the lower object, in line with the gravitational trope associating height and "weight," or dominance. Thus, "belowness" is equivalent in a much broader sense to victimization and, for men specifically, of feminization.

To lose, to be beneath, to be emasculated, crushed, violated: we see in this collapse of experiences the power of core metaphors to define the inchoate subject (Fernandez 1986:31–32). The emotional power of the topographical model lies in its conflation of sensory dimensions by means of a unified and readily visualized metaphor, and to displace all the attendant fears psychologically, or "fix" them within an overriding apprehension about losing one's position or balance within the resultant architecture. This global fear of losing control in any single dimension, ramified as it is by every image within the linked system of images, therefore becomes magnified into a universal fear of extinguishment, of bodily diminishment in all dimensions: social, sexual, moral.

Verses and Reverses

Normally held in check by strictures of masculine decorum, these deeply held anxieties of men in Andalusia, like everything else that truly matters, find expression in the carnival copla. The power of the encima concept is expressed in the following specimens, extracted from carnival coplas about the stock female villain in the Andalusian domestic comedy, the mother-in-law. These verses relate specifically to a woman's capacity to usurp power, to subvert the sexual hierarchy, and to appropriate "aboveness." The following lyrics, taken from a longer poem, express one poet's fantasy of "getting her off from on top":

Le compró un vestido a la moda	I bought her a fashionable new gown
Y la peló a lo garzón	And gave her a new haircut,
Pa' que no me conozca,	And to make her forget about me,
Y me la compré un gachón,	I bought her a fashionable gown,
Y me la quite de encima	And to get her off my back,
Pa' que me tiene muy malos ratos	I even bought her a pretty boy,
Que se tienda panza arriba	Just to get her off of me,
Y araña como los gatos.[2]	Because I really suffer when
	She rolls over and scratches like a tomcat.

One revealing "upside-downing" about women's position is the following oft-repeated carnival copla. Like the ditty above, it was written by Juanillo "El Gato," one of the most celebrated local maestros, around 1965. The lyrics perfectly voice the fears men have about status reversals, their anxieties about loss of position, emasculation, and sexual subjugation:

La mujer, como el aceite,	Women are like oil:
Siempre quiere estar encima,	They always want to be on top,
Y al hombre que lo consiente,	And the man who countenances this
Le hacen tragar la quina.	Will be made to pay the price.
Y a todas horas encontraran	We always hear that
Lo que el hombre suele mandar,	The man should be in command,
Pues no acertamos a comprender	So we cannot even begin to
Esa manía, esa manía de la mujer.	Understand this obsession, this obsession
	Of women to be on top.
Si el marío sale,	If the husband goes out,
Es un callejero;	She calls him a street bum;
Si se queda en la casa	If he stays inside,
Es un casolero.	He's a house bum.
Hasta en el trabajo	Even in the work that men and
Que jacen de acuerdo	Women do together
Achucha el "pa' bajo"	He gets crushed beneath
Y ella hacia el techo.[3]	While she's up near the ceiling.

The poet alludes to "work" done together, meaning, of course, sex, but also implies other instances of sexual mingling discussed above, such as the olive harvest and house construction. Defined by the geometry of sex and gender in Andalusia, copulation becomes a perfect metaphor for political relations. Someone must be "on top" and therefore in command.

We have explored the meaning of this metaphor with regard to homosocial labor relations and public politics, and we have seen the trope not only defining perceptions of domestic dominance — the eternal question of who wears the pants — but extending into the realm of speech and rhetoric itself. For the silence or muteness of women, so often remarked upon and debated in studies of Mediterranean societies (Harding 1975; Ardener 1981; Herzfeld 1985a, 1985b, 1991; Dubisch 1991), is turned around ironically to become an acted-out "mania" to gain "topness," conflated thematically in the verses with both sexual dominance in a literal sense and the domineering voice of the shrew who belittles her husband no matter what his qualities.

In the copla, the woman has a "mania" to usurp the symbolic realms of hierarchy: work, the home, sex itself, the spoken word. Toppled, the man is reduced to servility, "crushed" like a thrall underfoot, flattened by the weight of his maniacal wife, whose words and body equally diminish him to nothing. As in English, the Castilian verb *achuchar* (to crush) can mean to crush either sediments or a sports opponent. Dominance, expressed stratigraphically, is at once rhetorical, sexual, and geometric. Whoever is on top has both power and voice to circumscribe the other, in a demonstration of the reciprocal effect that occupants of different positions in a hierarchy have. A person is either above or below, either on top (encima) or subservient (pa' bajo), and every relationship is defined by antithetical contiguous relations, as with objects in astronomical space.

The most important polarities of Andalusian culture join in a tiered cosmology, the orientation points of which are at the same time moral, political, and sexual. In carnival genres, the operative principle in this universe is the symbolic inversion of the established order. As Barbara Babcock (1978:20) argues, this inversion is always possible in tiered systems because their polarities are so stark; and this ease of reversal is in fact the source for the humor in the copla cited previously. Babcock points out that cognitive or symbolic reversal is an inherent quality of social hierarchies, because as clear-cut scales or ladders, they can easily be turned upside down in the imagination. This idea mirrors Freud's concept of the indestructible negative in the unconscious. In his short work "Negation," Freud remarks that the inversion of existing structures, or negativity, is indeed inevitable and necessary for mental processes in general and for intellectual creativity, for it represents a temporary escape from the work of repression (1953:182–184): "Negation is a way of taking account of what is repressed. . . . By the help of the symbol of negation, the thinking-process frees itself from the limitations of repression and enriches itself with the subject-matter without which it could not work efficiently. . . . This view of negation harmonizes very well with the fact that in analysis we never discover a 'No' in the unconscious, and that a recognition of the unconscious on the part of the ego is expressed in a negative formula."

When inversion occurs, the consciousness recognizes in the form of a negative symbol, or mirror image, that which has been repressed. Order is replaced not by chaos, but by a form of disorder or reordering, the opposite of the previous state. This dialectical phenomenon represents, as Davis (1978) has argued, both the value of and the danger to the established hierarchy presented by the topographical model, and in fact it constitutes the central contradiction of the model's reductive linear imagery. For things are not simply negated; they are instead turned upside down. The vertical model provides a convenient visual representation of the social order and justifies it by analogy to natural forms — and in so doing, stimulates the imagination to contemplate its reversal, in equally direct and schematic terms. This arrangement corresponds to Dumont's (1979:809) conception of hierarchy as "the encompassing of the contrary." One simply turns the model on its head (Babcock 1978:25). Terrence Turner (1977:58) also notes this aspect of hierarchy: "When the higher-level transformations must be controlled and therefore in some way formulated or described, from the standpoint of the lower levels, the description will tend to be couched in terms of paradox, or the negation of inversion of lower-level criteria such as normative definitions of categories, relations between statuses and groups, etc."

Many psychologists, such as Piaget (1962:229), have argued that such cognitive "reversible operations" create *Spielraum,* an imaginary play space in which to experiment with revolutionary ideas and images. Erik Erikson (1972:165) has called this Spielraum a means that all people have to infuse reality with "imaginative potentiality," that is, to experiment without limits. In his study of rites of rebellion such as carnival and proletarian festivals, Kertzer (1988) shows how such ludic antitheses work in political rituals, much as Davis demonstrates the paradoxical effect for sexual relations in European cultural history.

Metaphors We Live By and the Carnivalesque

Phrased in a vertical metaphor, scales of value, like top-heavy ladders, are inherently unstable. As a deformation of the normal order, the power of the carnivalesque must be seen in the light of this inherent tension within the discriminating faculty of the mind. The work of carnival is to experiment with such scales and yardsticks, to explore their metaphorical and moral possibilities, and in this way to make evident the logical inconsistencies of the world so that we can better understand them. In this sense, the work of carnival is undoubtedly universal and human rather than Latin or Mediterranean or Spanish. Latin carnival is simply one of the ways in which such experimentation and reordering occurs; other societies have other art forms to accomplish this necessary function.

So the question remains how "Spanish" or "Andalusian" the data presented here are. Good arguments can be made for both specificity and universality. Certainly in Andalusia a spatial metaphor seems particularly germane because of the regional consciousness, with its geographical anchor, the physiological distinctions between social classes, vertical niche burials, male anxieties about female usurpation, and so on. None of these things, however, is unique to Spain. Indeed, arguments can be made for the universality of the situation from several perspectives. Considering the Andalusian evidence comparatively, for instance, Brandes (1992:120) stresses the global ubiquity of such vertical representations, implying near-universality: "Up and down, high and low, tall and short — these vertically ordered spatial dimensions seem to provide metaphors for opposing moral, social, and other qualities in Western civilization as elsewhere. . . . One has only to consider the Japanese custom of bowing, whereby the higher-status individual remains more elevated than his or her inferiors; or seating arrangements in Balinese household courtyards, wherein numerous pavilions, each mounted on sandstone of a different height, provide 'a hierarchy of sitting places.'"

Perhaps the most compelling argument for the universality of the hierarchical view is made from a phenomenological perspective by Lakoff and Johnson in *Metaphors We Live By* (1980). They argue that up-down and other orientational metaphors are "grounded" in human biology and phylogeny — that is, they arise out of humans' erect posture and the "motor programs of everyday functioning" (1980:56). Rejecting epistemological foundationalism, they conclude that "human categorization is constrained by gross reality, since it is characterized in terms of natural dimensions of experience" (1980:181). In other words, everything derives ultimately from the primary human experience of the most fundamental force, gravity; from a perpendicular axis; and from human anatomy and sensory apparatus. It is true, of course, that humans do stand upright, unlike other animals, that they depend on sight rather than smell, that taller people are generally stronger, and that the brain (or mind) is anatomically "up" while the excretory (lower) functions are "down," so that spiritual "up-reaching" does reflect morphological and physical constraints.

From a psychoanalytical perspective as well, the data on expressions of domination and submission lend support to classic Freudian notions of oedipal ambition, castration anxiety, and sado-masochism. One can argue also for the relevance of Adlerian "masculine protest" in interpreting the male response to the threat of a "lowering" that is equivalent to feminization. From a slightly different perspective, Percy Cohen provides novel psychoanalytic support for universality on the basis of his work with children. Asking, "Why is higher . . . superior?" he answers: "All men have experienced childhood; and all children have experienced adults as more powerful, more prestigious, and more experienced than they are; all children have also experienced adults as higher than they are and have come to recognize or, at least, to suppose that greater height has much to do with greater advantage" (1980:59). Applying this idea to Andalusia, Brandes concludes that "it is the experience of childhood that makes such semantic formulations understandable and intuitively true" (1992:133).

Some clues to the ambivalent nature of the Spanish carnivalesque can be found here. We spoke of carnival as bringing together both sides of every issue, juxtaposing affects, and bringing into consciousness both a wish and a fear attendant on that wish. The wish to subvert hierarchies is self-evident, as is the desire to gain "aboveness" in relation to women; but accompanying the wish to turn things upside down is a very powerful anxiety: that of chaos, extinguishment, and loss of control.

Male resistance to "belowness" in political terms is eroticized as a polymorphous experience in which an inferior position stands not only for social subordination but also for a sexually "acted-upon" status. Rather than challenge or subvert the system of relations prescribed by public culture, male genres dealing with sexual reversal encapsulate anxieties about descent further into the depths. In this context, Adler's masculine protest certainly makes sense as a motivation for the misogynist carnival verse. The ease of such inversions also implies the potential instability of *all* hierarchies and structures, including those of sex, age, family, and politics. If women, like oil, having risen to the top, can now be cast down through the trick of carnival burlesque, then men can also be dethroned and degraded to the simultaneous states of infancy and womanhood. In the carnival imagination, the hierarchical model is right-side-up and upside-down at the same time. The masquerader in drag, regressing to oneness with the mother, becomes both woman and child, and those conditions are both fraught with ambivalence, negations of manhood. The lesson is perhaps that all behavior, no matter how seemingly monolithic, is always ambivalent, that all hierarchies are reversible, and that men and women are both on top and on the bottom at the same time, for there is no negative in the imagination. Carnival, the imagination in festive form, has no "no."

Here and There
The Geography of Sex

A whole history remains to be written of spaces — which would at the same time be the
history of powers . . . from the great strategies of geo-politics to the little tactics
of the habitat. — Michel Foucault, *Power/Knowledge*

So men are up, women down. That way men can have the "upper hand,"
at least in their mind's eye. This third dimension, sex, is indeed an invented
landscape of the mind: conceptual, imaginary, a figment of male reverie, a
vision of how things should be. In reality, of course, no one is really encima,
above, or on top of, anyone else in real physical space, except maybe during
the sex act or in physical combat. But the second dimension of reality, that of
flat geography, where people are on the ground, is divided equally into male
and female domains, and not only in the imagination.

In Spanish pueblos, more than in many other places, men and women live
apart. In the typical Mediterranean pattern of separation of the sexes, male
and female are "two separate worlds that pass without touching" (Duvignaud
1977:16). No trespassing is permitted here, no upside-downings: nothing is
left to the imagination! In sociological jargon, the separation of men and
women in two-dimensional space is known as "the gendering of space" (Spain
1992); as in much of the Mediterranean world, this gendering of real, physical
space seems deceptively clear-cut and unyielding at first glance. As usual,
though, on closer inspection, things are not quite what they seem. We have

examined the symbolic topography of sex, its verticality, the "ladder of man," as it were. It is now time to consider the physical geography of sex, its horizontality, and the consequences of this second dimension. This geographic dimension of sex, too, undergoes some curious metamorphoses during carnival. These, however, are not conceptual; they are real.

What I am referring to here is not to the division of labor by sex (who does what kind of work) or the distribution of power (who wears the pants) or any other behavioral distinction between the sexes. Rather, I mean the actual physical separation, or distancing, of men and women in the built environment. This includes the rules about where men and women are supposed to be, the "little tactics of the habitat" as Foucault puts it, and the symbolic associations with spaces in the architecture of the village. In a recent paper on power and place in Costa Rica, the anthropologist Setha Low (1996b) applies the term "spatialization" to this notion.

"Spatialization" means that everywhere in the physical environment there exists a moral geography governing the placement of persons. This placement constitutes what Shirley Ardener (1981) calls the social map, or the ground rules for the "where" side of life, and the context for interactions between the sexes on a daily basis. The rules relate in part to identity and to status. Granted, a sex-based architectural formula, or cognitive "mazeway" as Anthony Wallace (1970) once called it, operates in all cultures, but rarely does it operate with such pervasiveness as in many Mediterranean societies. In parts of Spain, Andalusia, for example, a gendered geography shapes the daily routine of most people at most times, because men and women genuinely fear being caught "out of place." The following observations, then, apply to the *sexual ecology* of experience in the rural communities of southern Spain and the psychological ramifications of such a gendering of the environment.[1]

A notion of sexual ecology encompasses the spatial context of behavior — where men and women should be geographically at specific times of the day. But it also includes the cognitive realm: the forest of symbols and ontological metaphors that form the familiar cosmology for both sexes, the mental blueprints that people use to navigate. I take it that these orientational rules in Spain are not Mediterranean universals (perhaps Lévi-Strauss might see them as part of some broader binary system)[2] but rather represent a variant of something more global, but different elsewhere in intensity and in form.

Female Seclusion and Exclusion

We have to begin with one of the visually most striking aspects of the Mediterranean world, that of female seclusion: women's confinement to interior or enclosed spaces. Certain areas of the built environment in rural communities are thereby defined implicitly as either female or male territory; "frontier lines" as Lévi-Strauss (1961:397) has said, are strictly drawn. Consequently, prohibitions and proscriptions pertain about sexual trespass in and outside these confines, and men and women are punished if they are out of line. The ground rules affect both sexes, but I think they have a more onerous impact on women: women's appearances in "important" places like parks, plazas, and public buildings are strictly limited by the barbed wire of convention, which excludes women from public life. Severe sanctions are brought to bear against women more often than men.

When in public places, women in rural Spain usually maintain a stance of "submission and silence" (Herzfeld 1991). That is, their bodies and voices take on a veiled or "muted" quality — although their deference rapidly disappears in places controlled by women, like the home, the marketplace, and other incontestably female spheres. (Incidentally, in Andalusia, where most men are anticlerical and refuse to enter a church, the female domain includes the interior of the parish church: an exception to the rule about public spaces' being male.) I am in no way alluding here to the Islamic practice of veiling the face or covering the body with opaque clothing, but rather to the distinct but obviously analogous practice of sequestering women out of sight.[3]

In Andalusia women can be observed scurrying through public areas of the villages. They must not be seen stationary or seated in any public place. They must not pause outdoors; they must always be moving, as though on some errand. Unless accompanied by a male kinsman, most women, and especially unmarried girls, avoid lingering in plazas, parks, and streets and until about ten years ago women never entered the bars, casinos, or taverns unaccompanied. Since the 1960s, respectable married women have begun to enter bars on Saturday nights, but only with their husbands. Some forward younger women may cautiously enter the most brightly lit, higher-class sort of café on holidays, but no well-bred woman will appear alone in a bar, and no respectable woman would ever enter a working-class taverna without a male consort. Many older women still refuse to set foot in any bar, no matter what the occasion (except for carnival, as we will see). Most anthropologists who have worked in the area of the southern rim are familiar with women's avoidance of bars. Even today, the practice is only beginning to change slowly in the backwaters of western Andalusia, and certainly not in smaller pueblos bereft of tourist attractions. I remember vividly one incident in 1973 that alerted me early on to this phenomenon of spatial constriction.

I came upon an old woman dressed in black outside a tavern in a small village with her face turned toward the wall. She looked very uncomfortable and seemed almost on the verge of tears. As I passed into the bar to get a cup of coffee, she stopped me and timidly asked me to convey a message to her son, who was drinking and playing cards inside, and I hastened to do so. Later, this man told me that like most older women his mother would not step into a bar even in an emergency, and because of this she had to find some man to transmit messages within (this was in the era before telephones were widespread in that part of Spain). Her discomfort had been due to the conflict between her need to get in contact with her son and her anxiety about entering the forbidden male world.

Moreover, when women and girls do appear outside in Andalusian pueblos — for example, in the agricultural work gangs, as they do quite often, incidentally, because of a shortage of male laborers — they are garbed from head to toe in layers of covering not normally seen in the village. Their hair, normally brazenly exposed during evening walks and on festive occasions, is ritually covered in the presence of men during the olive harvest, for example. It is as though some danger, normally under control, were recognized in this promiscuous mixing of the sexes with the men up above, so that the lustrous hair of the women down below has to be hidden.[4]

Indeed, I have felt the anxiety of women caught in the open — on an abortive errand, for example, when they are stared at intensely by the rows of men sitting outside bars (Figure 14) — as a kind of agoraphobia, a fear of open public places, a fear of crowds, of assemblies, as though being seen were equivalent to being naked. Women, of course, have their own folk methods of coping with these restrictions and with their confinement.

To give one example from personal experience: the husband of my neighbor Filomena, a peasant woman in her early fifties, a hard-working farmer, was absent virtually all the time, either at work or in the neighborhood tavern. Filomena had four grown sons, also wanderers, and no daughters to keep her company. Because of this abandonment and the dearth of female neighbors on the small narrow street she lived on, Filomena was restricted basically to the home and, on Sundays, the church. People pitied her because of this isolation and called her *pobrecita* (poor thing). Normally a woman, confined to the home, has at least her daughters, old mother, sisters, and nieces to keep her company. These kinswomen work together, sew at night, gossip, and clean house together in merry, gossipy groups. They are confined, but not lonely. Poor Filomena, however, had no living female relatives, and she was surrounded by absent males, if such an oxymoron is permissible.

But being clever — not to mention desperate — my neighbor found an ingenious way to compensate for her misfortune. One day in May, I found her leaning rather theatrically outside her front door with her wrist on her forehead, looking pale and tense. Breathing deeply and clutching her heart, she

14. Men seated on street; note woman (right), shopping, 1980.

breathlessly told me and my wife, who was, as she knew, a medical doctor, that she had developed "an allergy" to her own house. Not to a part of the house, she said, but the "whole damned thing." She could not abide remaining inside for another minute and had to "take the air" or die. It was serious and getting worse. To complete the obviously rehearsed performance, she gave us a tearful look of utter misery.

Filomena suspected that her illness had something to do with the nasty chemicals her husband used for his farming and then brought into the house on his clothing, traces of insecticide or fertilizer maybe, she wasn't sure. She was convinced that he tracked these awful chemicals throughout the house, men being such careless and unregenerate slobs. But the doctors could find nothing wrong with her, and her husband scoffed. So she asked for some corroborating support from my wife, so that her husband might bow to foreign medical authority and let her take the air on occasion just to counteract the allergy to the house. Having handled such requests before, we promised to speak to her husband, and shortly afterward we did so.

A gentle, tolerant man, he smiled indulgently, nodded knowingly, but said nothing. Afterward, Filomena began to take restorative walks around the block, which I believe did her much good. When she met us on one of these perambulations, she laughed out loud and thanked us profusely for helping her back to health. But what stuck in my mind was that our neighbor needed medical justification to get out of her own house for a few minutes a day. Other women with more rigid husbands, or stronger superegos, were less fortunate.

Sexual Quarantine

What I have seen with my own eyes in Andalusia is corroborated by legions of ethnographic reports; sexual quarantine is an unambiguous empirical reality. As such it must be accepted as a fragment of life as it is personally experienced in Andalusia. I had occasion to witness cases where the depth of commitment to sexual segregation led to occasional incongruities between reality and conviction. Visible evidence was elided or openly denied. Men would tell me emphatically, for example, that women never venture outside the home except to market, while, not more than fifty feet away from where we were talking, hundreds of women could be plainly seen picking cotton or weeding sunflowers — more women in fact than men, given that most of the male laborers were then in Germany or Switzerland. When alerted to this fact, the men would simply dismiss it as a sort of statistical deviation, by assuring me that what I was witnessing (and would witness time and time again) was anomalous, unusual, rare, out of the ordinary, perhaps a mirage, or due to special circumstances never clearly explained. But it was obvious to me that this discrepancy between what I saw and men's idealized view of the "place of women" represented an example of wishful thinking. "Women are of the home" (*la mujer es de la casa*) became a kind of mantra that if repeated often enough might become true or at least allay male anxiety about women's straying from their proper place.

The sequestration of women, which amounts to a masculinization of exterior space and occasionally to a distortion of empirical reality, is a part of the "public/private" dichotomy so often referred to in literature on the Mediterranean region (Sciama 1981). It is at the same time conceptual, moral, social, and in a little-understood way, territorial. That is, is has to do with the social construction of spatial boundaries and frontiers, with gender identity, with principles of exclusion and inclusion, and with domains of power. A cleavage in the geophysical world, this spatial dichotomy between men and women creates a kind of Einsteinian relativity in the village, an astrophysical "bending" of dimensions. It makes for a situation where a particular physical space is inhabited at most times by men only; one example is the bar or tavern, which is exclusively male until closing time, when it gets cleaned by women, thereby becoming temporarily female — or one might almost say hermaphroditic.

This masculine terrain is open, or accessible to all men — in fact, rather like the spotlit proscenium of a stage, as Herzfeld (1985b) notes in *The Poetics of*

Manhood. Here men "perform" the daily rituals of manhood on the public stage, again to use Herzfeld's terminology. Sometimes a parallel interior dimension is folded into the wings of the community theater. This secondary "invisible" realm is closeted and dark, reserved for women and girls. The central marketplace, for example, indoors and enclosed, is "female," except that tradesmen come and go, doing the heavy lifting and provisioning.

Such a sexual spatialization, with all its complexities, has been approached in many different ways in the past twenty years in the literature on the Mediterranean. Indeed, the subject is a major component of an entire subspecialty in Mediterranean ethnography, gender study, and of course it is grist for the mill of theorists of many persuasions: Marxist-Leninist, Marxist-feminist, structuralist, and Freudian, to name just a few. In her book *Gendered Spaces,* Daphne Spain perhaps best summarizes the prevailing feminist position, by far the most often encountered in the literature (1992:15–16): "Spatial segregation is one of the mechanisms by which a group with greater power can maintain its advantage over a group with less power. By controlling access to knowledge and resources through the control of space, the dominant group's ability to retain and reinforce its position is enhanced. Thus, spatial boundaries contribute to the unequal status of women." Yet in a book of three hundred pages, the author never once even mentions the erotic side of life; nor does she allude to the role of sexuality in establishing spatial boundaries or to the pleasure men and women derive from being with members of their own sex at times. Spanish men, at least, do not go to bars in order to dominate women, although that might be a side effect (Driessen 1983). In her book, Daphne Spain (to take one example) regards sexual reproduction as a purely political process, as though humans were reproduced through mitosis or in test tubes, like Dolly, the Scottish sheep-clone. In this way, the hard facts of sexuality are expurgated from some politically correct gender studies, much as gender used to be expunged from sex studies, in the days of the Kinsey Report. We are back to a pre-Freudian, even pre-Enlightenment image of humanity as disembodied spirit, an image as bloodless, lifeless, and sexless as it is pedantic. As Melford Spiro (1979) once plaintively asked, "Whatever happened to the id?" Where is humanity recognizable in such an interpretation? Even though the feminist position that spatial segregation oppresses women and privileges men is the most economical, and probably true (insofar as any sociological theory is true), the spatial dimension of sexuality is too rich to be exhausted by any one sociological theory or any one political agenda.

For one thing, the sexual division of space does not merely buttress male dominance that merely oppresses women and empowers men. I have heard men lament that like the Flying Dutchman, they are eternal wanderers who are never able to return to the home shore. It is almost as if they are sentenced to exile by the exigencies of their unforgiving style of manhood, a harsh code that the Portuguese anthropologist Miguel Vale de Almeida (1996) calls hegemonic maleness. Lidia Sciama (1981) noted this paradox about male privilege in her paper on public and private domains in the Mediterranean. Just as women are denied entrance into the political space of the outside world, so many men, diverging from the stereotypical masculine extroversion and aggressivity, are wounded by their culturally enforced expulsion from home and hearth. Their satisfaction with gender boundaries depends on personality.[5]

The public-private divide or domestic-political split has been the subject of much debate in anthropology, beginning with the first symposium on Mediterranean studies ("Mediterranean Countrymen: Conference on Mediterranean Studies," organized by Julian Pitt-Rivers), held in Aix-en-Provence in 1959. I can think of at least four valuable approaches to the question. The first and most influential is that of Pitt-Rivers, who in *The Fate of Shechem* (1977) seems to look at Mediterranean sexual separation as a manifestation of a larger structural balance governing "the politics of sex" wherein male honorableness rests insecurely on a corresponding female shame. The honor-shame syndrome thus lies at the root of female confinement, for men obviously need to "protect their flank" by limiting access to their women — that is, by hiding and protecting them.

The Schneiders extend this approach in their work on political economy in Sicily. In their first book (1976), as in Jane Schneider's groundbreaking article, "Of Vigilance and Virgins" (1971), we find a powerful heuristic model. The authors place the Mediterranean basin within a broader geopolitical context by showing that the local system fits within the global framework of regional place, space, class, and dominance inside the world capitalist system. The subordinate "position" of women can thus be seen as analogous to the subordinate position of the regions of the periphery. This international model does provide a plausible and satisfying symmetry. The Schneiders (1976:97) also speak somewhat obscurely of "wife-capture" by the metropolis, or center, as playing a role in the hiding away of women, but I find the notion too abstract.

Whether Pitt-Rivers's structural interpretation or the equally imaginative insights of the Schneiders are true is, however, unimportant. The rightness or wrongness of such pioneering work makes little difference; one can never know for sure, anyway. The point is not that the theorists have solved the problem but that they have forced us to think about it in a fruitful way and have thereby ignited much insightful commentary. Pitt-Rivers and the Schneiders paved the way for the rest of us by joining the debate in the first place. As current jargon has it, they should be given credit for "problematizing" the phenomenon of sexual segregation.

I can think of others who have also bravely stepped into the fray to examine

Mediterranean sex codes. Jacob Black-Michaud (1975) regarded the whole apparatus as stemming from segmentary politics, but his point of view, which he is no longer here to defend, today seems antiquated. Jill Dubisch (1986, 1991, 1993) and Renée Hirschon (1981a, 1981b) have written about the issue from a reasonable feminist position, to the effect again that sequestering equals oppression, and Michael Murphy (1983a, 1983b), James Taggart (1992), and George Saunders (1981) from various psychological perspectives, focusing on childrearing practices and oedipal tensions between the generations. All these interpretations add useful perspective.

It is possible to analyze from a neo-Freudian standpoint certain kinds of ocular activity relating to concealment: voyeurism, scopophilia, and visual searching out. A woman's body is regarded in the Mediterranean lands as being especially vulnerable to *ocular* attack. The eye is conceived to be an organ of both predation and penetration, so that to see is both to eat (to devour) and to invade; staring is therefore a rape or ravishment of the object. "In these parts to see is to steal" (Duvignaud 1977:228). So the eye is both bipolar and bisexual, both masculine and feminine. The art historian John Richardson (1991), in his recent book on Picasso, takes up the convergence of visuality, sexuality, and power as an obsessive and formative element in Picasso's character and art.

Richardson shows that the artist, who was born and nurtured in Andalusia and was very Andalusian in some ways, especially in his love for flamenco and bullfights, was obsessed with the human eye as an organ of almost supernatural power and prescience. "Why not put sexual organs in the place of eyes and eyes between the legs?" he once asked (Richardson 1991:10). Picasso liked to direct a smoldering stare at people, especially women. He did so often, sometimes to their discomfort. "The eyes of that Andalusian are killing me," one of his mistresses is reported to have said. He once told Françoise Gilot, "You should wear a black dress and put a kerchief over your head so that no one will see your face. In that way you will belong even less to the others. They won't even have you with their eyes" (Richardson 1991:11).

In the same sense in which women can be "had" by sight, a man's property and his manly force can be wrested from him through the act of observation, in a society where concealment and secrecy, as Pitt-Rivers (1971) has pointed out, are essential to reputation and good character. For to see is to know and to know is to gain power over the object, to possess it, as Picasso knew so well. In "The Secret Society," the sociologist Georg Simmel made the following observation: "Secrecy is its own sociological purpose: certain insights must not penetrate into the masses; those who know form a community in order to guarantee mutual secrecy to one another" (Wolff 1950:355). Ernestine Friedl

(1961) comments obliquely on the meaning of concealment when she speaks of life in the Greek town of Vasilika as being an endless game of hide-and-seek. All anthropologists of the Mediterranean have experienced this "game" in the course of their fieldwork.

Women Out of Place

We have some inkling, then, about why in Mediterranean villages the sexes are kept separated, beyond the point required for sexual modesty. Barriers are erected between men and women to reduce the occasion for sexual "theft" of a particular Mediterranean kind. But why are women denied access to the crowded places like bars, and why are men, conversely, encouraged to seek out public arenas where they can be appraised by their fellows? What does it mean when a man or women transgresses and is caught "out of place"? What actually constitutes a sexual-spatial barrier, which is after all an immaterial marker, or as Germaine Tillion says, an "invisible frontier" (1983:167)? And what does spatial transgression mean in terms of the broader systems of social categorization we have looked at?

The notion of frontiers and "women out of place"[6] brings to mind Mary Douglas's (1966) definition of dirt and pollution: matter out of place. Any object or person out of its assigned place is dirty and polluting. Out-of-place things cause anxiety, a sense of disorder. The same metaphorical mechanism is at work here: women out of place are both polluted and polluting, and so are men who are caught out of place. They are, metaphorically speaking, "dirty." But what is it that is being contaminated? And what are the sanctions and punishments for the violation? And what are the ramifications in the moral universe of the Andalusian agrotowns? What does it mean to say that a representative of one sex is in the *place of the other*? And, at the next level of abstraction, what does it mean to say that a place, or a spot in the world — a locus arbitrarily defined by architecture, not an object at all but simply empty air — is either male or female?

The question about the meaning of contamination touches on the sanction against being out of place and the broader meaning of such sanctions in other cognitive contexts.[7] How are men and women punished by public opinion for gender trespass? First, we have to answer the question, What is the crime? Let us take the obvious case of a woman who enters a bar alone in Andalusia. No matter what her intentions or her inner character, she becomes a loose woman; instantly, her sexual modesty is thrown into question. In the minds of male onlookers, she becomes fair game and at the same time becomes a sexual predator herself; she is regarded as possibly promiscuous, out-of-control.

Thus she loses her cultural shield against sexual trespass by trespassing on men's territory. It is an aggressive act leading to moral confusion, symbolic disorder, and punishable by the Furies of public opinion.

I knew of one case in the town of Carmona involving an inseparable married couple. In their forties, the man and his wife, childless, went everywhere together, unlike other married couples, who spent only a few hours a day in each other's company. The woman, whom we shall call Augustina, used to follow her husband to the neighborhood bar, where the two of them sat silently in a corner drinking beer every night. They greeted other men in the bar, but mainly kept to themselves. The husband, Ernesto (a pseudonym, like all names mentioned here), did not play cards or dominoes, avoided the men's ritualized exchanges, and spoke mainly to his wife. Men in the bar indulged the couple but kept their distance. Ernesto was a loner, a cobbler who worked alone out of a shop in his house, and Augustina, who was not a local woman but a native of a small mountain village in another province, was never seen except in his company. The two were nicknamed "Romeo and Juliet" and were considered harmless but "crazy." People avoided going near them as they sat holding hands in the dark corners of the bar. The men felt uncomfortable around them and the couple's presence inhibited the general merriment. Ernesto alone would have been accepted, but not in tandem with his wife. As a mixed couple, they were "wrong." Eventually, the bartenders asked them to leave, and they moved to Seville, probably locked forever in their mild folie à deux. My informants could point to no other example of a woman "regular" in a bar. I have never encountered another example of an Andalusian woman's frequenting a bar. Romeo and Juliet broke down the spatial barrier between man and wife, between man and woman, and consequently they were placed in a category by themselves, in an androgynous no-man's-land.

What about a man who lingers in the marketplace or at home at night? He is likened to a women or a mother-hen or some other personification of effeminacy and passivity, so that his punishment in the court of public opinion is to be redefined sexually, turned into something else, something less than a man, something bad. To give one example: Salvador, a man in his thirties who shopped for himself in the marketplace, squeezed fruits and haggled over the price of chickens like an old woman. He was a young widower, and he had no sisters to care for him, although people said he could have relied on his mother, as most men would do, for the most feminine tasks, like shopping and cooking. Another oddity was that he often wore an ascot around his neck, something never seen before or since in this part of Spain. Because he could be found in the marketplace buying eggs, with the women, and wore such strange attire to boot, Salvador became known as a *maricón* (queer), although the calumny was never proved. The men avoided him, but he seemed indifferent to ostracism. He apparently enjoyed shopping and cooking. Unlike most men, he just did not care what the others thought of him.

Let us pause at this point to take stock. The woman who is found out of place is thought of as a kind of man, or rather is *like* a man; she is endowed with an aggressive sexuality which can destroy her; by contrast, a male transgressor like Salvador is deprived of his masculinity. He is persecuted for passivity, she for assertiveness, neither for an *act* of defiance against the rules, but rather both for a *solecism* involving place: they have crossed to the "other side," broken through a geographic Maginot Line, assaulted the ramparts of convention. The reproof for being out of place, out of time, for representatives of both sexes, reflects a curious symmetry. The reproof is born of the underlying tensions and conflicts of an insecure sexual identity, which though certainly not unique to Spain, is highly polarized there. Being out of place is an indication of contagion or disturbance in the sexual order of the village. But the defect in the sexual balance of the village itself is one built into the system as the ever-threatening contrast, as sun is to shade — the inevitable obverse, that which is repressed. The woman in the bar is the female side of manhood, and the man in the market is the male side of femininity. The deviant embodies a universal fantasy of entering forbidden places or appearing naked, and in ostracizing the deviant who acts out the unconscious fantasy, the people banish from their own psyches the disturbing unconscious thought.

Spatial arrangements and taboos of this sort institutionalize one of the primary means by which society's order is communicated to individuals and "felt" by them. The semiotic power of space is that it functions as a "morphic language" (Hillier and Hanson 1984:198), a primary means by which society is both interpreted and experienced by its members. The accommodation between sex, status, and space arises from the constant renegotiation and reenforcement of historical patterns of differentiation, exclusion, and hierarchy. As Bourdieu (1977) has noted, the power of a dominant group lies in its ability to maintain social constructions, images, and norms that make the present order of things "natural" (see also Spain 1992:18). And what could be more natural than space? Thus the erection of barriers in space must be seen as much as a projection of barriers against the "other" within as against the one without.

Why Sexual Segregation?

Bearing these conclusions in mind and taking the bar as the prime example, we return to the question why women are excluded from male spaces. On the basis of observations about how bars are used by men to create a society of equals, we can make a few inferences, none of which is completely valid by itself. First, the bar is the place where informal exchange of commodities takes place. Such exchanges constitute a kind of shadow economy. To say that women are excluded from the world of power brokering because they are excluded from taverns is to state the obvious, but the question of why this should be so remains. For one thing, why do men guard the high ramparts of convention to such an extent that women, normally desirable, at least as visual objects (most Spanish bars display semipornographic images and icons), should be bodily barred? It is necessary again to think of the identity-bolstering aspect of exclusion and inclusion; for every space that is denied to one sex becomes a prison as well as a lair for the other. In exchange for their power to exclude, men must accept its inevitable downside: visual deprivation. What could be more depressing for heterosexual men than having nothing to look at all day but other men?

But remember that the bar, like everything else in Andalusia, undergoes a status and sex change during carnival. Carnival "opens" everything. The rules of bar etiquette also undergo changes. For one thing, women gain entry both in groups and singly. During carnival, the bar becomes a stage where the murgas pause to sing their coplas. Having wandered out of the bar down the street, the gaily clad troubadours ceremoniously enter the next bar, beating their drums and tooting their horns. The doors of the bar are thrown open, men and women mingling and drinking promiscuously, the men in drag, the women costumed according to their fancy. The band performs, the audience lustily applauds the "spicy" lyrics. The crowd reacts as one. During carnival, men are women and women are men.

Of course, we must not forget the economic motive in all this. Being mainly poor men, and mainly unemployed, the troubadours expect remuneration. They accept drinks, but they also pass around a hat for loose change. Sometimes, in crass coplas, the singers make direct appeals for money. An example from the early 1980s blends such an appeal with a political message about the regionalist struggle:

Hoy le saludamos con muchos cariño	Today we greet you affectionately
Y con alegría le vamos a cantar,	And with great joy we sing to you,
Y le deseamos a ustedes y su familia	And we wish you and your family
Que pasan felices este Carnaval.	A most enjoyable carnival.
Nosotros traemos bonitas canciones—	We have some lovely songs
Seguro que a ustedes le' van a gustar.	That you're sure to savor,
Si damos un piciaso, perdonen ustedes	And if we screw up, forgive us:

Por el poco tiempo que han sido ensayá.	We haven't had much time to practice.
Esperemos un regalo,	Now, we expect a gift,
Por su propria voluntad,	Which of course you'll part with voluntarily
Lo menos dos mil pesetas	At least two thousand pesetas [twenty dollars]
Que eso para usted no es ná,	Which is nothing at all to you,
Y le damos las gracias	And small recompense for the
Con muchísima alegría,	Pleasure we give you,
Estos murguistas presentes.	We, the murguistas assembled here.
Un viva le damos a Fuentes!	So, "Long live Fuentes!"
Luchemos juntos por to' Andalucía![8]	Let's all fight for our Andalusia!

Women in large numbers masquerade, promenade, and pack the bars. They participate, at least as an audience, in the show and throw money at the singers, although they do not themselves sing or compose songs. No one objects to their presence. In fact, since the male clowns are all in drag and the women revelers are also costumed (though not in drag) and masked, with their hair and faces covered, no one really knows the sex of the masqueraders. In this promiscuous mingling of sexes and bodies, all barriers against women collapse; the sexes are indistinguishable. The "invisible frontier," though still invisible, is no longer a frontier. Carnival erases the sartorial as well as the moral, psychological, and spatial boundaries between the sexes. The bars lose their masculine character. Indeed, they temporarily become female, in the sense that virtually all the masqueraders appear female, being either transvestites or exotic women. On this day women are therefore not out of place in bars. They belong anywhere.

Subtle changes occur, too, in drinking and invitational rituals. Men no longer invite other male barflies to share drinks and cigarettes. Instead all are focused on the murga bands. For their performances, the musicians expect and receive endless rounds of drink. All exchanges occur between the two groups, performers and bystanders. Some men take advantage of this reversal to escape paying their bar bills. The bartenders accept the loss as a cost of doing business on carnival day.

But let us take another tack, and examine the act of the *invita,* or "invite,"[9] itself. In and out of carnival, bars are places where men slake each other's hunger and thirst—ply each other with bodily sustenance. These exchanges should be regarded as the male counterpart to the female monopoly over alimentation. The bar then serves as a substitute kitchen, where men provide food for other men, normally a woman's job. Driessen's (1983) view of the bar as a place of male refuge takes on added appeal when one thinks of the bar as a parallel, masculinized larder. How else can men seduce each other but through the exchange of food and cigarettes? In this ritualized way, men "mother" each other. In this way lifelong bonds are forged.

The bar, drinks, and cigarettes, therefore, which are perceived as quintessentially masculine, take on sexually ambiguous, compensatory overtones. The bar can be seen as a sort of substitute for the breast. Perhaps the idea of the "male breast" is the real meaning behind women's exclusion. The all-male bar gives men a chance to nourish their fellows, to indulge their feminine side, to take over the female role in life, to usurp, in symbolic ways, female nurturing. Far-fetched? Perhaps, but everything about carnival is far-fetched.

What about the alcohol use as a prime factor in sexual divisions? Drinking is of course associated with loss of control and sexual abandon in many cultures (Marshall 1979:85). Alcohol works as an inhibitor to the moral sense, so that drinking often precedes sexual indulgence; it must therefore be denied to women, except on special occasions like carnival. Yet the fact that alcohol is served in the café does not seem an adequate explanation for women's exclusion in and of itself. As in other parts of Spain (Brandes 1979), most men in Andalusia will sit for hours over a coffee or soft drink in bars, and some regulars do not drink at all but simply smoke and play cards — although that is unusual. I knew a man in his seventies in the town of La Campana who spent most of his waking hours in the local tavern without ever drinking anything stronger than chamomile tea, thus earning the nickname El Camomilo.

During carnival, men feed each other, and the sharp lines between male and female collapse in chaos. In erasing boundaries and in superimposing opposites, carnival brings about a unification of bodies and provides a polymorphous experience that is deeply pleasurable. In addition to inverting hierarchies and reversing time, carnival also obliterates distance — both in the metaphorical sense of social distinction and in the real sense of physical space. The power of carnival overwhelms all human dimensions of contrast: time, space, sex, and status.

10

The Mayete as Carnival Caricature

How close together lie festival and warfare. — Marcel Mauss, *The Gift*

We now turn to politics, by which I mean struggles over power and privilege in the public, or male, realm. A prime target for carnival verse is the *mayete,* a fixture of rural society in western Andalusia with deep roots in folklore. The word *mayete* is the colloquialism that people use to describe the middle-class farmer that Marx called the petty-commodity producer, in other words, the rural bourgeois. In Spain, the mayete is not much more than a middling peasant, really — not rich, but not poor either, certainly not dirt poor like the vast majority of landless farm workers, or *peones.* The latter live side by side with the landowning mayetes, without however entering into any lasting commerce with them.

In the Franco period, the working poor could not attack the rich land-owners openly in their songs, nor could they vent their anger at the authorities, who were often the selfsame oligarchs. They had to refrain from direct attack on the latifundists or the Franco government and its functionaries, for example, because of the severe state censorship.[1] Instead, they directed their venom against that respectable middle-class target the pompous bourgeois, the may-ete, both because doing so gave them a substitute pleasure and because they truly despised the alternative target. This secondary theater of class warfare gave rise to a special genre of rhetorical vilification which pitted the lower orders in verse not against the big landowners or Franco officials, who were in a position to retaliate through lockouts and blackballing, but against the relatively lowly peasants. Through the carnival coplas in this chapter we examine this curious war between the bottom and the middle.

Fuentes de Andalucía[2] (Fuentes for short) is a farming town of about eight thousand people located in the classical *latifundio* country of the Guadalquivir River basin. Like most of the other pueblos in this zone that I have mentioned at various times, Fuentes is sharply divided into rich and poor. A central feature of its social life under the Franco regime—indeed, since the 1800s—has been the fierce class struggle between the latifundists ("señoritos" in the classic Andalusian usage) and the seasonally employed farm workers, called *peones* or *jornaleros* (day laborers) or simply *trabajadores* or *obreros* (workers).

For the most part, the uniformly rich and powerful señoritos were politically reactionary, pious, and elitist. Having come to power through their victory in the Civil War (1936–1939), this landowning elite autocratically wielded the cudgel of Francoist power, keeping the poor in check. The poverty-stricken workers, who were largely anticlerical and politically left-revolutionary, mainly espoused a range of mildly socialist or agrarian doctrines, but a sprinkling of anarchists and nihilists among them leavened the mix; however, many shades of political opinion were represented, of course, including the clerical right. But the leftist workers uniformly, even unanimously, held populist or egalitarian beliefs rather than doctrinaire Marxist ideas and aspired toward a classless society where each man might own the land he tilled, as private, inalienable property. Given the degree of hostility throughout the region between the extremes of this sharply drawn class structure, as well as the bitter history of violence before the Civil War, many observers regarded western Andalusian rural society as basically a two-class system, without a viable middle (see Bernal 1974; Calero 1976; Tuñón de Lara 1978).

This bipolar approach was very common in both native and Anglophone historiography, but there was excellent evidence of much more complex systems of stratification and of political alignments in many areas. The systemic complexities included various intermediate strata of peasants, agrarian bailiffs and agrarian specialists, shopkeepers, and bureaucrats (see Moreno Navarro 1972; Luque Baena 1974). It was almost a scholarly tradition in political science, for instance, to discount the social significance of these petty-bourgeois types, especially the small peasants, who were often pigeonholed as inconsequential "minifundistas" (see, for example, Roux 1991), and to concentrate only on the much more conspicuous groups of landowners and laborers—that is, the very rich and very poor who had furnished the operatives at the extremes of the political spectrum (see Martinez-Alier 1971; Artola et al. 1979).[3]

Although many observers have acknowledged the existence of the middle strata, especially the commercial bourgeoisie, few anthropologists have spent much time examining social relationships between the *agrarian* lower and middle classes;[4] there seemed, indeed, to be little to say about the relations between autonomous peasants and the landless proletarians.

Like many other observers of western Andalusian agrarian relations (both Spanish and foreign), I made this same mistake of omission while doing field-work in the early 1970s (Gilmore 1980). I also neglected the role of the small but substantial agrarian middle class in the Fuentes area and overestimated the importance of class struggle between señoritos and jornaleros. Like so many others, I downplayed the role of the mayete in class relations (see Henk Dries-sen's [1982] compendium of my sins). Here I want to rectify the mistake, not to placate my critics, but because it needs to be done. The best way to correct the omission is through an analysis of carnival verse.

The mayetes, the peasants, were — and still are — socially important. They historically formed a kind of social buffer zone between the oligarchs and landless laborers; and they too, as it turns out, had both social and economic ties with the politicized workers, figuring prominently in proletarian percep-tions about society and labor relations. For the most part apolitical and self-sufficient, these middling peasants stood somewhat aloof from the ongoing class struggle between uppers and lowers. Yet they were nevertheless involun-tarily drawn in by forces beyond their control.

This chapter describes the situation during the period from the end of Civil War (1939) to the early 1980s — that is, the heyday of the dictatorship and its aftermath. While increasingly obsolete at the end of the twentieth century, much of the imagery discussed here lingers on as an element in proletarian consciousness and folklore even today, as we shall see. Some very recent car-nival verses still enthusiastically disparage the mayetes.

Mayete: Etymology and Ethnography

In the flat, fertile area to the west of Seville City, the smallholding farm-ers have their own linguistic label, attesting to a regional class formation of considerable longevity and salience. I am speaking here not of rich landlords, but of subsistence peasants, small- to medium-sized market-oriented cultiva-tors, and *hortelanos,* or small-scale vegetable gardeners (people with less than fifty *fanegas,* or twenty-five hectares of arable land). These hardworking farm-ers cultivate their properties with family labor, selling their wheat, olives, sunflower seeds, and vegetables in local markets. Occasionally they have the surplus capital to hire additional help at harvest time, but just as often they rely on family muscle power.

People in Fuentes, La Campana, Carmona, and the neighboring towns and villages call such modest farmers "mayetes," a term not heard much beyond the local area, the *comarca*. On the lips of the landless, the curious expression "mayete" (with the *y* heavily aspirated: almost "mazhete"), is a term both of abuse and of envy. Owning land, the mayete is slightly better off than a worker (after all, he has property), but he is by no means rich. He is self-employed, which also means a great deal to a landless laborer. Most important, the term implies that the man can avoid day labor. The mayetes also speak of themselves in this way, as "autonomous" or "free," although it is just as common for them to refer to themselves as *propietarios,* property owners.

What is the lexical provenance of this expressive colloquialism? Its semantic and historical origins are indeterminate, lost in time. No one I spoke to in town could trace its etymology; it is not standard Castilian, and nobody knew of its meaning anything other than "middle-class farmer," or "peasant." Since "mayete" is a localism, the concept also provides townsmen of all classes with a rare sense of parochial uniqueness and, to some degree, unity. "Mayete," known in structural linguistics as a semantically empty phoneme, may have no more extended meaning, but the term captures the essence of a collective representation and plays a key role in the elaboration of group identity.[5]

Often explained to outsiders as *propietario pequeño* (small owner) or *el que trabaja su propia tierra* (a man who works his own land), "mayete" has very different connotations from *labrador* (capitalist farmer) and *terrateniente* (big landowner). Although some sophisticated people speak of the *campesinado,* referring to all rural people who work with their hands, *campesino* (standard Castilian for "peasant") is seldom heard in this part of Spain. The more technical "propietario" is rare, although it may be occasionally used by mayetes or sophisticates.

A cognate, *mayeto,* is found in Malaga and parts of Cadiz Province and environs. Because in Fuentes and its neighboring villages residents have a tendency to turn final vocals into an "e" sound (*pesete* for *peseta*), an obvious phonetic link exists between the variants. A synonym for "mayete" is the curious word *pisguarero,* apparently a corruption of the venerable Andalusian term *pegujalero,* meaning small-scale cultivator. Written *pisguarero* by the literate people in Fuentes, the word is pronounced "pi'huarero," in one of the common elisions, or phonetic conflations, of southern speech. A pisguarero, then, is a classic mayete, a "real mayete."

As we have intimated, "mayete" carries a rich and resonating rhetorical load. So layered are the nuances of the word that it inspires different images in the minds of the latifundists on one hand and the workers of Fuentes on the other. To the rich, it signifies a "true peasant," a *tio del campo,* an ignorant country bumpkin who is "stuck to the land," as they say contemptuously. A wealthy interlocutor defined "mayete" as a man of the earth who plows with mules rather than tractors, whose fingernails are dirty, and who has earth stains on his trousers, "a mule."

Conversely, in the view of the lowly laborer, the mayete is something entirely different. He is a man of distinct and enviable economic security, even of leisure. For the jornalero, the mayete is "a man who works less than I do," a man who is "rescued from wage labor by a few fanegas." The mayete, far from being disdained, is a man to admire and, above all, envy, perhaps to hate a little, an autonomous man who enjoys middle-class dignity and is spared the disgrace of hard manual labor. He is *un autónomo,* the workers wistfully remark, articulating their greatest aspiration.

Sometimes severe conflicts, although not of the same political intensity as those between the very rich and the very poor, do arise between workers and mayetes. Most such fights stem from the exigencies of the labor market. Some of the better-off mayetes must hire temporary help at harvest time. Unlike the señoritos, who avoid personal contact with their workers, the mayetes do their own hiring, often favoring less advantaged relatives, neighbors, or simply workers whom they trust on the basis of previous experience or reputation.

Also, most mayetes work alongside their hired hands in the fields, as supervisors or additional labor. Working with their own hands, the mayetes cannot be denounced — as the latifundists are — for being lazy parasites or shameless exploiters. Some of the "little" (poorer) mayetes, instead of holding reactionary views about the elite, share the workers' democratic sentiments and are not in political opposition. (Some better-off mayetes, however, are violently right-wing; many supported Franco in 1936.) Yet conflicts do sometimes arise when mayetes and jornaleros work together. The mayetes are notoriously niggardly, and of course labor disputes inevitably erupt over wages, working conditions, and especially petty grievances — about the food provided during work hours or the precise quitting time or the arithmetic of piecemeal (*destajo*) weights and measures.

Most important, however, is the influence of the personality stereotypes that circulate among the workers. The farmworkers maintain a highly negative image of the typical mayete, "el mayete mayete." The stereotype is almost the distillation of all that is greedy, selfish, egotistical, and "closed" in the human character. In their folklore, workers portray the mayetes as crafty, self-important, and avaricious, indifferent to proletarian suffering, cruelly calculating, concerned only with minute details of their own finances (all summarized as *guriche,* another Andalusianism, meaning "stingy and grasping"). According to this disagreeable stereotype, the mayete is also petulant, complaining, and closed or "shut off" in personality—all qualities disdained by the workers, who pride themselves on being open and generous. And thus arises a straw man of class that enters into the poets' repertory of carnival defamation.

This mocking image has some basis in fact. The mayete is known for, and would not deny, his stern austerity and habit of vociferously agonizing over every little expenditure. Much of his obsessive thriftiness derives from the economic demands of small-scale agriculture, where one bad season can lead to ruin; but the workers, believing that twenty fanegas of olive orchard or wheatfield is enough to support a family in style, have no sympathy with the mayete's complaints. Moreover, with their acute sense of the hedonistic satisfactions that money affords, the workers of Andalusia find it not only inexplicable but disgusting that the mayetes hoard their money and, to use the stock phrase, "eat worse than a common laborer."

All this cultural dissonance, of course, is fair game for the proletarian satirist and the working-class carnival troubadour who set their sights on the human comedy. During the annual carnival, the mayetes of Fuentes are lambasted in songs, jokes, riddles, and burlesque. They represent a prime and inexhaustible target.

For their part, the mayetes harbor corresponding grudges, which arise mainly from financial squabbles, against the notoriously demanding workers. The mayetes must bargain in the labor market for the services of the workers. Being able to offer less work for shorter stints to employees, the mayetes cannot compete with the better-off señoritos and must pay a little more for the jornalero than do the richer farmers who can offer weekly or monthly work. In the period of 1980–1982, for example, this difference amounted to only about 5 or 6 percent of the day wage (about two thousand pesetas at that time, or about twenty-five dollars). But even so small a differential served to anger the mayete employers, because they were put at a disadvantage. The mayetes continually complain about the unrealistic attitude of the workers, always demanding more than the impecunious farmers can afford, when it comes to wages and working conditions.

Given all these misunderstandings, the mayetes seem to have adopted an outward show of indifference to their workers. This may be partly a self-defense mechanism to avoid provocations. This clash of styles and personality traits fuels the satirical coplas. We now examine some of the more famous examples of anti-mayete verse.

Proletarian Protest Songs

The following song specimens about mayetes were collected between 1972 and 1990, mainly in Fuentes. The lyrics date from the 1950s to the mid-1970s. In every case, the words were written (or dictated) by the usual working-class artists. Even when the brief commentary that accompanies each example is in the present tense, it is necessary to bear in mind that we are speaking of the Franco period and the mid-1970s. The following copla is typical of the genre attacking the mayetes for their closed, mercenary personality:

Los mayetes con el tiempo	With all the bad weather of late,
Estaban desesperao,	The mayetes are getting desperate,
Y con la falta de agua	And with the drought we're experiencing,
Poco crecían los sembraos.	All their crops are withering.
Si algodón no sembramos	If the cotton crop fails
Y tampoco hay maíz,	And the corn dries up too,
Creemos que mucho' de ello'	Most of these mayetes
No van a poder dormi'.	Are going to miss some sleep.
Aquí nuestro Director	Our bandleader here
Oyó una conversación:	Overheard a conversation
Dos mayetes se contaban	Between two mayetes
Cada uno su dolor.	Recounting to each other all their woes.
Uno le decía al otro:	Says the one to the other:
Yo ya lo tengo pensao	If it doesn't rain damn soon,
Si no viene el agua pronto	They'll drag me off to the canals!
¡Al caná me voy tirao!⁶	

This song is self-explanatory, except for the reference to canals. Los Canales, actually referring to irrigation channels, is a cotton-growing area along the Guadalquivir River, near the town of Lora del Río. Workers from town emigrate there in the cold early spring months to pick cotton for a day wage when no other work is available. While earning a few pesetas, they live in squalid, unheated shacks, eat cold bread, drink brackish water for weeks, and suffer from chilblains. Being somewhat financially secure, the mayetes never have to experience the degradation of working in such sordid conditions. The canals represent the utter despair of the poorest workers.

The next example pillories two particular mayetes, one nicknamed Perico

Mateo and the other Juanito "El Calero." These were two close friends, known in Fuentes for their miserliness and their financial scheming. Perico Mateo was so stingy that he refused to pay for maintenance on his farm machinery, instead making his unqualified son, Leonardo, do all the work, just to save a few pesetas. El Calero, Mateo's associate, was just as much of a peseta pincher.

One day, in an incident that soon became part of carnival folklore, the bumbling Leonardo got his fingers caught in the spokes while greasing the wheels of a rick. He ran yelping in pain right across town, all the way to the infirmary, making a spectacle of himself, much to the amusement of the workers. One of the maestros wrote a ditty to celebrate the event:

Los mayetes de este pueblo	The mayetes of this town
Están aburrios,	Are a ridiculous lot,
Y lo vamos a decir.	And we're going to give you an example.
Uno vive en la calle El Bolo	One of these mayetes lives in Bolo Street,
Y ha comprao un carro,	And he bought himself a cart,
Y lo vamos a decir.	And this is what happened.
Todo el dia se lleva	This guy is too cheap to get it serviced,
Engrasando; su Leonardo	So he has his son Leonardo
Se pilló los de'os:	Greasing it up all day,
Y al Postigo	Until the poor dope gets his fingers
Se fue dando gritos.	Caught and goes whimpering in pain
Este quién lo entiende	All through town.
Es Perico Mateo.	Now, the guy who really understands all this
	Is Perico Mateo.
Todo aquel que sea mayete,	Anyone who needs more information
Que no sepa lo que es agonía,	About what true agony is
Le pregunte	Should consult Juanito "El Calero,"
A Juanito "El Calero"	Who has been an authentic peasant
Que fue un pisguarero	All his life.
De to'a su vida.[7]	

Such verbal barbs were often followed by rehearsed burlesques, almost like a dramatic postscript. In a particularly crude one, which I witnessed in 1973, a clown in typical mayete attire, the boots and the signature blue cotton work clothes, appeared out of a bar. He carried some old farm implements, a hoe, a rake, and a sickle, as though to make the reference even clearer. The "mayete" showed off his ample derriere for a time, strutting pompously through the streets; then he leaned over, and with a flourish, began pulling fake money from his "anus," throwing it to the laughing crowds. "Money is only shit to a real mayete like me," he shouted, as the people clapped appreciatively. Carnival humor, as usual, appeals to the lowest common denominator.

Our next song takes a slightly more confrontational tone. Using provocative language rather than farce, it attacks the mayetes for their insensitivity to the plight of the workers. Here the poet makes a clear political statement about unfair labor practices and exploitation. Since many mayetes are descended from workers who by luck or hard work escaped poverty, the poet makes the point that mayete indifference to workers' poverty is a betrayal that will be punished in time by the powers that be. All it takes is "one bad year" for the mayete to wind up broke, unemployed, and back where he started. This warning bespeaks the need for all to recognize their common humanity and show sympathy to the less fortunate.

En Fuentes, con la maíz	In Fuentes, all the mayetes
Se han llenado de billetes,	Did pretty well in corn this year;
Y no se pueden sufrir,	They're loaded with greenbacks.
Estos pícaros mayetes.	Oh, those rascally mayetes.
Compran yuntas y tractores	They're buying ricks and tractors
Se jacen de su labor	With all their money
Y se burlan cuando pue'en	And having a good laugh at us poor workers
Del pobre trabajador.	Whenever the opportunity arises.
Luego que llega el verano,	Then in the summer, they
Siegan con los forasteros,	Harvest their crops using outside (blackleg) labor
Porque dicen que nuestros	Because they say we locals ask too much.
Pedimos mucho dinero.	But let them remember this:
Pero que tengan en cuenta	Once they were workers, too,
Que ellos han si'o jornaleros	And come just one bad year, we'll
Y en veniendo un año malo,	Be seeing them on the unemployment line.
En el paro los espero.[8]	

Like many other songs, the preceding plays on a favorite image in the carnival coplas: the *pícaro*, or rascally, mayetes. The poet brings them down to earth with an earful of spiteful scolding. Despite their superior airs, he cries, these smug property owners are just inches away from falling back to lowly worker status. Come one bad harvest, one drought, one crop failure, and the mayete will return to proletarian misery. The powerful egalitarian theme found in proletarian culture in Andalusia is highlighted here. The poet knows that superior status is an illusion that nature will eventually dispel. The song is a warning as well as a satire. Another song, written during a year of low prices, expresses the same idea:

Mayetes y labradores de Fuentes,	Mayetes and landowners of
De este pueblo de Fuentes,	This town of Fuentes,
Los precios de las cosechas	The prices you get for your crops
Mas baratos cada dia.	Are falling every day.
Este año la Cooperativa	This year the Cooperative
Se ha tardao en pagar el algodón;	Is late in paying for cotton:
Los mayetes no cogían el sueño,	The poor mayetes can't get any sleep.
Muchos de ellos no han cobrao del to'.	Some are getting no payment at all.
Este año son los precios mas baratos:	Yes, this year the prices are low:
Lo hemos visto nosotros en un boletín,	We heard about it in a bulletin,
Labradores y mayetes de este pueblo,	Mayetes and farmers of this town
No sombrais ni una mata peregil.	You can't even grow a sprig of parsley.
De esta forma no se puede comprar gas-oil	So how are you going to buy Gas for your wonderful new tractor?
Pa' que pueda labrar tu tractor.	If your precious land can't support you,
Si tus tierras no pagan los gastos	Then you'll soon be emigrating just like us,
¡En Suiza y Alemania os están esperando![9]	And we'll be waiting for you in Germany and Switzerland!

The lyrics warn that with the overproduction this year, the mayetes will soon be emigrating to northern Europe, looking for jobs, just like the workers: all brothers in need, reduced to the same misery.

Next we look at another example from the same poet who composed the previous ditty, Marcelino Lora, a native of Fuentes and a famous bard. He baits the mayetes once again with the same ironic message. This year, 1967, the problem is too much rain. Here Lora depicts the northern city of Barcelona, another emigration terminus for the unemployed, as the yawning mouth of doom when the crops fail.

Ay mayete, por Dios, ay mayete, por Dios.	Ay, mayete, for God's sake,
Tanta agua es nuestra perdición.	So much rain is our perdition.
No sembrarás, no cogerás, que malo este tempora'a.	You can't plant, you can't harvest

Ay que ruina: los mulos tengo
encima,
¿Y si no trillo que comen mis
chiquillos?
Ay Mayete, por Dios, ay mayete, por
Dios.
Si no hay trigo, cogerás algodón.
Me se murió la mula ya es de no
comer ceba'a,
No tengo verde por eso se me muere.
Y lo que debo también lo tengo
encima,
Ya no me quedan ni pollos ni
gallinas.
Ay mayete, por Dios, ay mayete, por
Dios,
¡Barcelona nos espera a to'!¹⁰

Oh, how terrible is the weather.

Ay, what ruin is crushing down
On my poor mules, and
Without wheat, what will my little
ones eat?
Ay mayete, for the sake of God,
If there is no wheat, you'll have to go
to work
Harvesting cotton for a wage.

My mule died because I had no
barley.
I have no forage at all and it died.

With all these debts crushing down,
I'll soon have neither chicks nor hens.
Ay mayete, for God's sake,
Barcelona is waiting for you.

Note again the use of the loaded term "encima" in the verses, with all its implications of being crushed, weighed down, humiliated.

Some songs have an even more caustic tone, some going so far as to impugn the mayetes' honesty. For example, the following ditty, composed during the Republic (1931–1936) by Félix "El de La Gazpacha," makes a stinging accusation against a specific individual, using the man's well-known (and detested) nickname. The rebuke is particularly galling because in using the word "desenguía" (misspelled in the original broadsheet), which carries the sense of money paid to a whore, it likens the mayete in question to a prostitute. It is, of course, an inflammatory insult to any man in Andalusia to compare him not only to a woman, but to one of the worst sort.

The song refers to a policy instituted by the liberal government of the Republic (probably in 1933 or 1934) when an effort was made to provide low-interest loans to small farmers. Many of these highly sought-after loans were apparently subject to rampant corruption and fraud at the municipal level, at least according to the envious workers, who were not eligible for them, not owning land. Defamatory lyrics like those below often led to pitched battles between the workers and the mayetes. After the war, of course, these verbal darts had to be toned down due to government supervision, and in some cases, due to the fear of litigation.

Y este verano que viene
En vez de algodón

So this year, they are going to pay
The mayetes to grow sugar beet

Serán remolacha.	Instead of cotton.
Dan el dinero en delantera	If you're a mayete
Que el mayete hoy	You can get the dough;
Les hace falta.	Just lie and say you need it.
Eso es una ignorancia	This is a scandal and a disgrace,
Y el que quiera cobrar "desesguía"	And anyone dishonest enough to collect
Que le informe	This whore's money,
A Manuel "La Quilina,"	Can just go and
Que estuvo cobrando	Ask Manuel "La Quilina,"
Hace pocos dias.[11]	Who's been priming the pump for days.

I imagine most of the lyrics above speak for themselves. The meanings are simple and unambiguous, the intentions clear. Most interesting about the sentiments expressed is what they show about proletarian social consciousness in Andalusia. Taking a high moral tone, the poet reveals a nuanced awareness and as deep a concern with cultural values as with politics and economic issues. In the years before democracy, the workers' deepest resentment came from contemplating moral and ethical issues (rather than class exploitation in the usual sense): the mayetes' pretensions and their smugness about the workers' difficulties. Throughout, the theme is "You are just like us, so don't put on airs," expressed through ironic warnings about a common fate.

Many anthropologists of Spain, both native and foreign (for example, Moreno Navarro 1972; Brandes 1980b; Collier 1987), have observed that the strongest political belief among Andalusian farmworkers during the Franco years was not so much politically sophisticated anarchism or socialism as a cultural attitude that can only be called a folk, or populist, egalitarianism. Resembling the "deep popular utopianism" of *Don Quixote* that Bakhtin (1984:25) constantly remarks is the mainspring of Cervantes's political thought, this sentiment, too, is a rather apolitical form of egalitarian feeling. It is not so much a revolutionary creed as a vision of moral unity of the worthy: a hatred of hierarchy and pretension in any situation. Although painful for the poor, poverty itself is not an evil, nor is the wealth of the rich, if used properly. The real evils are forgetting one's basic humanity and brotherhood with the poor, repudiating commonality with the disadvantaged, withholding charity, being stingy, ignoring one's obligations, engaging in ostentation or luxury in the face of misery. The poets assure us that such unmitigated evil will be miraculously punished by public opinion in the pueblo or by some ill-defined fate — God or some other unforeseen power. The worst and most intolerable human traits are smugness and superciliousness vis-à-vis the less fortunate.

Poetic Justice

Sometimes, of course, the forebodings are realized and the high and mighty are brought low, providing a most satisfying form of Andalusian schadenfreude. The following song rejoices at the long-awaited downfall of some particularly arrogant mayetes. It celebrates an epochal event that occurred in 1971 in Fuentes, a vengeful hope fulfilled. Soon becoming a carnival legend, the actual story is as follows.

Since the 1920s, a group of mayetes had rented smallish plots in a great estate owned by an absentee landlord, the duke of the Infantado, one of the biggest landlords and richest men in Spain. It was in an area called El Cuarto de Caza, located partly in the municipal territory of Fuentes, which covers about fifteen thousand square hectares. Apparently the modestly well-off rentiers came into town occasionally and, with their money and airs, lorded it over the landless workers. "They would come into a bar and drink among themselves and say bad things about the workers," one told me, repeating a widespread complaint. "They were arrogant and closed. They thought they were better than we were because they had two fanegas of the duke's land. Hah, the duke's land. What fools!"

Then things changed. In the late 1960s, deciding to modernize and mechanize, that grandee of Spain decided to evict the mayetes from El Cuarto de Caza. They had no legal papers and were unable to provide evidence of squatters' rights, despite the efforts of numerous lawyers. Finally, their appeals exhausted, they were forcibly removed from the duke's property by the Guardia Civil in a very ugly episode. Never one for ceremony, the Guardia threw the peasants' possessions on the ground, amid the women's weeping and the men's cursing and calling for vengeance. The next February, Juan "El de La Harina," a local maestro, composed the following song to commemorate the poetic justice of the mayetes' downfall:

Aquellos mayetes	Those mayetes
Del Cuarto de Caza	Of the Cuarto de Caza,
Que con amenazas	Who were driven out
Salieron de allí,	By threats,
Y ellos se creyeron	They once thought
Que con el dinero	That with all their money
De aquellos terrenos,	That came from those acres
No iban a salir.	They'd never have to leave.
Ellos se juntaron,	So they joined together
Vieron abogados,	And hired a bunch of lawyers
Y a to's le sacaron	Who succeeded only in
Mu' bien el parné'.	Fleecing them of every penny.

Algunos en el pueblo	Some of them came to town to
Se han visto vender;	Sell their possessions;
Y unos van por tagarninas,	Others had to forage.
Otros por cisco comprao,	Others still are selling charcoal,
Otros tienen un zambullo	And yet others set up cafés and bars,
Y otros están arruinaos.	But some are totally ruined.
No te acuerdas el dia,	Mayetes, do you remember
Que cuando vendías el trigo	How swollen with pride
Que orgulloso tu vivías,	You were when you sold your wheat?
No te acuerdas el dia	You would never have believed
Que te tuvieron que echar	That you'd be thrown off
Despues de tu fruto dao.	Your beloved land before the harvest.
T'as quedas desengañao	Well, you were wrong, and now
Y en la cartera [*sic*]	You are in the street
¡No tie's un real!¹²	Without a penny in your pocket!

(*Tagarnina* is a local thistle, *cardo,* used for forage, and a *zambullo* is a make-shift bar or tavern; *acuerdas* is Andalusian for the proper Castilian *recuerda* ["remember"]. Otherwise the lyrics are self-explanatory.)

Even after Franco's death, even after the censorship was lifted, the poor mayete fell beneath the poets' scourge. Under the Socialist government of Felipe Gonzalez (1982–1994), for example, the poets continued to applaud the mayetes' troubles. During the agricultural recession of the mid-1980s, Juanillo "El Gato" composed the mocking verses below:

Un saludo cariñoso	We have a very sweet image
Acude a nuestra memoría:	In our memory engraved:
El de Felipe Gonzalez	That of Felipe Gonzalez
Grabado está en nuestra historia.	As a fact of recorded history [i.e., as out of office].
Hay un duelo establicido	The authorities have a contest established here
Entre el agua y la aceituna;	Between rising prices for water and oil;
Y esperanza no hay ninguna.	Oil always rises; there's no hope.
El petróleo y el café	Gasoline and coffee, I have heard,
Segun tenemos entendi'o,	Are also too expensive
Por lo mucho que ha subi'o.	Even to think about.
Tomaremos carbonato	So we'll drink cheap carbonated water
Pa' jacé la digestión,	For the digestion,
Y a Juan Carlos lo tenemos	And we'll show Juan Carlos
Tan negro como el carbón.	That we've turned black as coal itself.

Unos con el desempleo	Some of us suffer because of
	unemployment
Y otros por enfermedad,	Others because of illness,
Y los mayetes en el paro	But with this recession,
¡Tiene la gloria gan'a![13]	At least the mayetes have
	Gotten their just deserts!

Politics, Culture, and Mayetehood

What the carnival coplas do, then, is set up the "rascally mayete" (the pícaro, scoundrel, or rogue) as a community straw man ripe for puncturing. The pícaro mayete himself becomes a buffoon: Sancho Panza–like, pompous, and puffed up, he is rebuked by the Fates in the guise of mocking proletarian clowns. The bourgeois farmer, depicted as a monster of swollen pride, becomes for everyone a cautionary example of pretentiousness and complacency, an inviting target awaiting retribution in carnival's court of public opinion. Mayete pride, the songs assure us, "goeth before a fall," as the maestros adapt ageless folk wisdom to the local context.

The risible stereotype constructed through the use of mockery and satire affords a measure of comfort to the workers, whose envy and resentment find a perfect object in the caricature of the oaf soon parted from not only his money but also his grandiosity. While the hated señorito could not be ridiculed publicly (and would not listen, either, being absent during carnival), the relatively comfortable mayete was vulnerable, an easy target for venomous character attacks.

Ironically enough, in the case of the Cuarto de Caza mayetes in the song above, the scourge of the mayetes and the engine of their destruction is not God or nature, but a much richer man, a duke — in fact, an exalted grandee of Spain, historically one of the biggest villains of local folklore. So carnival politics makes strange bedfellows of rich and poor. The opulent duke, comfortably ensconced in his palace in Madrid, finds himself an instrument of *proletarian* vengeance. In this ironic twist of fate, the maestros deliciously appreciate the uniting of social extremes against the middle! As in the morality tales of the Middle Ages, the absentee aristocrat and the masses unite to punish the smug bourgeois. But such ironies are not uncommon in Spain, where the richest and poorest segments of society have for centuries participated in a curious "symbiosis" (Mitchell 1991). We will deal at greater length with this alliance of uppers and lowers in the next chapter.

The mayete stereotype is the product of fierce proletarian pride, which in Andalusia transcends local political issues. The superiority of the honest poor over the fatuous bourgeois is an entrenched theme in Spain that can be traced back to Cervantes's mockery in *Don Quixote* of middle-class social climbing personified by the land-greedy Sancho Panza, as well as in the populist tradition of such classical Castilian dramatists as Lope de Vega and Calderon de la Barca. Thus, despite their poverty, ignorance, and lack of refinement, the semiliterate poets of Andalusia trace their inspiration to the deepest wellspring of Spanish popular culture. Not poverty but arrogance is evil; injustice lies not in wealth per se, but in inhumanity; and the people have faith such wrongs will ultimately be righted.

During the darkest days of the Franco dictatorship, the proletarian poets of Fuentes were surely a mouthpiece for vox populi, for the landless and the oppressed. Their voice was not one just of crude mockery or of class hatred but a polyphonic chorus informed by a complex and profound irony, spiced with laughter and gaiety, ennobled with hope and the quest of the honest poor for self-respect and dignity.

11

Copla Politics
Ideology and Counterpoint

God sets us nothing but riddles. Here the boundaries meet and all contradictions exist side by side. — Fyodor Dostoyevsky, *The Brothers Karamazov*

The carnival songs deriding mayetes are a leading form of political theater — they literally number in the hundreds. Instead of "inverting" the class hierarchy, they pull out its center, causing the entire structure to implode and conflating its two extremes. Carnival is always political; even its sexuality is political, because it has to do with power relations and status, not to mention "who's on top." But carnival in Spain is political in specifically Spanish terms. These are nothing if not ambivalent, as poetic justice is meted out through the agency of the rich duke and his minions, the bullies of the Guardia Civil. But what of the carnival poets' view of the upper strata of society, the rulers, the Church, the current ruling ideas, the moral and intellectual baggage of the plutocracy?

Authors of many accounts of European carnival see an unambiguous revolutionism at work. Some, like Le Roy Ladurie (1979) and Kertzer (1988), describe incidents of class warfare and insurrectionary violence. Such incidents have occurred during carnival throughout Spanish history, too. Kertzer notes in his survey of politics and ritual that throughout European history, carnivals, whether violent or not, "provided an occasion for the powerless masses to gather, an occasion that was otherwise lacking" (1988:148–149). By its very nature, therefore, carnival always had powerful revolutionary, anti-elite overtones, according to many observers.

Yet we made mention early on of other approaches. Some observers, while acknowledging carnival's class overtones, take a more functional approach. In concert with Gluckman's "ritual of rebellion" model (1963), a second interpretive school sees carnival as essentially a means of letting off steam and paradoxically of maintaining the status quo. In this view, carnival, acting as a ritual "safety valve" (Kertzer 1988:149), defuses rather than encourages revolution. Carnival is, in the expression of Stanley Brandes, "the symbolic means through which the governing powerholders provide the commoners of their town with a sop" and "pull the wool over their eyes" (1980a:90). As Kertzer (1988:149) notes, the debate over whether carnival acts as a safety valve or revolutionary theater continues without closure, for much of the evidence is ambiguous and can be used to support either view.

There is a third view, which is more synthetic than alternative, that of the Russian critic Mikhail Bakhtin (1984). Rather than taking an either-or approach, Bakhtin sees carnival as both-and: subversive and conservative at the same time. Bakhtin's main point is that by its topsy-turvy nature, the carnivalesque mingles incompatible symbols and affects and juxtaposes latent moral and ideological contrasts and political symbols that are present within both mass culture and elite culture. The fierce mockery of the carnivalesque, like all folk humor, is therefore not unidimensionally condemnatory but politically *ambivalent,* incorporating both derision and renewal, degradation and veneration. For Bakhtin, carnival at once "asserts and denies . . . buries and revives." In this view, carnival does invert the world's hierarchies, but the effect is transitory and not *merely* negative: "We find here [in carnival] a characteristic logic, the peculiar logic of the 'inside out' . . . of numerous parodies and travesties, humiliations, profanations, comic crownings and uncrownings. A second life, a second world of folk culture is thus constructed. . . . We must stress, however, that the carnival is far distant from the negative and formal parody of modern times. Folk humor denies, but it revives and renews at the same time. Bare negation is completely alien to folk culture" (Bakhtin 1984: 11–12).

Conceptualizing the carnival's political voice in this way, not as "bare negation" but as counterpoint, as ideologically polyphonic, signals a post-Marxist acknowledgment that proletarian consciousness is many-voiced, disorderly, and largely inconsistent. This idea supports the discovery that when it comes to existing hierarchies and norms, working-class subculture, like any other, "both affirms and denies at the same time," and that carnivalesque discourse resembles a dialectic negotiation of contradictions rather than a statement of unequivocal dissent (Bloch 1985:41).

Drawing on some insights from political anthropology in this chapter, I would like to examine some coplas with political themes dealing with subjects other than the mayetes. The texts presented in this chapter, dating from 1900 to the present, show the subversiveness that we expect of the Latin carnivalesque. But they also demonstrate a curious contradiction, rarely acknowledged by other anthropologists working with this kind of material: a fusion of ideologies, "praise-abuse" toward the constituted authorities (Bakhtin 1984:416).

This mixture of sentiments subsumes what Mitchell, in his study of flamenco politics, has referred to as the "rich-poor symbiosis that has characterized Andalusian expressive culture in general" since the Counter-Reformation (1994:99). A dramatic illustration of the same ideological ambivalence, so characteristic of political Spain, is seen when anticlerical Andalusian workers, who fulminate against the priests and who burnt churches during the Civil War, participate in Holy Week parades and venerate patron saints (Moreno 1985; Mitchell 1990).

I do not dispute that Spanish carnival was a ritual of resistance; it certainly was that. Rather, I want to point out that this quintessentially popular festival has always been thematically and morally *multivocal:* it is an ideological hybrid, not monody but polyphony; its tone is subversive and conservative at the same time. In Spanish carnival, as in most theatrical verbalizations, vox populi pronounces not a monotone rejection of elite values or of the mayetes, but a much more powerful *ambivalence* toward these things.[1]

When it comes to carnival's political context, Marxist and communist scholars — especially Anglophone scholars — have promulgated a monolithic (and I believe overly romanticized) view of the Spanish festival. In one of the earliest instances, Hobsbawm in his classic study of anarchism, *Primitive Rebels* (1959), cites carnival coplas to illustrate the revolutionary fervor among the anarchist farmworkers of Andalusia. In the corpus of work in English on Spanish politics (for instance, Kaplan 1977; Mintz 1982; Collier 1987), rarely has acknowledgment been made of any ideological ambivalence or inconsistency on the part of participants in carnival culture. It is as though all working-class masqueraders were identically predisposed and of the same mind (like the scholars?). But this naive view presupposes an inordinate degree of cultural homogeneity that exists nowhere in the world. Mitchell (1990:88) has termed such stereotyping of the poor in Andalusia as noble revolutionaries a kind of scholarly "mythopoesis of class consciousness," Marxist iconography. Carnival coplas attest to a much richer, more nuanced, and more heterogeneous subculture than has been previously assumed.[2]

To be sure, carnival discourse included angry political protest. Much of the protest was indeed revolutionary: anticlerical, anticapitalist, and certainly antibourgeois (anti-mayete). Much of the satire and profanation in carnival songs and skits reflected class struggle against latifundism, *caciquismo* (bossism), exploitation, religious oppression, and other injustices. But another, equally insistent voice of carnival projected a rather different and more complaisant worldview.

This gentler voice corresponds to what Bakhtin has called "the carnivalesque upside-down" (1984:410), the reversal of the reversal, the negative negated, which we have already seen in the case of imagery about women. In this contrarian voice, the working classes celebrate rather than denigrate the classic values and norms that form the backbone of Spain's specifically Castilian Great Tradition: conventional morality, nationalistic enthusiasm, bourgeois sentimentality, and Catholic traditionalism. Hierarchies seem to be accepted, even praised, rather than assaulted. This counterpoint will become apparent in the presentation here of contrasting lyrics.

Early Twentieth-Century Politics

Let us start with the earliest copla contributed from memory. This ditty dates from the period of the Torno Politico, or "rotating" government (1880–1920), when by tacit agreement liberal and reactionary regimes in Madrid alternated without much electoral input. To judge by the names mentioned, this verse dates to either 1909 or 1910, the first of which was a year of intense political agitation, culminating in the infamous "Tragic Week" in Barcelona — seven days of class violence and church-burnings. My sources did not know the name of the author, a rural proletarian from the town of either Osuna or Marchena.

Denouncing politicians from across the ideological spectrum in simple, even stark, terms, the poet expresses the hatred of the "small for the mighty" and the disgust for the state that Le Roy Ladurie (1979:105) speaks of as a recurrent feature of European carnivals. The invidious comparison of corrupt Spanish officials with foreigners is of course the worst insult.

Local people throughout the region adopted this little ditty as a kind of unofficial subversive anthem. For decades, they elaborated on the lyrics, changing the names of the politicians and the foreign countries to suit the times (Communist Russia replaced Portugal in the 1930s); they recited it during carnivals right up to the Second Republic and even during the Civil War (the 1930s), when such expressions were dangerous.

Ni La Cierva, ni Mauregui	Not La Cierva nor Mauregui
Ni Cañalejas, ni Maura,	Nor Cañalejas nor Maura,
Ninguno tiene vergüenza,	Not a single politician
Que no defiende a su patria.	Has any shame at all.
Fijarse en Inglaterra,	Not a one defends his country.
En Francia, y en Portugal.	Look abroad, look to England
Y vereís a sus goviernos	Or to France, even Portugal,
Con protección vigilada.	And you will see governments that
Aquí se protege al vago	Vigilantly protect their people.
Al granujo y al ladrón.	But here who gets protection?
Y todos están protegidos	Only the lazy, the cheats and thieves,
Menos el trabajador.[3]	Everyone is cared for, except the
	workingman.

Contempt for the Spanish government is a constant theme of Andalusian carnival songs (Rodríguez Becerra 1992). This song represents a gem of the popular genre. But hostility toward the Madrid government is not unalloyed — it does not carry over to wholesale condemnation of the state. Even under the Franco dictatorship, when workers were largely antigovernment and anticlerical, many songs expressed love of country and pride in Spanishness as well as in Spain's Catholic tradition and its elite nationalistic manifestations, despite the association of these allegiances with official oppression and Castilian tyranny. As is the case with expressions of religion — Spaniards often express anticlerical and pious sentiments simultaneously — it is important in Spain to distinguish between aspects of a (to foreigners' eyes) apparently monolithic phenomenon.

Carnival coplas, while condemning the state, often uphold the very moral virtues, obligations, and notions of patriotism and *Hispanidad* that have been an integral part of statist propaganda about "La Raza" since the nineteenth century. Rather than see such bourgeois sentiments as examples of the "imposition" of elite hegemony, as Abner Cohen (1993:148) does in his study of London carnival, it is perhaps wiser to acknowledge workers' general ambivalence about these issues, which are deeply rooted in primordial loyalties and self-identity, in the Eriksonian sense of feelings and needs that transcend politics. One song lavishing fulsome praise on Castilian notions of nationhood goes as follows:

Eres España querida,	My beloved Spain,
Orgullo del español.	What pride we feel in being Spanish.
Tu bandera cuando ondea	Your unfurled banner
Brilla mucho mas que el sol.	Is more brilliant than the sun.

El mundo entero te envidia	The entire world envies you:
Como tu no hay otra cosa igual,	There is nothing equal to you,
Y por muy lejo que estemos,	And though we may be far distant,
No te podremos olvidar.	We can never forget you.
La belleza en tus mujeres [es]	The beauty of your women
Como rosa en el rosal.	Is like the rose upon the rosebush,
Los labios como claveles	Their lips [are] like marigolds and
Y su cuerpo escultural.	Their forms more shapely than flowers.
España te veneramos	Spain, we venerate you,
Por ser nuestra Madre Patria;	You, our adored Motherland,
Gustosos damos la vida	And we would gladly give our lives for you
El día que te haga falta.[4]	Whenever the need arises.

War and Nationalism

Andalusian workers' ambivalence about the Castilian state and its programs is reflected in the following pair of songs about the colonial war in North Africa during the 1920s (against the Rif rebels led by the Berber chieftain Abd El Krim). Marked by sharp swings between abject defeat in 1921 and final victory in 1926, this war against the Moroccan guerrillas was highly unpopular with the Spanish Left — especially in Andalusia — which constantly fulminated against imperialism. But typically, workers' attitudes wavered between pacifism and jingoism. Of course, their reactions depended in large part on the current performance of the Spanish army against the rebels, who were dismissed as a ragtag band of bandits until the humiliating Spanish defeat at Annual. But the swings in public opinion also reflected some degree of ambiguity among the masses concerning the potential benefits — both economic and emotional — of victory.

Dating from 1922, the first carnival after the rout at Annual, the song below, ostensibly a letter from a doomed Spanish soldier, delivers an antiwar message coupled with an indictment of the managerial class that has gotten Spanish conscripts into this predicament. The poet denounces the battle as being not for the glory of Spain but for gold (the Rifian mines), said to benefit the ruling class. The "thieves and bandits" are of course the capitalists and their lackeys, not the Berber guerrillas.

Melilla, tres de enero;	Melilla, third of January;
Querido amigo,	Dear friend,
Un favor de ti espero;	I ask a favor of you;

Que no digas lo que escribo.	Do not repeat what I am about to write.
Hace tres días me encuentro	Three days ago, I was
En un hospital metido,	Taken to the hospital badly wounded:
Que defiendo un convoy,	Trying to defend a convoy
De un balazo caí herido.	I fell, shot down.
Los soldados, a montones,	Our soldiers fall in droves,
Mueren cuando entramos	And die like flies.
En cualquier acción.	In any military encounter.
Y aunque tenemos cañones,	Although we have the artillery,
No hay vergüenza ni valor.	We have neither shame nor valor.
Tambien en los campamentos	Even in the bivouacs,
Pasamos hambre y tormentos,	We suffer from hunger and torments —
Nada a mis padres lo digas.	Do not tell my parents, please.
No tenemos ropa ni comida;	We have neither clothes nor food;
La miseria nos come	Misery eats away at us
Y nos mata;	And finally kills us;
Nos llevamos toda nuestra vida	We're wasting our lives
Defendiendo minas,	Defending mines,
Granujas y piratas.[5]	Thieves, and bandits.

Finally, with the assistance of the French Foreign Legion, the Spanish pacified the Rif in 1926. The following song commemorates the Spanish victory in a playful way, using animal imagery as in fable or allegory, but nevertheless evidencing a certain pride in Spanish arms and in a satisfying conquest over an ancient enemy, the Moors. The contrast of the celebratory mood to the lyrics of dissent and despair above is marked. The lyrics sound a definite note of imperial self-congratulation.

Será verdad,	It's the unvarnished truth,
Esa guerra de Marruecos,	The expeditionary army in Morocco
El ejército terrestre	Had an adventure, which we'll
Y ahora se lo explicamos.	Tell you all about now.
Llevan cañones	They have cannons
Y alguna ametralladora;	And a few machine guns;
Van divisando al moro	The Moors begin to appear
Y va llegando la hora.	And the moment of truth fast approaches.
Un batallón de ratones	A battalion of mice
Lo dirige un cigarrón;	Pull a big grasshopper;

Detrás chicharras	Behind them, a bunch of crickets,
Detrás de un melon.	Following a melon.
Y una mosca borriquera	And a fly, leading the mules,
La acompaña un abejorro	Is accompanied by a beekeeper,
Y la avispa con su lanza	And the wasp, with his stinger,
Se hizo el amo del moro.	Makes himself the ruler of the Moors.
Ganó l'Alhucemas	He won Alhucemas
Y las minas de oro.[6]	And the gold mines of the Rif.

The theme of the Moor as "other" and as enemy (Arabs and Muslims are all lumped together as "Moors" in Andalusia) continues as a foil for Catholic Spanish national identity in ritual performances even today throughout the region (Rodríguez Becerra 1984). Many towns and villages still perform the ancient parades of "Moros y Cristianos," complete with mock battles and military imagery from the medieval Reconquest (Amezcua 1995). These ancient stereotypes are used creatively today for carnival purposes. The following song about "the Moor," for example, dates from the carnival of 1991, which coincided with the Gulf War against Iraq. After some indecision, Spain joined the allies by sending a few sailors and some token patrol boats to the Gulf. Absent any national interest in Kuwait to speak of, opinion was very divided on this policy, but since the Spanish public still regards "the Moor" as generically dangerous and threatening, most Spaniards acquiesced to the government's anti-Iraq stance.

Sung by Los Palmitos (Hearts of Palm), a group dressed in palm tree costumes, the lyrics playfully poke fun at Saddam Hussein, meanwhile interweaving the venerable Moor-as-enemy motif with jokes about the sexual prowess of the troubadours and the superior quality of the local delicacy, the heart of palm. The political intent, minimal to begin with, is further blunted by the rapid-fire burlesque:

Los Palmitos de mi pueblo	The Palmitos of my town
Cada vez tienen mas fama.	Are more famous every day,
Si buenos están en el campo	They're good in the fields,
Mas bueno están en la cama.	And better still in bed.
Entre pencas y forraje	Between the cactus and the forage
Salta la felicidad.	Is where happiness lies.
¡Ay, que higa tan hermosa!	Oh, what a beautiful little fig
Dice el mozo a la moza,	You have there! said the boy to the girl.
Pa, pará, pará, pará.	Pa para para para.
Esta murga aquí presente	This murga here present

Le dice al señor Serra:	Says to foreign minister Serra:
Manda palmitos al moro	Hey, send hearts of palm to the Moor;
A ver si acaba la guerra.	Maybe that will end the war.
Que nuestros pobres soldados	Our poor soldiers over there
Están to's mu' asustaos.	Are just dying of fright—
Por curpita [*sic*] de ese moro	It's all the fault of that Moor,
Que está loco y amargo.	That crazy and vicious Moor.

The Republic and Proletarian Themes

Opposing beliefs, mixed sentiments, and clashing loyalties often commingled during carnival celebrations, even during the height of revolutionary fervor in the 1930s. During the Republic, workers and peasants expressed a variety of political views through carnival coplas, commenting caustically on local political events.[7] Although most of the poor in Andalusia were firmly leftist or anarchist, many were quite conservative and even reactionary because of deeply held Catholic beliefs, personal ties to the rich (Corbin and Corbin 1984), or simply unaccountable idiosyncratic conviction (see Maddox 1993 for a review). These conservative workers were often called squirrels or billy goats by the revolutionaries; but it would be a mistake to ignore either their importance or their numbers merely because they were despised by the Left. I reproduce three carnival coplas, two from the 1930s, one more recent, expressing very different political views. All three were written by workers.

Our first two songs, composed fifty years apart, salute the Casa del Pueblo —the Socialist trade union dissolved by Franco in 1939 and re-created in 1977—and threaten class enemies and conservatives. The third song, also dating from the Republic, takes a very different, in fact a right-wing, position, condemning the Republic and its socialist ideals as ill-conceived and decadent.

Casa del Pueblo te visitamos	Casa del Pueblo, we visit you
Y a tus obreros vamos a saludar;	And salute your brave workers;
Al Presidente y la Directiva,	We salute your president and the party secretary
Por ser la base más principal.	Because of their
Gran organismo tiene este Centro	Excellent work in organizing.
Todos sus miembros contentos están,	This great workers' center
Porque le agrada aquel impuesto	Has made its members proud and happy;
Que su Maestro suele implantar.	They are even happy to contribute
Aquí no hay esquiroles	Their dues to the labor leaders.
Que protegen al burgués,	There are no scabs here,

Que con sus interventores	No scoundrels who protect the bourgeois
De la Escuela de Ferrer,	With their anarchist machinations and tricks,
Nosotros elegiamos su proceder,	We have chosen our leader freely,
Y aunque seamos murguistas	And although we are carnival singers,
Todo el mal que profesamos,	The only malice we profess today is to
Es darle un ¡viva! al obrero	Shout, "Long live the workers!"
Y ¡que mueren los traidores!⁸	And "May the traitors perish!"

This type of song extolling the Casa del Pueblo unites labor and progressive political themes, condemning class enemies while lauding working-class heroes and organizations. After the Civil War such songs were naturally prohibited by the Franco government. By the late 1970s, however, after Franco's death, some workers returned to the old themes. A particularly fierce example from 1981 from Fuentes de Andalucía is this:

Queremos Casa del Pueblo,	We demand a Casa del Pueblo,
Todos los obreros de Fuentes.	All the workers of Fuentes.
Hoy por hambre tus obreros	Today we suffer such hunger
Están cerca de la muerte.	That we are near death.
Si te declara en huelga	If we go out on strike,
Te quieren ametrallar.	They want to machine-gun us.
Darse cuenta, compañeros,	Note it well, comrades,
De esta vida explotación;	From this daily exploitation
Ahora nos protegen menos	Our rulers defend us less
Que el miserable Borbón.	Than the lousy monarchy did.
Es muy triste y muy humilde	It is both sad and humiliating
Que tengamos que entregar	That we have to surrender our lives
Nuestra vida a la injusticia	To this injustice, as did
Como la entregó Galán,	[Antonio] Galán.
Y en alta voz gritaremos	At the top of our lungs we shout,
¡Que viva la libertad!	"Long live liberty!"
Tenemos que hacer un bloque,	We must organize a united front,
Todos los trabajadores,	All we workers,
Que nos quitaron lo nuestro	So we can get these inquisitors
Aquellos inquisidores.⁹	Off our backs.

These songs are typical of the proletarian protest genre from the late 1800s right up to the present and, as we can see, showed remarkable consistency through the years, during different regimes. Still, the theme was always counterbalanced by other coplas expressing opposing ideas and sentiments, often written by the same poets or their brothers or comrades. Some of the counterprotest ditties are rightist political propaganda excoriating the disorder of the Republican period; others are more ambiguous, expressing caution and disillusionment, like the song below, which sadly contemplates the Republic as presaging both good and ill. Through tropes about shining beacons and fragrant bouquets, democracy is portrayed here as an overidealized, a false panacea doomed to bring failure and disappointment.

Tu, República Española	You are the Republic we have
Que en mi pecho te abrigué,	So longed for and imagined,
Tus colores amapolas	Your thrilling [tricolor] banner is
Es una estrella polar.	A beacon like the north star.
Esparciendo tus olores,	Spreading your fragrance,
El catorce de abril	You were born among flowers
Tu naciste entre flores	On April 14th,
Por impulso popular;	Created by the popular will;
Tu que odias la monarquía,	You, who despised the monarchy
Símbolo de esclavitud.	As a symbol of slavery.
El hombre en la melodía	Mankind followed your sweet melody
De tu música sonó,	With greater and greater hope,
Y ha causado grandes daños,	But in the end you caused great harm,
Y el deseo se agrandó	As our desire for you grew.
Al pueblo que te engendró.	Both life and death
Vida y muerte	Have you given to the people,
A tu pueblo le estás dando	Your way is one of half-measures,
Con tu proceder parcial,	And your promise is tarnished
Y en la suerte	By false starts and partial successes.
Que se llama en este mundo	O, the poor masses!
el poder circunstancial.	Your labor and your struggle
¡Pobre pueblo!	Have finally borne fruit,
Tu trabajo fue fecucundo [*sic*]	But all has gone for naught,
Aumentando tu sufrir,	For your suffering has only grown,
Y hasta que el dolor profundo	Until the deepest agony
Se propague a todo el mundo	Engulfs us all, and
Y nos haga sucumbir.[10]	We all perish in the end.

Another song, written in 1933, reflects an even more strongly right-wing position, at odds with the new liberal democracy. The antirepublican diatribe below reflects the views of some Catholic workers who fiercely opposed the Republic as not only anticlerical but also subversive of discipline, patriotism, tradition, and good order. Although a minority, these working-class conservatives made their dissatisfaction felt through various means, including carnival coplas that directly condemned democracy as an assault on Spain's patriarchal heritage:

Yo no se que pasa	I don't know what is happening
En esta preciosa villa.	In this fine little town of ours.
Nunca se ha visto aquí	Never have there been so many
Tantos disgustos en famila.	Outrages in our families.
Ya se pelean los hijos,	Now children fight with their own parents,
Hasta con sus mismos padres	Even with their own fathers.
Ya se riñen los hermanos,	Brothers fight among themselves,
Aquí la culpa de to' la tiene	And the cause of it all is
Os le voy a decir:	Easy to see:
¡La República funesta	It's this damnable Republic
Que se ha establicido aquí![11]	They have set up here!

In line with the carnival practice of criticizing whatever regime is currently in power, these lyrics condemn the Republic as "damnable" or "dismal" (*funesta*), interestingly enough, from a decidedly reactionary position fully in concert with the old hierarchical order that the Republic undermined. Some Spanish workers, like the unknown author of this ditty, were on the right of the political spectrum for their own idiosyncratic reasons. Workers might hold collaborationist sentiments either because they were pious and offended by the leftist anticlerical agenda or, equally often, because they associated liberalism with an attack on patterns of authority with which they felt comfortable.[12]

The Authorities

The next two songs are examples of praise lavished on people and institutions that are usually anathema to the Spanish Left and to many workers: the rural police and the Franco family. The first song, dating from 1925, actually sings the praises of the Guardia Civil—the paramilitary police force that so often violently crushed workers' strikes and protests and that most revolutionary workers regarded as the civil arm of the Devil. In this case, the Guardia had performed an act of public service during a natural catastrophe the year before, winning the gratitude of all, regardless of their politics:

Lo tendremos en memoria,	We will never forget the main
Como recuerdo del venticuatro	Event of 1924,
Una familia se ahogaba	A family was in danger of drowning
En una choza sin tener amparo.	In their hut: no help came.
Dieron parte a los civiles	Then the Guardia Civil stepped in,
Y el comandante, que se hallaba enfermo,	And the commander, though ill,
Pronto dispuso el viaje.	Left his sickbed immediately;

Para salvarlos,	The entire barracks mobilized
Todos salieron.	To save the peasants, every man helped.
Ese buen comandante	This kind commander
Que a caballo montó,	Jumped on his steed
Con sus subordinatos	With all his men in line
Pronto llegó.	And arrived in the nick of time.
¡Viva la Guardia Civil!	Long live the Guardia Civil!
¡Viva el sargento!	Long live the sergeant!
Ganaron cruces a salvamento	They should win medals for bravery
Y a los muchachos	For their good deed, and what's more,
Los obsequiaron,	For providing all the children
Ropa y comida y unos zapatos.[13]	With food, clothes, and shoes.

The next song is a paean to the daring young aviator Ramón Franco (the dictator's brother). The lyrics commemorate his heroic nonstop flight to Argentina aboard the hydroplane *Plus Ultra* in 1926. Despite his association with ultra-right-wing politics and militarism (he was the Gabriele D'Annunzio of Spanish fascism), Ramón Franco caught the public's fancy. His gesture made him the Spanish Lindbergh and put Spain on the international stage in a rare favorable light. The lyrics clearly express support for pan-Hispanism as well as for the bravery and vision of the pilot. The tone is patriotic and worshipful.

Allá en mil cuatrocientos,	In fourteen hundred and ninety-two,
Allá en el noventa y dos,	Columbus set out from Puerto de Palos,
Salió del Puerto de Palos	And sailed across the sea.
La embarcación de Colón.	
Quién se lo iba calcular,	Who would ever have imagined,
Ni eso lo esperaba nadie,	Who would ever have hoped
Que a América se marchara	That you could travel to America
Hoy volando por los aires.	Today by air. Commander Franco (we even like his name) [*franco* means "frank," "honest"] took off,
Salió el comandante Franco,	Along with two companions,
Que hasta su nombre nos gusta,	
Con dos compañeros mas,	Into the sky,
Volando en el *Plus Ultra*.	Flying aboard the *Plus Ultra*,
Y la nación argentina,	And the entire Argentine nation,
Aunque son americanos,	Although they are Americans,
Tienen deseos de abrazar	Wishes to embrace their
A sus queridos hermanos.[14]	Beloved [Hispanic] brothers.

Rather than degrading the high and mighty, some carnival songs, like the one just cited, praise people, places, or things of widespread national appeal, regardless of their political identifications, class status, or social connections. Patriotism and local pride have always lurked beneath the irreverent surface of carnival satire. Distinctions of class and status can be either transcended or intensified by carnival poets, as the mood strikes them. Sometimes, local murga poets have praised the rich and powerful of the pueblos (the señoritos) rather than attacking them, especially when they acted in ways compatible with dearly held folk ideals of charity and generosity. In his book on carnival in Cadiz Province, Jerome Mintz (1997:9–10) cites several examples of such extravagant praise for a rich woman in a small pueblo who was known as a generous patron of the poor in times of need.[15]

Another example of this sort of elegy for the generous rich and the deservedly powerful, from our area in Seville Province, is the following paean to the Duchess of Alba. The song takes as its subject a tragic air crash that occurred in 1961 during a charity drive in Seville City. Bobby Deglané was a news announcer for the state-run television station that was covering the event, and the Duchess of Alba was the patroness of the relief operation. The two celebrities remained in Seville for some time after the tragedy to express condolences and to attend the funerals of the victims; in this way, the elite were united in grief with the commoners.

Sevilla viste de luto	Seville today is dressed in mourning;
La gracia de Andalucía;	The beauty of Andalusia is obscured.
El arroyo Tamarguillo	The Tamarguillo, overflowing its banks,
Le ha quitado su alegría.	Has taken away our happiness.
Cuantos cristianos	Those Christian souls, taken in their prime,
En una tomba sagrada	Rest now in their holy tombs,
Pa' esas madres no hay consuelo,	But for their grieving mothers, weeping piteously
Llorando sin esperanzas.	There can be no consolation.
Sevilla estaba impaciente,	All Seville was excitedly waiting,
Toda llena de alegría,	Full of joy, waiting expectantly
Esperando la caravana	For the relief caravan
Que de camino venía.	Approaching by road.
Delante una avioneta	Leading the way was
A la alegra caravana,	A small chartered airplane,
Cuando de Madrid salieron	The harbinger of joy
El periodista un milagro [sic]	For the happy occasion,
De los que da Dios en la vida.	The motorcade coming down from Madrid.

Al caer en el suelo ardiendo	Then tragedy struck without warning;
Una mujer le dió vida.	We saw the plane falling, plummeting,
El dia de los funerales	The earth burning, death raining
Sevilla de velo negro,	Down on those to whom a mother's
La Giralda y sus campanas	love gave life.
Lanzan el sonido de duelo.	On the day of the funerals
Bobby Deglané llorando	All Seville wore black,
Y la Duquesa de Alba	The cathedral tower and its bells
Al pie de la Macarena	Shook the sky with doleful peals.
Y al frente su caravana.	Bobby Deglané wept openly,
Señor Bobby Deglané	As did the Duchess of Alba
Y la Duquesa de Alba	At the foot of the Macarena Church
En memoria los tenemos	Before the shrouded motorcade.
Como lo mejor de España.[16]	Mr. Bobby Deglané and
	The Duchess of Alba,
	We cherish your memory
	Among our most sacred images of Spain.

We now turn to a eulogy invoking Christian charity and the institutions of the Church. The example is representative of a genre that speaks of forgiveness and universal brotherhood as opposed to airing political grievances or promoting class consciousness. This type of sentimental encomium often acclaims public agencies or offices — in this case the Catholic charity services provided by Franco — despite their connection with the state and Church.

Es tan amable la vida,	Life is so precious,
Como tanto la apreciamos.	Something to be deeply cherished.
Hay dos cosas en este mundo	There are two things in this world
Que nada diferenciamos.	That unite us all.
Cuando venimos al mundo,	When we come into the world,
Venimos encuero y descalzo.	We are all naked and barefoot,
Y a la hora de la muerte	And in the hour of death
Somos todos fiel cristiano.	We are all good Christians.
Que alegría es la salud:	What a joy it is to have health,
Pa' mi sería el mas grande capital.	I think it more precious than money:
Si la pierdo ya no hay remedio	If lost, there's is no recovering it;
Ni cirujano que puedan curar.	There is no surgeon who can cure you.
En Sevilla un sanatorio	Now, in Seville there's a clinic
Que lo conocemos tó,	That we all know about,
Donde hay tantos niños enfermos	Where many sick children go,

Llamado San Juan de Dios.	Called San Juan de Dios.
Inválidos de piernas y brazos y sin alegría	Unhappy invalids with broken limbs
Otros ciegos por desgracia,	Go there for help, as do the blind,
Que no ven la luz del día.	The halt, and the lame.
¡Darse cuenta! el padre que allí lo tenga	Note it well! How the father worries
Con que pena vivirá y ¡que dolor!	About his sick child, how great his distress,
Dá una limosna si te la piden	And so give alms, if you are asked, to
Pa San Juan de Dios.[17]	The Hospital of San Juan de Dios.

Of Two Minds

Clearly, the poets of Andalusia are of two minds about the institutions that govern them and mighty ambivalent about the elites they serve. They feel hatred and defiance, but also grudging admiration, gratitude, and collaboration, and rampant envy, accompanied by the inevitable imitative impulse. Long ago, Robert Redfield (1956) spoke of the syncretization of great and little traditions as constituting the essence of peasant culture. In rural Spain, this Redfieldian blend of upper and lower is certainly complex from the standpoint of religion, taste, and morality; a comparable amalgam is evident in the realm of ideology and politics. The domain of ideology, where everything seemed so clearly defined and monolithic to many Marxists, is extremely convoluted in Spain, thanks to the split rhetoric just discussed.

Timothy Mitchell has described the curious symbiosis between the highest and lowest segments of Andalusian society in his treatise on the history of flamenco culture. He refers to this affective mutualism as the "interclass emotionology" of rich and poor. He notes that the upper classes in Seville and Malaga, the señoritos, imitate the downtrodden poor, and as a matter of style, have developed a highly romanticized discourse about them, just as the poor take on the manners and trappings of the rich. Consequently, the two extremes of this castelike society — the gentry and the paupers — had always felt "a reciprocal and semisecret attraction for one another" (1994:104).

Indeed, starting in the eighteenth century, the upper classes of Andalusia began to show a remarkable interest in the artistic performances, dress, and lifestyle of the poor, the picaresque lumpen becoming a model for rich and bored young playboys. "Upper-class interest in under-class expressive styles goes back a very long way in Spain, especially in southern Spain, where the symbolic and religious aspects of poverty played a key role in the ideology of aristocratic Catholics" (Mitchell 1994:99). A similar and reciprocal process has been at work throughout the twentieth century at the other end of the spectrum. Despite their political antagonism to the señoritos, the revolutionary day laborers of Andalusia found much to their liking in the aristocratic style, especially the lip service paid to Christian virtues, to the glorification of sociability and hospitality, to patriotism, and to a specifically Spanish masculine camaraderie.

Here we see the "basic ambivalence" (Pérez-Díaz 1993:302) of the Spanish working classes toward their superiors throughout the present century. Such naked political ambivalence was still prevalent in the mid-1990s in Spanish workers' attitudes toward the elite, toward the capitalist system, and toward business, according to studies of worker attitudes carried out by the Spanish sociologist Victor Pérez-Díaz (1993). He writes that "a similar ambivalence existed in the relationship between the workers and the capitalist order as a whole" (1993:303), meaning that most workers interviewed could not make up their minds whether they disapproved or approved of capitalism and the profit motive. In a curious conjunction of class and culture in Spain, the upper and the lower orders of society, even as they literally fought each other to the death, sang each other's praises. Only in the February carnival could Spanish workers find a suitable vehicle for the expression of such blatantly contradictory feelings.

12

Bars, Bards, and Bawds

Under a bad cloak, there is often a good drinker. — Miguel de Cervantes, *Don Quixote*

Carnival discourse celebrates a Spanish code of manhood and a corollary model of social equality. It unites these Platonic ideals through the community of song, laughter, and above all, good fellowship and drink. Alcohol is itself a commodity honored during carnival. The village makes an "offering" to the Muse, for instance, through invitations to the already tipsy poets to take a *copita,* "a cup of cheer"; and of course alcoholic overindulgence is the chief lubricant for the merriment itself, as well as the primary means of keeping warm on cold February days. Drink and bars figure inseparably, for people do not tipple socially outside bars in Spain (though in the home alcohol is part of meals). Wine, especially pale dry sherry (*fino*) and *manzanilla* (the "little apple," lightest of all fortified wines), is the sacred festival liquor in Andalusia, especially for carnival, and the bars are the founts of this sunny liquor. One cannot fully understand carnival, ritual, or for that matter anything else in Andalusia without first considering bars, the protocols of drink that unite men as brothers, and bar etiquette, which bind everything together.

In many Spanish-speaking societies, bars are a kind of surrogate home for males, a men's club, a secret society, a lodge. In the neighborhood taphouse, men unite, having escaped the oppression of the wife-dominated, mother-in-law-infested home. Alcoholic beverages are more than merely "drinks" in this context; they constitute an important substance of exchange, a fluid social currency through which men forge, renew, and manipulate relationships. As George Foster (1979) and Brandes (1988:175) have observed of Tzintzuntzan, Mexico, where many similar conditions prevail, drink is virtually the only consumable (apart from cigarettes) that men can produce for exchange, given that they do not cook or prepare food. "Since men do not cook, they are denied opportunity to express affection and friendship to partners by offering them food. . . . But they *can* offer drinks, which represent the same symbolic values. . . . Undoubtedly, many Tzintzuntzan men drink more than they really want to simply because they are caught in a trap in which only through offering and accepting liquor can they maintain important social relations" (Foster 1979:222).

In Spain, the same might be said for cigarettes, which also figure prominently in bar protocol. Virtually all men smoke and drink at the same time. If they refuse one indulgence, they are sure to enjoy the other: to do neither would be considered truly deviant (Aguilera 1990:145–148).

But this "need" to indulge and share has other justifications. In Andalusia, serious puffing and tippling are hallmarks of manhood or *hombría* (Gilmore 1990a). All men are expected to use and to exchange drink and tobacco, publicly in the many bars of the pueblo, and no masculine interaction is complete without them. Consequently, male relations in public places may be regarded as a bibulous brotherhood defined by the continuous circulation of perishables, consumed in fraternal assemblies in bars shrouded in clouds of tobacco smoke and lubricated by free-flowing liquors.

The obligatory exchanges are conducted in bars and taverns through ritualized invitas (offerings), which men announce in stentorian tones of expansive bonhomie. Only men participate; women do not enter the bars, except on special occasions — on Saturday nights, during fiestas, and of course during carnival. At home, women may sometimes smoke or drink in moderation, but the public and ritualized exchange of alcohol and tobacco is considered entirely and exclusively male. (This homosocial aspect is very important to the following discussion and will be examined in detail.)

As in Mexico, entrance into the public arena of male sociability in Andalusia necessitates entry also into a continual exchange of commodities, the material component of friendship, whose deeper value all men appreciate and cultivate. "In Andalusia, 'speaking' (*hablando*) is equated with sociability," say Corbin and Corbin (1984:18), referring to both sexes in the town of Ronda (Malaga Province). For men alone, so are smoking and drinking — equally oral activities, and equally communicative. The same seems to hold true in the north, in Old Castile (Brandes 1979) and Catalonia (Hansen 1976). To drink and smoke in rural Spain is to "talk," to be a man among men, a participant in the drama of everyday life.

Not only do tobacco and alcohol represent the principle currencies of masculine society (being cheap, "male," and as liquid as money), but they are also used to initiate, accompany, and ratify most important social contracts, not just the murga performances in carnival. No formal bargain or casual agreement is complete without a ritual drink and an exchange of cigarettes. Even more important, given their prominence in public life as prelude and accompaniment to friendship, such transactions also convey powerful moral messages about a man's character and his sensitivity to shared norms of public behavior. While ulterior motives — manipulation, profiteering, image-making, and the like — are sometimes suspected, these are discretely disregarded through a formulaic discourse emphasizing the selfless virtues of generosity, dependability, and openness, which ritualistically reproduces the desiderata of male character.[1]

In one very important context, however, the exchange of tobacco and alcohol is absolutely taboo. This is the father-son relationship. Between fathers and adolescent sons, a rigid protocol forbids both use of and reference to the two commodities, to which the son cannot even allude in the presence of the father. Unmarried sons, especially, should not light up or drink in the presence of their fathers; just as they must not refer to sex, they may not mention or refer to their own use of cigarettes or alcoholic beverages. Observation of this rule varies somewhat depending on personality, but as a normative ideal or generality, the proscription has been noted in passing by virtually all fieldworkers in Andalusia, rural and urban (Pitt-Rivers 1971:114; Press 1979:110; Murphy 1983a:654; Corbin and Corbin 1984:32–33). It is clear that the commodities in question represent something beyond the "friendliness" of the person and that their exchange reflects deep values about masculine interaction in a more general sense. So rigid is the prohibition that fathers and sons usually frequent different bars, to avoid even the possibility of cognitive dissonance. Murphy goes so far as to call this practice father-son avoidance (1983b:659).

Bars, Taverns, Casinos, Bodegas, Mesones, Tascas, Cafés

Every barrio and almost every street in every Andalusian pueblo has a neighborhood bar or tavern where men congregate. According to official designations for tax purposes, "bars" and "cafés" are distinguished from "taverns" on the basis of amenities and services. Bars and cafés are cosmopolitan, offering tables, waiter service, and hot food. Less fashionable and frequented by a rougher clientele, taverns (*tabernas*) and wineshops (*tascas*) offer spartan interiors, only cold *tapas* (hors d'oeuvres), coffee, and only the cheapest brands of wine and liquor (Gilmore 1980). *Casinos* are registered as private clubs, usually with a specific theme or focus, such as bullfight clubs, flamenco music clubs, or reading societies. Like their simpler analogues, these "elite" establishments always feature a bar and drinking room as well as a reading room.

In any of them, men and youths aged about twenty and older—the "regulars"—meet every night for rounds of merriment and tippling. Nightly card games and domino matches may go on for weeks and involve dozens of friends. Also, a good deal of business is transacted at bars over both drinks and coffee, and many tradesmen make use of the crowded public spaces as unofficial "offices" for initiating and sealing brokered contracts, both during the day and at night (see Hansen 1976 for a Catalonian example). If you are looking for any particular man in the evening, you are sure to find him at "his" bar. Consequently, in a society where private homes are often off-limits for entertaining, drinking establishments furnish a stable arena for virtually all forms of male interaction, from business to gambling to snacking to nightly guzzling to infrequent *juergas* (drinking binges, often culminating in a drunken visit to a brothel).

Wine, Men, and Song

Men deeply love their bars. The women say "men live in the bars," which I found to be not only a profoundly true statement but a summation of my own experience in Spain. Naturally, as with all such important matters in Andalusia, bars figure prominently in the carnival events, both as subject of ditties and as public stages where the coplas are sung and recompensed with libations. So infatuated are men with their neighborhood dives, in fact, that the murga poets celebrate the love affair in verse, belonging to a recognized genre of bar ballad–cum-elegy. The ballads are reminiscent of the love poems that the Nuer pastoralists compose about their beloved cattle (Evans-Pritchard 1940) or the sentimental songs and epics in which other peoples honor heroes, spirits, and other instances of outstanding virtue and import. Great art always accrues to objects of central cultural value. In Spain, bars are way up there on the scale of cherished things. Having committed their favorite bar coplas to memory, men will sometimes spontaneously burst into such a song when contemplating an aperitif, or just reflexively at the advent of tippling time. I often found myself listening to men singing the praises of their favorite bar or tavern as we marched off toward the very place in question. Men sing of women, too, but sometimes bars take precedence: they are that important. Some examples of this genre of bar-panegyric follow. The first dates from the 1960s:

Tenemos un bar en Fuentes	We have a bar in Fuentes
Que se ha puesto popular.	That has become very popular indeed.
Está en la calle Cruz-Verde	It's up on High Street,
Donde todo el mundo va.	Where everybody goes:
Van cazadores, rebuscaores,	Hunters, gleaners [impecunious workers who survive by gleaning],
Esparragueros y cantaores,	Asparagus pickers, flamenco singers,
Allí de juerga están todo el día.	All of them wasting the day on binges.
Marcelino, tu tienes	Marcelino, you have
Tus tapas y tus vinos	The town's best tapas and wines,
Son las que se prefieren	You serve the top brands,
Y con buen paladar,	And like your superb larder,
El cante que tu tienes	Your flamenco singing can't be beat.
En ningún lao lo habrá.	There's just one thing I'd like to ask:
Tu me harías feliz	You would make us all very happy
Si nos diera probar	If you would just let us
El vino que tienes	Sample your delicious wines
Metío en el barril.[2]	Right out of the barrel.

A similar specimen from 1984 jokes lovingly about the service in a centrally located bar, which is always so crowded that the owners rush about haplessly trying to meet the demand:

Hoy he vuelto a pasar	One day I was walking down
Por la calle Cruz-Verde,	High Street,
Que en El Postigo se pierde	The one that gets lost in the
Y a la calle Lora da.	Postigo ward and ends at Lora Street.
Cuando llego hasta el final,	When I got to the end, I took
Cojo calle Mayor arriba,	Main Street up the hill
Me meto "an cá" Matildita	And finally ended up at Matilda Avenue,
Y allí me pongo a pensar.	And there I started to think:
Que en mi pueblo	There's a public house in this town
Hay un patio mu' particular,	That's a true delight to behold,
Que lo lleva el paneto	Where they have the best grub
Con facilidad.	And where the service is top-notch,
El servicio es muy bueno	
Y se puede ver,	Because if you order
Si le pides un tinto	A glass of red wine
Te pone un café.	They serve you an espresso.
Agárrate, porque vamos a entrar,	Clear the way: we're coming in,
Los niños del Ciruelo	The Plum Tree boys [local club]

Te queremos cantar.	Want to hear you sing, so let's go.
Corre, corre, Rafaelillo,	Run, move it, Rafaelillo, get going,
Saca tapas, buen vinillo.	Bring us some tapas fast, a little wine too;
Segundo va y le dice a Rafael,	You're too slow, Rafael,
Resulta que no tiene un papel	You're not doing your job.
Y una puerta falsa quiere hacer	What you need is a trap door
Que le cae frente al Cuartel.	To drop you to the supply room.
Si el negocio es tan bueno,	If your business is this good,
Lo vamos a ver,	We'll have to wait
Cuando al que está en Caracas	Until your brother, the one in Caracas,
Se l'acabe el "parné."	Runs out of money and returns to wait on us.
Entérate, no te vayas a enfadar,	Hey, listen, don't get mad,
Porque estás son las cosas	Because these are just
Que lleva el carnaval.[3]	The jokes of carnival.

Bars have character, too, just like men. Like men, they also have their political affiliations. During the politically frenzied Second Republic (1931–1939), bars served not only as meeting places for tipplers, but also as unofficial headquarters for the various political parties, trade unions, and occupational and status groups. Each bar had its own reputation as a socialist, communist, anarchist, reactionary, or monarchist stronghold (Gilmore 1980). Some bars were reputedly "working class"; others were "mayete houses"; some were known as haunts of "big landowners," "day laborers," or "elitist lackeys," and so on, and often each had its own specific party representation. The following song, dating from 1934, celebrates the various bars and taverns of La Campana, providing a rundown of their political and other distinguishing stereotypes:

Con gracia vamos contarles	In the spirit of fun we're going to relate
Lo que nos "vemos enterao":	Something we've learned
A varias tabernas de La Campana	About the various taverns of La Campana,
Creo que las han "cristianao."	Which have all been "civilized" [improved, that is, not cheap tascas, but real bars].
La primera es la Fila:	First on the list are
Bajo el Cielo de Montecarlo,	Under the Skies of Montecarlo and
Y el Huerto del Tio Martin,	Uncle Martin's Garden; the latter, with

Que con mucha gracia
Es el Republicano.
La Casa de Troya
La Taberna de Vito;
La de Pepe Hidalgo
El Secreto del Vicio;
y los Socialistas
El Huerto El Frances,
Porque quien allí entra
Sale sin el "parné."

La Cueva de Los Hurones
Es la taberna el Pedrero;
La de Paco "El del Postigo";
La "Posa" del Gato Negro;
El Castillo del Silencio
Es la taberna del Parro,
Y es la agrícola
La Banda de Los Capuchones
     Negros,
Los terratenientes y los
     "paniaguaos."[4]

Much grace, is our official
     Republican bar.
Then there's the bar owned by
The Troya family, Vito's Tavern,
And don't forget Pepe Hidalgo's
     place,
Pleasure Palace — all good Socialist
     hangouts,
And then there's Frenchy's Garden,
Which is unforgettable anyway,
Because whoever enters that place
Leaves without any money.

Then there's the Heron's Cave,
Which is run by old Pedrero, and
     don't forget
The bar owned by Paco, which is
     called From the Postigo [personal
     nickname],
The Inn of the Black Cat;
The Castle of Tranquility
Is the name of old Parro's tavern,
Which is the haunt of the well-to-do
     farmers.
Then there's The Black Capuchins,
Which is for the rich landlords and
     their lackeys.

With its centrality in the male consciousness, the bar gives passage to another dimension. The glass-bead curtain of the Spanish bar is the doorway to a wonderland of symbolism, the communicative basis of masculine camaraderie. No self-respecting man enters that masculine fortress without carrying a pocketful of change and a pack of cigarettes. These are the admission tickets to a world apart. Drinking patterns follow a very pronounced etiquette, replete with "consumption rituals" (Gell 1986:111), in which most men cheerfully participate. Men who, for personal reasons, wish not to imbibe, or recovered alcoholics, are at a severe disadvantage in this insular world. Indeed, most teetotalers are forced to adopt a carefully defended pose of congenital illness to avoid alcohol, claiming dyspepsia (a favorite excuse), "liver problems," or "doctor's orders" — vaguely defined and often challenged.

One older man named Alfonso, in the town of La Campana, about five miles north of Fuentes, a recovered alcoholic, drank only chamomile tea at his bar.

This peculiarity earned him the irritating nickname Alfonsito El Camomilo, as well as a reputation for eccentricity. He was well known, and avoided, for his habit of enumerating his various ailments in bars. Nevertheless, by consuming alternative forms of liquid, by smoking, and through prudential displays of generosity, such disadvantaged men are often able to participate still in the ritualized exchanges that underwrite male sociability.

The cycle of imbibing begins early in the morning, at approximately eight o'clock. Many working men stop off at their neighborhood bar before work for a quick pick-me-up consisting of a cup of black espresso with *aguardiente* ("ardent water"; "firewater" would be a good English equivalent) or a chaser of inexpensive brandy—or a combination of these two, served in a small snifter. Aguardiente is a raw anise-based liquor similar to Pernod, ouzo, raki, and other clear aniseed liquors found throughout the Mediterranean region. Many larger pueblos in Andalusia produce their own brands of this corrosive moonshine for either local use or commercial distribution. With a slight admixture of water to achieve the desired milky effect, it is traditionally knocked back in one or two long gulps, followed by sips of strong, sweet coffee. An interesting variation on this effective morning eye-opener is the notorious concoction *sombra y sol* (light and shade), ostensibly named after the division of seats at the bullring. The aptly labeled mixture consists of a base of dark brandy topped off by a layer of aguardiente, which, lighter in weight and color, floats temptingly on top. To be fully savored, the synergistic brew must be consumed in one gulp. This is considered a real man's drink; coughing and wheezing afterward draw reproachful frowns. Like bullfighting, mastering this potent drink without flinching is a skill acquired only after a long and strenuous apprenticeship. For many men, who will have eaten dinner the previous night at eleven or later, this morning jolt suffices as "breakfast."

At lunchtime, men repair to their favorite haunt. The midday meal is the main one, followed by a two-hour siesta—and then it's back to work until about eight in the evening. At lunch, many men will content themselves with a preprandial beer or sherry, coffee, or a soft drink, while amiably conversing with cronies. After work, most men return to their favorite bar for some serious sherry sampling and conviviality, including a round of cards or dominoes, the price of one drink giving a man the right to linger most of the day and night. Even if they interrupt their socializing and rush home to eat a light snack for dinner, the same men may return to the bar in the late evening to continue their card games while sipping coffee or the ubiquitous aguardiente (sherry is not drunk after dinner). Frequently, avid gamblers and *juerguistas* (bingers) will gamble and drink until thrown out by sleepy publicans at two or three o'clock in the morning. Despite all the drinking, public displays of drunkenness are rare, and Andalusians pride themselves on their ability to retain "formality" even in a pickled state (Aguilera 1990).

Noting the long hours spent in public establishments, many visitors to Andalusia mistake the fondness for bars as simple hedonism, a weakness for strong drink, or (if the observers are unaware of the chronic unemployment in the region) an ingrained idleness. Others attribute the crucial role of the bar to a masculine desire to escape the female-dominated world of the home and shore up their manly self-respect (Driessen 1983). These interpretations may be partly true, but there are other, more practical, reasons for loitering late over drinks. For many landless workers, and for the many men without permanent employment, the bar or tavern serves as an unofficial union hall and labor exchange. Traditionally, the farm bailiffs who do the hiring wander from bar to bar in the evenings recruiting workers for the next day's agrarian campaigns. For very practical reasons, then, even if not for the pleasure of masculine revelry, most workers spend their evenings in the bars where they know work opportunities might appear. In addition, without other public meeting places, men involved in politics or in trade-union activity have always used the bars as convenient forums for organizing and proselytizing. Most men with an interest in public affairs cannot afford to absent themselves from these nodes of activity and information.

Protocols of Male Exchange

"My friend, I invite you to a snort." "No, man, *I* invite *you!*" Such aggressive verbal exchanges, or close variants of them, are heard in any Andalusian bar at any time where groups of men congregate. "*Hombre,* have a copita with me!" Or, in the economical Andalusian way, a man will simply raise his hand to his mouth, his thumb forming a spigot and the pinky outward, to designate the double-spouted Spanish drinking jug, or *jarra*. The meaning is clear: time for refreshments — come on, it's on me! These phrases and gestures represent the ritual prelude to a series of invitas. The time to share a cup of cheer has arrived. Who can say no?

Such invitations are frequently initiated silently but conspicuously, and accounts are kept by the barman who makes chalk marks on the wooden bar directly in front of the customer. When the drink is served, no one pays immediately. This would be considered crass — a slur on a man's honesty. "Only Americans and Germans do that," they say, shaking their heads sadly at such vulgarity. Infrequently expunged, the chalk tabulations generally grow until a man is ready to leave. Occasionally, the barman will come along and suddenly, with a flourish of the damp dishrag kept at the ready, erase a man's account. The barman says nothing, only smiles or winks, leaving any response up to the customer. Naturally, this happens often to newcomers, but it can occur at any time. The appropriate response is, of course, a disingenuous protest, followed by a resigned shrug and polite inquiry as to the responsible party. The barman leans over, speaks above the din, and indicates the silent benefactor: "He invited." Thus begins what Arjun Appadurai, in a study of commodity exchange, aptly calls a "tournament of value" (1986:21). Longtime friends, of course, dispense with such formalities by simply picking up the tab in lengthy Alphonse-and-Gaston routines of treating and countertreating, which often grow more and more tumultuous as the evening wears on.[5]

A formulaic exchange of cigarettes follows any invitation to drink together. The use of tobacco in Andalusia contrasts markedly with smoking practices in many blue-collar American bars, for example, where most men place their pack with matches or lighter on the bar for personal use. If a man runs out while in the company of friends at an American bar, others may offer him smokes, but tobacco exchange, at least in my experience, follows no preordained formula. Also, I think that in many U.S. bars, for a man to offer a cigarette to another man, especially a stranger, might be misconstrued, because many American bars are an arena for sexual dalliance. Indeed, this is a major difference between traditional Andalusian bars, American drinking places, and British pubs. Until recently, Andalusian bars were patronized only by heterosexual men.

Equality, Manhood, Exchange

Most ethnographers of Andalusia, since Julian Pitt-Rivers first wandered into a bar in Grazalema back in the late 1940s, have noted the importance of informal male sociability and superficial "friendship" in knitting men together, given the relative paucity of formal contexts for association and assembly (Gilmore 1975, 1987; Press 1979; Brandes 1980b; Corbin and Corbin 1984; Aguilera 1990). Most have also noted the mutual suspicions and distrust that have to be overcome in order for men to form lasting friendships based on *confianza* (trust) and *compromiso* (commitment). Andalusian men, both peasants and landless field laborers, usually work in solitude, only occasionally in cooperative groups or harvest gangs. In the solitary pursuit of an agrarian livelihood based on economic familism, these men are more often rivals than allies, for peasants sow and harvest independently, their families forming communities much like Marx's "sack of potatoes," his term to describe their individualistic nineteenth-century French counterparts. Workers, too, are independent operators for the most part, seeking day labor in competition with other men. Their numbers have historically depressed wages for labor to the point of bare subsistence, and often below (Martinez-Alier 1971; Gilmore 1987). As the Corbins point out (1984:17–18), the ambiguity and tension borne of such social atomism are initially dispelled through the reciprocal offering of petty courtesies and commodities, of which cigarettes and drinks are the most obvious and convenient.

Although the commodity exchange rarely leads to any calculable material benefit, it symbolizes several good personality traits: courtesy, generosity, an agreeable "openness" of character that is the basis of trustworthiness, and the maintenance of social networks. Such exchanges also convey an important ideological implication to working-class people. Andalusians, like most Spaniards, maintain powerful norms of masculine equality, an avowed "ideological egalitarianism" (Moreno 1972), which is a constant theme in literature on Spanish proletarian politics and folklore, as we saw in the coplas reproving the pretentious mayetes. The radical moral egalitarianism in Andalusia derives partly from a historical class struggle against political oppression and economic deprivation, and partly from sexual solidarity (Brandes 1980a; Driessen 1983). In rural Andalusia, despite (or perhaps because of) perspicuous signs of political and socioeconomic hierarchy, one frequently hears expressions such as "All men are equal," "We are all equals here," "A man is just a man," and so on — social ideals that parallel the tenacious political beliefs in justice and fairness voiced so vividly in political coplas and mayete-baiting (see also Mintz 1982, 1997).

The fierce pride in the inborn social equality of all men has an equally powerful obverse: a pervasive hatred of masculine subordination and of sociopolitical hierarchy as bitter injustices, emotionally akin to emasculation (Brandes 1980b; Collier 1987; Gilmore 1990). Such beliefs attain daily expression in the homosocial arena of the bars through *acts of sociability,* consecrated by material exchange. Through these transactions, no matter how seemingly trivial, men reify moral relations by means of symbolic values that circulate through a reciprocal generosity. Thus, because virtually all men can afford a pack of cigarettes and a drink, the swapping of such items makes for an artificial *equality of the act* that metaphorically sets a "starting point" for masculine parity, negating prior claims to precedence based on differences in material wealth or position. To drink together is to realize a conceptual equality — the common denominator of manhood. So, for example, when workers and mayetes drink together, a rare enough occurrence, distinctions in wealth and status are overridden by the act of commensalism. Beyond this starting point, of course, men, now identified as equals, compete for prestige in the tournaments of generosity that follow.

It is therefore not surprising that men who eschew such exchanges are criticized not only for stinginess but for haughtiness — for holding themselves "above" their fellows. A man who keeps to himself, drinks by himself, or fails to initiate or reciprocate invitations is said to *mal tratar a la gente* (treat people badly), to snub or insult others. Aloofness is perceived by many Andalusians as a claim to superiority; failure to enter into the exchange is considered an expression of contempt — and it is a sin of symbolic commission rather than omission. Thus, given the emphasis on ritual exchange as the moral basis for male equality, introversion, the failure to get involved, is a moral deficiency rather than a quirk of personality. Indeed, I was surprised to hear many solitary drinkers and smokers vilified not so much for being elusive or unsociable, as I had originally thought they would be classified, but for being "superior" and arrogant.

I was, in fact, shocked to hear one of my neighbors — a timid and gentle youth — being brutally abused verbally for his intolerable insolence and effrontery; all because he kept to himself at night. The young man, an intellectual, was pathologically shy and avoided the tumult and merriment of the bars. But his spending almost every evening at home instead of inviting his peers to drinks and tobacco seemed a slap in the face to them. "He stays away because he thinks he's better than we are: a real snob, worse than a cheapskate mayete," the men sneered, deflecting my feeble defense of my friend.

Fathers and Sons

Beyond mere courtesy and hospitality, then, bar exchanges can be seen as ritual endorsements of an ideology of masculine equality, an idiom of male comity based on the reduction of difference to arrive at the conceptual common denominator: manhood. The commodity exchanged is itself irrelevant and interchangeable; what matters is the "selfless" transaction among men, symbolizing commitment to the egalitarian ethic that unites all members of the male sex by denying any "baggage" of differences in material status. Thus, by logical extension, such exchanges that pare away differences in status are taboo between fathers and young sons. In Spain as in most places, relations between fathers and sons are, of course, ostensibly grounded in the established hierarchy (of paternal authority and filial obedience) rather than in a competitive equality. A certain superficial chumminess may exist between the men, but only after the son becomes a father himself and both men are on a more equal footing of maturity. Even then genuine camaraderie between the two is relatively rare, for both seek to maintain a certain "distance" (meaning, from the father's point of view, aboveness). Like most fathers everywhere, an Andalusian father expects his son to show him deference, and the son, for reasons of self-protection, social pressure, or residual oedipal feelings — if not out of a less ambivalent filial respect — usually accedes.

As we have seen, the exchange of "masculine" objects symbolizes and consecrates a conceptual framework of equality. In Andalusia, as elsewhere, of course, masculine equality implies the potential for competition and sexual rivalry; the ritualized invitas have a discernible component of competitiveness, as do all tournaments. Between father and son, the tourney of exchanges would contradict the "natural" order of familial ties that rely on distance (aboveness), and it would therefore threaten to subvert the most basic structure of kinship. Here is an area where strong moral norms of exchange intersect at right angles with incompatible norms of filial respect.

Thus, we begin to understand some of the affective reasons for the unusual degree of father-son avoidance in Andalusia in public places, especially bars. Some reference must be made at this point to the intersecting notions of honor and masculinity as they relate to the oedipal triangle. As Murphy shows (1983a, 1983b), much of the tension between the two kinsmen stems from the father's efforts to maintain dominance in the relationship — efforts which, if publicly challenged, would spell serious trouble for his manly image in front of his peers. As the son matures, his efforts to separate himself and adopt an autonomous masculine image threaten the convention of paternal control. It is the contradiction between the growing son's autonomy and the honor of the father, based on dominance over his family, that causes much of the difficulty between the two during the son's adolescence. "When an adolescent male seeks to make a bid for treatment as an adult, the 'manly' behavior expected of him is often interpreted by his father as a premature challenge to paternal authority and therefore an affront to honor" (Murphy 1983b:651). In the outside community, the stormy oedipal discourse takes symbolic form in the seemingly innocuous glass of wine and cheap cigarette: there could be no more evocative illustration of the metaphorical transformation of the trivial into the transcendent in culture.

Observers have noted that, given oedipal tension, the son's abstention from smoking and drinking in the father's presence is a formal "surrender" reflex — a signal of filial respect (Murphy 1983b:654). From a Freudian point of view, the sexual symbolism of the cigarette is obvious. In Spain as elsewhere, using tobacco and drinking alcohol specifically signify male maturity: a man who smokes and drinks is a grown man, meaning a sexually active man, a "true" man with an investment to defend in his erotic assertiveness. In this zero-sum setting, as Murphy argues, for an adolescent son to light up or drink in front of his father implies a *sexual* as well as social equality of persons, which in turn implies filial rebellion. The consequent avoidance between father and son in potentially dangerous public contexts is extreme, at least by urban American standards. It leads to some curious avoidance practices (Murphy 1983a), as we shall see.

The Son Also Rises?

Once I was in a bar in Fuentes drinking with some men in their late twenties. Suddenly, the ribald conversation came to a halt, and the men hastily squashed out their cigarettes on the floor. The drinking ceased (we had been sipping from sherry glasses on the bar). There was a noticeable shift in atmosphere, my young friends appearing suddenly taciturn and anxious, casting nervous glances at one another. They seemed distracted and off-balance as though some kind of electricity had passed through the assembly. They continued stiffly in this manner, warily surveying a smoky corner of the barroom where I saw nothing unusual, until finally a few minutes later two older men passed by the bar, nodded curtly, and left through the back door. At this, my friends relaxed noticeably, started laughing, and said, "Thank God, now we can smoke," and greedily grabbed their packs of cigarettes. A few seconds later we were as before, smoking, drinking, and chatting amiably about football, bullfighting, and sex. Naturally, I asked why and was simply told: "That was Juan's father and Julio's father with him. We can't smoke or drink in front of our fathers."

Why not?

"We have respect."

A more extreme case was that of the Medina brothers, Raul (thirty-seven) and Eugenio (thirty-four). Both were grown men with their own children. Their father, Juan, deceased in 1973, when I knew the brothers, had been a very traditional patriarch, demanding (and receiving) filial deference from his seven children. Reactionary in his politics, choleric and concerned about his public image, he resorted often to the belt to gain obedience from his sons. The two boys, of course, being as rebellious as any village youths, had smoked from an early age, but they had learned to practice deception to avoid paternal detection. Both had devised a method to hide their habit from their father: when catching a furtive smoke in the bathroom or bedroom, they held the lit butt between index and middle finger, but with the burning ember pointed inward into the cupped hand, the palm smothering the smoke. If surprised by the old man, whose sense of smell had been ruined by working with chemical fertilizers, they might escape detection long enough to dispose of the butt without incurring his fearsome wrath.

The two brothers continued to do this well into middle age, even after their dictatorial father had died. "A habit is hard to break," they said, explaining their curious behavior. As a consequence of their secretive mode of smoking, both developed serious epidermal carcinomas on their blackened palms, which eventually required surgery. Raul, in fact, came close to losing his hand to the surgeon's knife. Other men, like the Medinas, displayed similar nicotine stains and self-inflicted flesh wounds from concealing burning cigarettes — almost a kind of oedipal stigmata. Even in later life, for many of these men, to offer their father a cigarette (or to drink openly in his sight) was unthinkable — the moral equivalent of parricide.

Such observations seem to be corroborated by other ethnographers. The Corbins relate another interesting example from the town of Ronda, located not too far distant in the Malaga Province: "Smoking, drinking, womanizing in front of the father either threatens his authority or forces him to exercise it. . . . For example, a young man in his early twenties sitting smoking in a small bar ostentatiously dropped his cigarette on the floor every time the owner of the bar walked through the room, and picked it up to smoke again when the older man left. The sequence occurred five or six times. We later discovered the owner of the bar was the young man's father" (1984:32). And similar examples, somewhat less dramatic than these, can be found in virtually all ethnographies on southern Spain.

What Bar Culture Does

Bar exchange is more than mere courtesy, more also than a trivial prelude to networking and material calculation. In aggregate, the ritualized exchanges in the bars *are* the basic moral order of society, their bibulous trajectory outlining the structural contours of kinship and vitalizing a complex system of opposing values, such as equality and hierarchy, competition and deference. Acts of giving and receiving, and, conversely, acts of abstention among kinsmen, both reflect and transmit norms of comity and deference within a broader idiom of values. In this sense, the stream of cigarettes and drinks transcends the principle both of reciprocity and of individual calculation and represents, as Mauss put it (1974), the "movement of the whole society." Annette Weiner (1980:72) has expressed this well: "The processes of reproduction and regeneration are perceived as essential cultural concerns . . . exchange interaction is reflective of the kinds of symbolic and material values a society accords this flow."

In Andalusia, the mutual giving among men expresses also a political ideal that helps define both gender and community: the moral equality of manhood. At a deeper epistemological level, however, the concepts of both equality and manhood are open to question, as Herzfeld shows with regard to "honor" in Mediterranean societies (1980); for both are simply English glosses for ambiguous notions that may carry different nuances in varying contexts. Cognitively, among workers and peasants, the idea of equality in Andalusia implies both comity *and* competition, friendship *and* rivalry; likewise, manhood is a contentious concept that both unites men and sets them in opposition — especially sexually. If a man is another's equal, he can potentially compete with him for women. Here we find revealed the internal contradictions within the Andalusian ideal of egalitarianism, which is in part an ideological "cover" or denial for underlying anxieties and hostilities. As Aguilera (1990:160) astutely notes about drinking rituals in Almonaster, "The continuous drinking 'game' at the bar was aimed at creating superiority between relative equals." In this respect, I do not think Andalusian rules of masculine comportment differ in a *qualitative* sense from those in many other places where equals jockey for degrees of status. What matters, though, is the contrast with other powerful norms of male discourse governing fathers and sons where a hierarchy must be "fixed."

Obviously, the normative structure uniting "manhood" and "equality" is incompatible with the rules of family organization, particularly that of filial deference. In this important sense, given the emphasis on paternal authority (Murphy 1983a), an Andalusian man could not maintain "equality" with his peers if he permitted a filial challenge by engaging in exchange rituals with his son. His public acceptance as a man worthy of respect (and thus exchange) presupposes aboveness in that regard, which invalidates the ambiguous rules of peer exchange. So the pattern (of drink and cigarette exchange) makes total sense only when viewed from both perspectives; thus the "movement of the whole society" takes on its recognizable bivalent form. The object offered is insignificant; it simply reifies the act of giving, which is, at least in rural Andalusia, the expression of an entire moral universe.

Carnival and Bar Culture

The singing of the copla of course is rewarded with the offering of the copita, as bar protocol enters again into the matter of exchange. Singing and drinking are as intertwined and inseparable as eating and drinking in Spain, because singing causes a certain dryness of the throat that (as everyone knows) needs lubrication. Yet, as in other areas of life, carnival-time is witness to both a transformation and a universalization of bar rules. The bar, of course, is the prime locus for public performance and ritual, the place, aside from plazas and streets, where coplas are first heard, so that bars and cafés are the "stage," as it were, for carnival lyricism. They would be of great cultural importance for this reason alone, that they are the venue for carnival. As Mintz (1997:87) remarks, the tavern is the theater of the poor in Andalusia. Carnival and tavern culture interact in numerous ways.

First of all, all sexual proscriptions and distinctions between patrons disappear at carnival-time. Women enter the bars freely, masked and more or less unnoticed, unless of course, their attire is skimpy. Women drink at will, although there is little public drunkenness among women, except perhaps nowadays among liberated young girls — a scandalous new development roundly condemned by the elders. Perhaps more important, the father-son avoidance pattern breaks down, given that neither can recognize the other anyway because of the masks. No one pays any attention to the "rules," either of generational respect and authority or of basic honesty, and as already noted, some men take advantage of the anonymity and chaos to evade big bar tabs, a dereliction that no self-respecting man would even dream of during normal times.

But carnival also highlights crucial underlying themes in both the bar culture and the wider culture it reflects; and by making these themes universal, it subverts some everyday distinctions between people. During carnival, bar attendance becomes no longer a matter of sex or age or status or parochial identity or political affiliation but an exercise in festival communication. Carnival, first, universalizes drink and tobacco exchange, permitting women and girls to enter the public arena of men, tearing down the barriers of convention. With everyone masked and speaking in the same squeaky falsetto, how can one tell if the tippler offering you a cup of cheer is a man or a woman? Workers and mayetes jostle together promiscuously, as do Francoists, communists, anarchists, and Christian Democrats. The same breakdown of barriers is enacted between fathers and sons, united for once in the for now postoedipal protocols of drink and camaraderie. The father buys the son a drink, as the son does for the father; the father becomes the son, and the son the father; both are disguised as the mother — a confusion that Freud would have appreciated. So carnival turns the bar inside out as well as upside down. Bars, bards, and bawds are one, united in an ongoing, slightly tipsy ritual of renewal.

13

Carnival Evolving

The strongest and sweetest songs yet remain to be sung. — Walt Whitman, "A Back-ward Glance O'er Travelled Roads," *November Boughs*

Politically, Spain has changed greatly since the 1970s, the time when I collected most of the songs presented here. The older songs, those my sources could recite from memory, date mainly from the period between the Civil War and the 1970s. Only a few are from earlier periods. Most of the lyrics in this book are therefore reflective of life during the Franco dictatorship, which lasted until 1975. But even before Franco, Spain was never a real democracy except during the brief interlude of the Second Republic (1931–1939). The country had suffered through the somewhat more benign Primo de Rivera dictatorship in the 1920s and experienced continued abuse of power by politi-cal cliques before that. Most of the songs, therefore, except for the few dating from the brief Republican period (the Nationalists took over most pueblos in 1936 when the rebellion began), reflect an autocratic political environment.

After General Franco died in 1975, though, the Spanish people dismantled the old regime with dispatch. In the first general elections in 1977, they re-soundingly endorsed a democratic transition and have stayed the course most impressively. By the mid-1980s, Spain was already a thriving liberal democ-racy. The country today (1998) is a full-fledged member of the European Economic Community as well as a respected player on the international stage and a full partner in European affairs. In addition, since the late 1980s Spain has experienced an unprecedented economic boom that has lifted its people to the first rank of industrial powers. Since the complete break with the old regime (which can be dated from the election of the Socialists in 1982), all forms of censorship and political repression have been eliminated, including those affecting public celebrations like carnival.

The liberal government also curtailed the extensive powers of the Church, with ecclesiastical compliance and even support. Previously, as elsewhere in Spain (Behar 1990), parish priests could censor the expressions of their flock arbitrarily and autocratically. No more: virtually no limits remain to expression in speech and art. Furthermore, Andalusia, like all other recognized regions of Spain, now has a high degree of local political autonomy, boasts its own "Cultural Junta," and is free to regulate cultural life according to regional aspirations. How has all this political and social change affected carnival in the past few years?

In 1991 and again in 1995, I went back to Spain to observe how carnival was faring under the current liberalization. Aside from a new world of democratic politics, a subject that obviously concerns us here is changing sex mores in Spain. In the past, by lifting repressive norms, especially those affecting women, carnival permitted licentious behavior by both sexes. We have seen that along with the men, women parade (though rarely "in drag"), make obscene jokes, approach men, drink, carouse, and so on. Yet, despite these opportunities, women's participation in formal organizations has been virtually nil. Women perform no skits, sing no songs, and write none of the lyrics, either comic or serious. Unlike in the big city of Cadiz (Mintz 1997), there are no female poets in Fuentes, Carmona, or any of the other rural towns and villages I worked in. Country women have no "voice" in the public discourse of carnival. Women still abstain from carnival creativity; carnival lyricism remains a purely male discourse.

This invisibility can be explained by what we know of deeply entrenched rural Andalusian sexual standards. Carnival is public, and up until the 1980s women were not allowed to be leaders in the public arena. Yet, much of the old sexual segregation had already broken down in Spain by the early 1980s. The feminist agenda is not unknown even in the remotest farming areas of rural Andalusia, where women read newspapers, watch television, and receive an admirable elementary education. Does carnival now reflect changes in sex relations? Are village women and girls now beginning to participate formally in carnival oratory? Are they gaining a voice? Aside from questions of sex and participation, how else has carnival changed since the 1970s? Let us look at how carnival evolved during the 1990s.

Carnival at the Turn of the Twenty-First Century

By 1991, the festival's organization already reflected many dramatic changes. Let us take the case of the pueblo of Fuentes de Andalucía, which I know best.[1] Since the 1980s, the Socialist town hall in Fuentes has taken a lively interest in the celebration and its events. Previously, local officials restricted public subvention of carnival to a minimum, occasionally awarding a few cash awards for best lyrics (subject to severe prior censorship) and providing a small prize — off and on, depending on official whims — for best murga costumes. Before the Socialist tenure, the old town hall, in keeping with Franco's emphasis on "National Catholicism," made funds available for Holy Week, in which the wealthier and more conservative townspeople paraded, carrying religious paraphernalia. From the 1940s until 1967, for reasons that are unclear, the authorities mostly turned a blind eye to carnival, except for sporadic crackdowns in which local constables, to dampen spirits, might sweep up masqueraders or collar a few token clowns.[2] The parish priest fulminated from his pulpit against the lewdness and impiety of the festival — to no avail, of course.

But since the mid-1980s, the municipal government has gotten involved in promoting carnival as a "people's fiesta." The councilmen have implemented a number of new ideas to help out. The mayor and the councilmen informed me that official policy now is to take a passive role in "fomenting" local culture — that is, to act as a conduit for collective wishes. This is a conscious effort to extirpate Franco's autocratic "direction from above." Thus the town hall should "carry out the people's will and nothing more," the young Socialist mayor informed me in 1995. Although it may seem trivial to outsiders, the representative function of local government — translating the popular will — signals a sea change in governmental policy in Spain, a radical rupture with the autocratic past.

Let me describe how carnival has changed in the past fifteen years or so. First is the matter of timing. The scheduling of carnival has been completely altered. Previously, the celebration was compressed into a four-day period before Lent that culminated on Domingo Piñata. But the difficulty entailed for the far-flung emigrants returning to town to enjoy their favorite festivity was in itself a source of much grumbling among the working class, who made up the vast majority of both the emigrants and the masqueraders. So in 1982, the local administration spread the celebration out over the month of February in an arbitrary way, paying very little attention to the ritual calendar. In addition, the authorities provided for activities on nine or ten days rather than the previous four. In 1991, for example, carnival took place between February 6 and 17; in 1995 it took place off and on over a two-week period beginning on February 25 and ending on March 5 (Ash Wednesday was March 1). In a purely temporal sense, carnival is beginning to lose its traditional pre-Lenten overtones and is becoming entirely secularized — a movable feast. The last vestiges of Church influence, which practically speaking had to do only with the timing of carnival, seem now to have been nearly eliminated.

The most important change, though, affects the time of day for which festival activities are scheduled. Carnival now takes place almost entirely at night rather than during the day. Most events are scheduled to start at either nine or eleven o'clock in the evening, and some last until early morning. This change reflects political factors. Under Franco, disguises were outlawed at night as representing a danger to public order. So people paraded during the day and partied in street clothes at night, if at all. I was told, however, that the "spontaneous" wish of Andalusians was always for a nocturnal carnival. As it turns out, the new nighttime focus reflects a return to the situation as it existed during the Second Republic, when nocturnal masquerading was briefly legalized. Perhaps the current scheduling reflects a desire to recapture the lost freedoms of the Republican period, although it should be added that nighttime fiestas are now considered more "sophisticated" in rural southern Spain. By 1995, carnival had become entirely a nighttime event, lasting from sundown until sunrise. This made it more difficult for me to study personally, as my nighttime energy has declined in recent years!

Since the mid-1980s, the town hall has made new financial commitments. Now the local government supplies about five thousand dollars for a community-wide dance complete with rock band, colored lights, decorations, and refreshments. This is held from dusk till dawn on a Saturday night during the two-week carnival period. The town hall also provides additional funds (about a thousand dollars) for prizes, including best murga costumes, best song lyrics, best individual costume, and so on. The "best costume" category is divided into two award areas: best "traditional" costume and best free-form costume. The traditional costume is also called *máscara de colcha,* or "bedsheet disguise," in reference to the customary transvestite masquerade in which men dress up in their mothers' linens.

The local government has also sponsored two entirely new events since the late 1980s. One of these is the *mercadillo,* or flea market, which is held in the morning in the town's central marketplace. This is attended mainly by young children under ten. They arrive early in costume, set up stalls, and peddle their "wares," which may include real farm produce or, more often, humorous items such as pigs' bladders, broken tools, funny clay objects, stale bread, and the like. The second new event is the *pregón de carnaval,* or carnival "announcement," which takes place on the first evening of the festival, to mark its official opening. In 1991, the town hall hired a professional singer from a much larger neighboring town to make the public announcement, complete with a flamenco song cycle. Although the announcement is considered "very Andalusian," it has an ersatz feel to some older people.

Spontaneous events, especially ex tempore skits and routines, have not changed greatly. Still in colcha or witches' costumes, the male masqueraders, either in small groups or individually, enact outrageous sight gags and pantomimes. The skits remain, as before, mostly bawdy and scatological, though many criticize not the futility of repression but, ironically, the loosening of public morality in the post-Franco period. The principals continue to be entirely male; women watch and applaud but do not act in the skits. I will give a few examples from 1991 and 1995.

In one skit from 1991, two clowns appeared in the main street, one pushing a sanitation worker's portable dustbin, the other carrying a shovel. The shovel was piled with condoms and condom wrappers, which the two pretended to be cleaning from the littered streets. The clowns ambled through town, shoveling "used" condoms into the garbage, loudly lamenting the decayed state of the town's sexual morals. In another instance from 1991, three men performed a birthing parody, with one man playing the expectant mother and the other two assisting as midwives. After the "birth," accompanied by loud wailing and falsetto shrieking, the "baby," a black doll, was tossed around the crowd for public inspection.

In another act, a lone male clown performed a very credible, noisy defecation in a bar on the main street. He used a bucket as a chamber pot and threw wads of "used toilet paper" about the bar, commenting all the while upon the extravagant use of such luxurious papers rather than the newspapers used in the more frugal past. In 1995, a group of youngsters in masks pushed a trailer through town filled with little sheets of paper, which they handed out to bystanders (Figure 15). On each was written "ticket for free sex, please state orifice of choice." As in the past, all such burlesques were performed by men and boys, to an appreciative mixed audience.

The Reinvention of Tradition

The major event now celebrated during carnival is actually a newly minted ritual called the Burial of the *Entornao* (pastry-shell). It reflects some relatively new themes, blended with older traditions in an effort to lend "authenticity" to the festival and infuse it with both new life and a regional Andalusian patina.

15. Obscene skit during nighttime carnival, 1995.

The Entornao event dates only from the late 1980s, although people insist that the idea for its mock burial derives from ancient customs dating from the preceding century. I could find no evidence of so venerable a pedigree. My impression is that a brand-new "tradition" has instead been created and promoted for contemporary reasons. The choice of a food item to symbolize carnival accords well with typically Spanish associations of specialty foods with public events, for example sardines (or perhaps pork, as Mintz insists [1997:xxv]), as in Goya's painting of carnival, or the rituals of bread, oil, and salt that accompany the first pressing of the olive oil in March.[3] In Andalusia people say that foods provide the "taste" of the season.

The entornao (literally "turned") is a sugary confection in a distinctive half-moon shape, about six inches across. A specialty of western Andalusia, this rather ordinary little bun is made from a rolled circle of flour, dyed a rust color with ground pimiento and saffron, and folded over a layer of sweetened chopped apple or other fruit. The crescent is easy to make, cheap, and filling. Beyond the mild jolt of sweetness and whatever dubious nutritional value it might have, the russet pastry has some positive symbolic virtues for rural Andalusians.

First, it is the food of the common working person, the only available sweet in a normally restricted diet. Second, anyone can make a decent entornao, for it merely requires mixing and "turning." Just about anyone can "turn them out" is the usual pun one hears. Consequently, the entornao has taken on the moral significance of the poor person's treat, which explains, in part, its adaptation as a culinary symbol of carnival. Those who make the pastry are always women, who remain firmly in control of culinary aspects of Andalusian life, even during carnival.

The ritual "burial of the entornao" now sponsored by the town hall takes place on the last day of carnival and represents the planting of the seed of the next year. In keeping with Andalusian anticlerical tradition, it also takes the form of a mock crucifixion. A number of volunteers make a huge cardboard entornao (Figure 16), which is actually "crucified" (nailed) onto the frame of a wheeled wooden cradle. The cradle is then drawn through the town's main street in a funeral procession, taken outside town, burned, and then ceremoniously buried. The entire time, masked celebrants are engaged in wild lamentations, breast-beating and keening. Everyone is invited to the mock burial, and the solemn procession includes well over a thousand mourners, male and female. All try to outdo each other in the volume and pitch of their wailing. The mourners are separated into three groups, *parientes* (male relatives), "widows," and "heirs" (children), much as in a formal funeral procession from times past. Interestingly, although at contemporary funerals, generally, separation by social categories is less and less observed and mourners now mix at will, at the entornao burial older usage is in force: the sexes are segregated, but in farce. By taking elements from different eras and blending them together, carnival seems to telescope time, in defiance of chronology.

Another interesting detail of the revised festival proceedings is the emerging regional consciousness that accompanies the cultural reinventions or rediscoveries. The central components of the Fuentes carnival and in those of adjacent pueblos like Carmona and La Campana, such as the entornao and the murga, as well as the characteristic forms of transvestite masquerading, have now become self-conscious symbols of "Andalusianism." Now steeped in a strong regional awareness, Andalusians have a sophisticated sense of the value of their *cultura* as a reservoir of local values, from which each town draws deeply in a competitive fashion. People often made mention of this theme, arguing like good functionalists that the festival "serves a purpose" — that of rescuing threatened customs from disuse. And the rescue mission, they claim, serves to keep Andalusian lifestyles alive and healthy, despite the homogenizing effects of modern communications technology such as television and film.

Previously, people were quite aware of the proletarian themes in carnival, but the form of expression was different. In 1973, for example, Andalusian carnival exhibited virtually no signs of a regional awareness among the participants. Instead, most festival observations played on local differences in

16. The giant entornao, with the author (foreground), 1991.

status between the workers and the mayetes or with other entirely local concerns. Political oppositions were rendered not directly in a regional idiom but rather interpreted according to an undifferentiated model of local, or occasionally national, hierarchies.

Nor was the concept of a plebeian "culture" so highly developed as it has become since. The word "cultura" was used to refer to breeding, but not in the meaning now prevalent, of traditions of the common people. The new consciousness, I believe, may be the result of the very forces carnival is said to counteract: television and radio. Since the late 1980s, these media have largely been taken over by a local elite with a very developed regional ideology (see, for example, Moreno 1984). The trend-setters, supported by regionalist academicians, actively promote the view that Andalusia is defined not by its linguistic or ethnic differences (which are minimal), but by its powerful and unique "culture," with its Mediterranean and Arabo-Judaic influences. This ethnonationalist message from the newly sympathetic elite seems to have reached into the small pueblos with resounding success. Carnival themes now overwhelmingly reflect the regionalist influence, with its slightly ersatz overtones.

Political Themes

As we have seen, during the freewheeling period of the Second Republic, political commentary was the order of the day. Each political faction composed its own songs in a displaced parliamentary debate, each band trying to drown out the other. We have already seen a few examples of such lyrics. Some songs united anticlerical with militant themes. An example from 1931 (the first year of the new Republic) ridicules religious belief, attacks bourgeois anticommunism, and reviles women, all in one:

Para hacer guerra al comunismo,	To make war on communism, on
Para hacer guerra al comunismo,	communism
Y en el siglo de las luces,	In this so-called time of
Las mujeres en el pecho	enlightenment,
Llevan colgadas unas cruces.	The women are wearing
Esos tiempos ya pasaron,	Big crucifixes
	On their chests.
Que erán de Carlos Tercero;	But those times have passed and
	gone;
Que la mujer en España	Those were the times of Charles III
Se meta por beaterío.	[the eighteenth century],
La culpa tienen los padres	When women in Spain
Y la tienen los "maríos"	Became saints and nuns.
Que las mujeres en el pecho	The fault lies with the fathers,
Se cuelguen los crucifijos.[4]	And the fault lies with the husbands
	Because they let their women
	Wear the crucifixes.

After the Civil War, the Franco government suppressed all form of political debate. The lively political genre died out, to be replaced by songs persecuting the mayetes.

After Franco died in 1975, however, the fierce polemic returned, for a while. During the late 1970s and early 1980s, political themes began to predominate once again. This brief interval coincided with a period of extreme political and ideological dispute in Andalusia generally, during which the country was governed by a business-oriented conservative coalition (the UCD), with Adolfo Suárez, a former Franco minister, as prime minister. As the following protest song from the 1977–1982 period shows, many workers and peasants, still suffering from age-old economic injustices, felt excluded from power and identified the UCD with the repression of the Franco years.

Este Gobierno facista	This fascistic government
Que nos tiene amendrantao	Has us all intimidated,
A todos los españoles	All of us Spaniards
Que no tenemos trabajo.	Who are out of work.
Si seguimo de esta forma	For sure, if we go on
Potenciendo al UCD	Tolerating the UCD,
Tanto vamos a agacharnos	We'll become a pack of cowards

Que hasta el culo se nos ve.	And they'll have us by the ass.
Y nosotros pretendemos	We only speak the truth
Solo decir la verdad,	When we say that so long
Mientras mande la UCD	As the UCD rules,
La hambre vamos a pasar!	We'll have nothing but hunger!
A todos los fontaniegos	To all you people of Fuentes,
Pedimos unificación	We ask for unity, in order
Para resolver el paro obrero	To solve the unemployment problem
Que tiene nuestra nación.	That grips our land.
En Fuentes ya lo sabemos	In Fuentes we know
Como en toda la nación:	As in all of Spain:
Que dimita la UCD,	That the UCD must resign,
¡Viva la revolución![5]	Long live the Revolution!

But already by the late 1980s, this aggressive genre had entirely disappeared. Songs still of course commented on topical events, in particular the Gulf War, which coincided with carnival in 1991. But political denunciations and political songs were lacking. No abuse was directed at government figures or "class traitors." It seems that the atmosphere of confrontation has passed. In addition, the virtual disappearance of songs singling out specific individuals as targets for moral chastisement attested to a much "softer" (*suave*) tone in carnival lyrics. Instead of the usual picardía ("spicy" and malicious lyrics) attacking recognizable targets, both political and moral, the singers chose a more abstract idiom; a gentler humor, though still "spicy," prevailed. Songs took as their subject imaginary or fictitious characters, global menaces like Saddam Hussein, or general social "types," such as homosexuals or comedians, or personalities from the Spanish media. There were fewer songs, of either the chirigota or the estudiantil variety, denigrating or idolizing women. The focus had shifted.

The most noticeable new motif was sexual; indeed, the lyrics display an obsession with sexual expression — in particular, for reasons that are not entirely clear, with sodomy. An anxiety about anal intercourse has in any case been a central theme in Andalusian male discourse and folklore. In his book on masculinity codes in Andalusia, Brandes (1980b) argues plausibly that the "por detrás" theme attests to homoerotic anxieties and concerns over gender identity, as well as to eroticized political fears of oppression, common in many lower-class masculine cultures. Yet sodomy never previously found any specific genre of literary expression in carnival coplas in Fuentes or neighboring towns. Between 1930 and 1981, for example, I recorded only one indubitable instance of lyrics about anal intercourse — a rather inflammatory accusation of homosexuality made against a citizen of Carmona.

Yet in 1991 in Fuentes alone, I recorded numerous skits and at least three coplas specifically on the subject. The AIDS epidemic is not responsible for this phenomenon, because AIDS is still virtually unknown in the area. Moreover, not all the lyrics are about homosexuals; the first example I will cite concerns heterosexuals. All the coplas express salacious curiosity rather than merely outrage at the idea, although the erotic humor is admittedly tinged with both derision and fear, as well, one suspects, as attraction masked as "surprise" or "disbelief" at such goings-on. Yet after comparing the lyrics cited in this chapter with earlier ones about moral deviance, one can say that the moral condemnation expressed in the 1990s coplas about anal sex is relatively mild, even neutral, emphasizing instead the ridiculousness of sex "from behind" and the powerful male fear of being "tricked" by a transvestite. The first of two examples of the sodomy motif involves a man and a woman; the second, homosexual rape:

Fuimos una noche a la Discoteca	We went to the Discotheque last night,
Y allí vimos algo que nos asombró,	And there we saw something surprising,
Y si no lo veo yo nunca me lo creo	And if I hadn't seen it myself,
Que de esa manera se haga el amor.	I wouldn't have believed you could Make love in this way.
Resulta que el tio tenía a la parienta	The guy had the gal upside down,
Cabeza pa bajo junto a la pared,	
Y se meneaba mas que una tartana	And he was shaking worse than
En la carretera del paso a nivel.	A buggy on a railroad crossing.
Casi seguro le puso el culo	For sure, after what he did to her ass,
Pa que no cague lo menos en un mes.[6]	She won't be able to crap for a month.

In a copla sung in 1995, the man is tricked by a wily transvestite who brutally sodomizes the innocent victim. This theme of homoerotic trickery was an obsessive new element, brought up time and again (indeed, rather too often I felt) during carnival in 1991 and 1995 in jokes, jocular warnings, and reports of supposed actual incidents of "sexual camouflage." This concern reflects the deeper anxiety Brandes wrote about: male fears of being manipulated into the passive role in anal sex and thereby being feminized or emasculated. Those fears are of course heightened by the carnival custom of mass transvestism and intense bodily contact among males.

La Murga Los Raspandurri	We, the Raspandurri Band,
Ahora le paso a contar	Will now tell you what happened to this guy we know

Lo que le paso a éste
Un día de carnival.
Cuando tocaba la caja
Una rubia le preguntó,
Quieres venirte a mi casa?
Que vamos a hacer el amor.

Y éste que está mas falto
Que el camello Mohamé
Saltó la caja y la ropa
Y con la rubia se fué.

Cuando pasó media hora,
Este ya estaba escamao;
Cuando metió la mano
El pobre queo asombrao,
Y cuando sintió aquello
Tan grande entre sus manos,
El le levantó la falda
Y vió el peazo de aparato.

Entonces salió corriendo
Con gracia y con disímulo,
Y la entrecogió la rubia
Y se la hincó por culo.

Y cuando pudo escapar
De la rubia travestí,
Estaba mas escocio,
Estaba mas escocio
Que el culo de la Bibí.[7]

One day during carnival.
See, he was playing his tambourine
And this blonde came up to him
And she asked if he wants to go home
   with her
So they could make love.
And this guy, more gullible
Than the camel-brain Mohammed,
Threw off his costume
And ran off with the blonde.
Well, after about half an hour,
They ended up in bed,
And when he put his hand down
   there
Did he get a shock.
He felt something very big
So he lifted up her skirt
And he saw a big apparatus.
Well, he tried to escape
By hook or by crook,
But that big blonde
Caught him and started
Working over his ass.
Finally, when he managed to get
   away
From the blonde transvestite,
His ass was more painful and sore,
More painful and sore,
Than the well-worn ass of Bibí [a
   television drag queen].

General Impressions of Change in Carnival

New events have been added to the carnival repertoire, as we have seen, and the times of celebration have been altered to facilitate working-class participation. Carnival now receives the lion's share of the municipal resources set aside for celebrations, in keeping with democratic policies that seek to implement, not frustrate, the people's will. As people approvingly told me, carnival is now administered "from below" — no longer "from above" — in one of those typically Andalusian inversions. The form and shape of carnival now expresses more fluidly and more precisely shifting popular motifs. People feel that they are the masters in their own house, "on top" in politics.

Also, the aggressive tone of previous years has lightened somewhat. The song lyrics no longer pick out recognizable targets for hurtful mockery. There is less emphasis on the punishment of moral deviance. The songs and skits celebrate moral unity and community in an abstract and nonpersecutory way, with little political protest. In fact, it appears that consciousness has lessened of the rich and powerful as threats. As people told me, "Before, carnival was a time to molest others; now it is only for fun and pleasure." The targeted other, the object of vilification, is no longer the mayetes, who are not doing well anyway, or the rich, who have for the most part moved away to the provincial capital, but wily homosexuals who trick young men into sodomy. People say, somewhat ruefully, that carnival is now "softer" (*mas suave*); less malice is directed at local targets, and less ideological violence toward others. One can say that in Andalusia, the focus of group hostilities has shifted from defined political entities to abstract sexual predators who defile masculinity.

Still, the recent upsurge of interest in anal intercourse calls for some explanation. Psychoanalytical interpretations aplenty are available for Hispanic joking about homosexual rape; most relate the jokes to early childhood experiences and subsequent male sexual insecurities. Ingham's work in Mexico (1986:60–61) and my own work on male gender identity formation (Gilmore 1986; Gilmore and Uhl 1986) can be cited here. Brandes (1980b) contributes useful insight from a political angle, arguing that male fears are linked to a sense of political vulnerability. These ideas are summarized in Taggart's sensitive book on Spanish folklore (1990). Yet similar joking and similar anxieties occur in many other national contexts—for example, among adolescents in Turkey (Dundes et al. 1972; Delaney 1991:50). I do not want to digress into an elaborate psychological interpretation of what appears to be a ubiquitous male qualm. The point, moreover, is not the constant—the psychodynamic origins—but the variable: *increased* preoccupation with sodomy in the liberal atmosphere of post-Franco Spain. Indeed the recent obsessions seem somewhat at odds with the standard interpretations, given that the degree of political oppression has lessened, not increased, in Spain; fears of persecution and exploitation have declined. I will merely make some suggestions about why there is more rather than less apprehension about anal rape in contemporary Andalusia.

Psychological interpretations of sexual anxieties are usually based on the principle of ambivalence. Homosexual fantasies usually reveal both a wish and a fear (that the wish will be fulfilled). If repressions suddenly diminish and anything becomes possible, as occurred so abruptly in Spain, then hidden wishes may become dramatically less controllable, more accessible to consciousness. Perhaps the men of Fuentes have lost some degree of superego control as a result of the disorienting suddenness of liberalization. As ancient rigidities break down, long-repressed fantasies surge surfaceward. After all, carnival is a time for losing control, especially in crowds. As Parker puts it in his masterly study of Rio carnival, carnival is a time for "losing mastery over one's body and merging with the bodies of others" (1991:144). Thus the transvestism of carnival carries a new danger: the rediscovery of one's own bisexuality. The fearful object — the polymorphously perverse self — may now lie within.

I do not want to overstate the decline of aggressiveness during carnival in the 1990s. Some externalization, some scapegoating remains; there is still plenty of "spice," even if the scapegoat is an abstract one. In 1995, some aggressive notes of a generalized nature could be heard; they did not seem discordant but representative of the prevailing atmosphere. Packs of young boys still paraded through the town, bellowing such ditties as "¡Eso es el carnaval! ¡El que no diga olé, se corta los cojones!" (This is carnival! He who fails to say "Olé" gets his balls cut off). As always, the underlying motif of threatened masculinity is prevalent, although as in other areas of carnival expression the object is an amorphous projection, an imaginary opponent: anyone who would deny the primacy of the bacchanalia, anyone who would frustrate pleasure.

Forms of costuming show both change and continuity. Male transvestism still predominates. Yet the people have also gone in for more "modern" forms of costuming, with masks in both colcha and witch formats displaying more variation than previously. People dress not only as transvestites but also as donkeys, palm trees, Martians, and so on. A new fad among women is the majorette costume, complete with batons and marching boots, copied from American television shows. Both men and women are now markedly less concerned about covering their faces. In the 1970s, the face was always fully masked; thus, people told me, the masquerader lost "his shame" and was freed from all restraint. In 1995, faces were often uncovered, and recognition was often sought rather than avoided. The invariable explanation for the change was that people were "proud" of their expensive costumes and wanted to show them off. The old proletarian pride in frugality had given way to the capitalist opulence of the 1990s.

The object of carnival is no longer only to disguise oneself in order to attack others. It is also to present oneself in the best possible light — a transformation of objective from communal persecution to narcissistic diversion. Some gender differences emerge here. Women tend to gravitate toward "elegant" (improvised) costumes: flappers, princesses, majorettes, and so forth. Most men, by contrast, stick to the ancient colcha and witch motifs. In this sense, the men remain traditionalist, comedic, self-mocking; the women seek innovative, more dignified, more "modern" expressions, often adapting images taken directly from magazines and television. In other words, the women still strive to be beautiful and fashionable, the men to be funny — or solemn — as the case may be. The bifurcation had proceeded apace by 1995.

This brings us back to the matter of differential gender participation. As the reader will have seen, one area that shows little alteration is leadership roles. Previously, all the band members, all the poets, and the majority of masqueraders were men. None of these patterns shows the slightest degree of change. Even in 1995, there were still no female singers or composers. Every song was composed by a man, sung by an all-male group. Women participated in the same way as before: as decorative masqueraders and audience members. Women do not shape public festival discourse. As Bourdieu (1977, 1982) has shown, appropriating power through public discourse involves acquiring the power to command an audience. Why do no female orators take the stage? Why are no lyrics composed about the role of women in the new Spain?[8]

One must place women's reticence in perspective. Rural Andalusian women have no hesitation about entering the political arena. Remember that three of the democratically elected councillors of the municipal government in Fuentes are women; they are grasping real power, not just symbols of power. We should note also a breakdown in sexual segregation: young women enter bars in all the small towns and villages and carouse in the streets until dawn; during festivals, miniskirted girls drink boys under the tables of the local cafés and taverns. Feminine withdrawal from carnival presentations calls for some other explanation.

In both 1991 and 1995, I asked repeatedly about this, thinking that the answer might offer a clue to women's self-perception in the new Spain. Spanish women speak often about their new freedoms and their new equality, sometimes with considerable passion. Yet the local women remain virtually invisible in the leadership roles during carnival, the communal high point of the year. I sought answers from both young and old women during the carnivals in 1991 and 1995. Then in 1996, in order to provide a broader-based sampling, I conducted a random provincewide survey on the issue by distributing a questionnaire, which was filled out in writing by a hundred respondents (fifty men and fifty women of all ages) in the pueblos of Fuentes, Las Cabezas de San Juan, Pedrera, Aznalcóllar, Los Corrales, and a few others in Seville Province. I again asked why women did not sing in the murgas, compose ditties, or perform burlesques.[9]

The women respondents articulated their answers in terms of affect rather than politics or prohibitions. They responded by saying the same thing that women had told me previously, in face-to-face discussions: women could sing if they wanted to; no one holds them back; but they just do not "enjoy" singing ribald songs in public. Women do not want to march in a band; they do not "feel like it." They say they would feel uncomfortable and ill at ease with such self-exposure and posturing. Answering other questions, like "What, if anything, impedes the participation of women in murgas?" the women intimated that the leadership roles of carnival are self-deprecatingly comic; they involve a buffoonery and a slapstick self-mockery that seems incompatible with a specifically Andalusian femininity. "Only a man can be such a fool in public," one women wrote on her question sheet, articulating a common attitude. So, in sum, it seems that the women are still pretty much content to let the men be the performers in a "masculine" burlesque that women enjoy as passive observers. But inherent in the feminine discourse of liberation in rural Andalusia today is a tenacious feminine ego ideal that risks endangerment in the public indignities subsumed under the cultural category of "clowning."

Incidentally, most of the male respondents to my carnival survey echoed the women's sentiments on their questionnaires. Although a few men said that women could do "whatever they wanted," and many said that women do whatever they want, anyway, regardless of propriety or men's wishes, they (the men) had no explanation for women's abstention from carnival versification. One or two older men argued that what kept the women back was not moral inhibitions, but "lack of education [culture]" (*falta de cultura*), but I did not find such a theory credible in regard to the younger women.

I have no better answer than do Andalusians themselves. The male ethnographer gets an object lesson in the fragility of the cultural construction of womanhood. The freedom of Andalusian women to engage in public displays of ritualized obscenity is still abridged by the consuetude of a defended self-image. In Fuentes, as in most of Spain, women seem to have dissociated the political and the cultural aspects of feminist discourse. Although women's deeper motives can only be a matter for speculation, my impression is that the pressures operating on Andalusian women have to do with a sense of self tied dramatically to the inner need for an attractive public image, which is the basis for a guarded femininity. It is not so much moral pressure but image control that keeps women from performing.

Public mockery — the heart and soul of carnival — is still incompatible with women's gender image, whereas for males ritualized clowning has always been permissible, as have periodic bingeing, drinking, gambling, and sexual tomfoolery — all part of the ancient double standard. Perhaps this too will change in the twenty-first century, but sex roles still remain a powerful pressure in Andalusia. Only time will tell. I leave further speculation on this point to the reader.

14

Conclusions
Meanings of Carnival, Carnivals of Meaning

The web of our life is a tangled yarn, good and ill together. — William Shakespeare, *All's Well that Ends Well,* IV, iii

In the previous chapters we looked at carnival rituals both as self-contained events and as festival expressions that deform, deconstruct, and reinterpret the world as it is — that is to say, the noncarnival world — in various ways. Throughout, we have used carnival lyrics as a lens through which to view Andalusian culture in context, with all its inconsistencies and contradictions. Now that we have seen how the coplas "work," both in and outside carnival, and how carnival antitheses are repeated and sublimated in the rituals and routines of everyday life, it is time to take stock of the meanings of carnival and the broader significance of the Spanish carnivalesque.

We have seen that through its coplas, the Spanish carnival is, first, a rhetorical celebration of human differences, of moral boundaries and social cleavages, and that carnival vocabulary is a vehicle for lifting up the righteous and casting down the delinquent and deviant. But carnival songs are not only about erecting boundaries, overthrowing structures, or reinforcing existing barriers that divide people. To be sure, carnival commemorates and retraces the symbolic lines that separate people and things into classes, generations, and sexes and, at an abstract level, into good and bad, high and low, inside and outside, public and private, and so on; but the festival paradoxically also exalts the things that unite people and that transcend surface distinctions.

The poets create playful but invidious contrasts in order to punish transgressors against the popular will, to right wrongs, and to upend hierarchies. But the same poets, sometimes in the space of a single day or hour, also honor the common experiences that override such transient human distinctions; they contradict themselves without a moment's hesitation. They sing with *sentimientos profundos,* that is, feelings deep enough to transcend visible differences, about loss and love, childhood and motherhood, family, honor, friendship, and death. In other words, like all social poets from Homer on, they sing of shared concerns, of universal humanity. The poets cannot neutralize the contradictions of life, which are in any case irresoluble, but their carnival lyricism can and does merge them in the receptive imagination of the crowd, juxtaposing the opposites that bedevil everyone, laying out the contradictions of human contact gaily side by side, and thereby, through whimsical superimpositions, temporarily both highlighting and relieving the tensions they produce.

Carnival songs are most pointedly about man's (here I specifically mean males') rejection of the despised "others" who share his world. The coplas enact a masculine repudiation of the bad woman, the evil, grasping harpy, the avaricious wife, the wicked woman with her mania to jump "on top" and beat the overwhelmed husband. Other bad social examples are also targeted: the middle-class skinflint, the moral transgressor of either sex, the sexual deceiver, the dreadful mother-in-law, the corrupt official, the pompous farmer, the self-important and the benighted. All are traditional stereotypes that necessitate dissociation and disavowal. But with wholesale rejection of the other comes not only momentary purification and relief but also debilitating loss of a deeper nature. For in the act of repudiation, the singer denies the cast-out other's surrogate within: the polymorphous libertine, the dissolute reprobate; and the attendant desires and limitations — economic ambition, the desire for luxury, the wish for domestic power, the "feminine" feelings of dependency. Rejection of "woman" also endangers the tie to the beloved, all-forgiving mother and banishes her protective nurturing. This turning away from woman is felt at a deeper level as a threat and is negated through restorative rituals of mourning and regressive melancholia over the mother. The defilement of woman in the chirigota burlesques — which we might characterize as a form of verbal rape — depletes or coarsens the man. It entails the loss of the idealized tender side of woman; it implies a final good-bye to childhood, the serene memory of which is recaptured in nostalgic reveries of symbiosis, timelessness, and nurturing.

Carnival also means condemnation of the class enemy: the exploiter, the money-mad peseta pincher, the mayete. But with this casting out of the devil comes a poignant sense of envy for his affluence, his comfort, his leisure, and the ability to live the good life without having to work for the despised day wage. The bourgeois has sold his soul to the devil, for sure, but at least he had the opportunity, a choice that eludes the landless peasant. Carnival mixes class hatred with personal ambition and with the vindictive envy of the small for the just slightly bigger.

Carnival is therefore not simply about strength and weakness, goodness and badness, belonging and rejection, us versus them. Nor is it only about tearing down or negating of the noncarnival world or of hierarchy and authority. There is nothing "one-sided" about Spanish carnival (Eagleton 1989:188). Too vast and inclusive for such nugatory pigeonholing, carnival transcends politics and addresses the inseparable twins of the human heart: love and hate—or, to view it another way, the dual impossibility of achieving either purity or completion. In Andalusia, carnival is a window briefly thrown open on the concealed machinery of life's complexities, a sudden rendezvous with the shocking unity of the sexes, a face-to-face encounter with the strange oneness of triumph and tragedy, a sudden awareness of the disturbing linkage of dependence and autonomy. All these paradoxes, exposed and magnified bizarrely during carnival, are played out unconsciously every day in noncarnival ritualizations, among men in the bars, by women in their interior castles, in the endless negotiations between the sexes over power and privilege. Mostly, carnival is about the balance between alienation and identity, the "lowering" and emancipation of that which is both the self and not the self, that which is within and without, that which is denied and repressed, that which is cast off from the self.[1]

All these inner struggles are represented in pictorial imagery, as is true in dreams. In Spanish politics, the revolts of the lowly orders have always been referred to as risings (*levantimientos*). Rebellions of the poor are always "put down" or crushed by those "above," who are fearful that the lower orders "want to rise up and take our place" and "take away what is ours." The lower classes wish for the triumph of male sexuality, predatory and powerful, as they imagine the analogous rising of the poor and the castration of the rich symbolized by such revolutions: the usurpation of sexual primacy, the pushing "down" of the feminine, as well as the overthrow of the threatening father. All these wishes and fears about one's place in the natural or physical order, though normally intermingled, are starkly discrete in the pulsating rhythms of carnival, where time and place are overridden. Carnival has affective and symbolic ambivalence without shading or ambiguity. Carnival embraces all extremes: revolutionary, reactionary, profane and sacred, male and female all at once.

Recent studies of the communicative arts have pointed out that carnivalesque artistic performances represent a Bakhtinian dialogue between speaker and hearer—a dialectic between heard and unheard voices (Hirschkop 1989). Oral poetry of this sort is not simply a recitative or a monologue; it is a dialogue between its composer and the expectant masses.[2] Those who study expressive culture often do so as a means of highlighting the often "muted" ideology of oppressed groups. These observers argue for the importance of a full-fledged "poetics and politics of ethnography" (Bauman and Briggs 1990: 71). Such an approach could, it is argued, illuminate the conjuncture of ritual, voiced utterance, and mass culture in hierarchical contexts like that of rural Spain and help give a voice to the voiceless. But the data we have examined seem to suggest that the emphasis on proletarian oratory must, as in all other kinds of rhetoric, be adjusted to the diversity of voices and themes within the local speech community of workers or peasants.

From a psychological point of view, we can say that much of the high emotion of Spanish carnival derives from the sensation of inner tension—or technically, anxiety. People are in fact anxious about what might happen to them, for carnival negates all the rules, collapses time, and superimposes opposites. The resultant magical free-for-all leads to a commingling of desire and guilt on the one hand and anticipation and fear on the other. The heightened tension explains much of the thrilling emotional tone of the festival, in which the participants are in an electrified, even hysterical, state of mind for long periods. For psychoanalysts, the state of anxiety is the irresoluble inner tension caused by the conflict between a wish and a fear—that is, by the experiencing of simultaneous but contradictory affects: the coexistence of stark opposites in fantasy or imagination, the conflation of love and hate, which, as we have seen, is the sub-rosa text of Andalusian carnival.[3]

Freud originated the notion of anxiety as a sense of impending danger about the possibility that a thought or an act will break through the taboos of the superego and destroying the balance between repression and the ego. "The relationship of anxiety to danger is anticipatory" (Hallowell 1955:266); or, in Freud's own words: "one feels anxiety *lest* something occur" (cited in Hallowell 1955:266). Anxiety produces a marked sense of displeasure, which requires relief through some sort of compromise or other resolution. Here, the tension is relaxed through the consummate act of public utterance, the act of the copla.

Of course, neither the idea of psychic ambivalence (or, for that matter, anxiety) nor the concept of the reconciling of opposites in art or humor is new. It is a well-established fact that all powerful fixations carry both a positive and a negative valence. The psychoanalyst Kris, for example, notes that creativity in the comic arts originates "in the conflict between instinctual trends and the superego's repudiation of them," and that comedy occupies a position "midway between pleasure and unpleasure" (1952:182). Political ideology is no different in this respect from sexual or aggressive fantasies in that it incorporates divergent and discrepant sentiments. The notion of inner tension as an integral aspect of any organic structure is a standard tenet not only of psychoanalysis and Marxism, but also of the sociology of emotion (Merton 1976; Weigert 1991). In addition to incorporating Abu-Lughod's notion of discrepant sentiments (discussed earlier), the notion of ambivalence I rely on here takes as its point of departure the "heteroglossia" that Herzfeld (1991:81) discusses in his study of the inner tensions of Greek masculine poetics, along with the polyphony in Turkish arabesk songs that Martin Stokes (1992:13) describes.

Returning to the class model of Spanish ethnography, we see a similar contrast of opposites, a similar equivocalness of feeling. Numerous native anthropologists working in Spain (for instance, Moreno 1984; Llobera 1986) have derided the use of social stereotypes by foreigners, such as the image of the "Mediterranean" peasant and the old woman in black. But political clichés — for example, the proletarian resistance hero of Anglophone historiography — are equally a form of stereotyping or "mythopoesis" or hagiography within a Marxist framework, as Mitchell puts it (1988:88). As we proceed with anthropology in Spain, what is needed is a greater sensitivity to the contradictions and discontinuities within proletarian identity, an approach that goes beyond the rigidities of an outdated Marxist model that sees only "resistance" where a much more complex mixture of motivations is at work. As the anthropologist Michael Brown sensibly urges, it may be time to start "resisting resistance" as a "paint-by-the-numbers" model for explaining everything: "A myopic focus on resistance, then, can easily blind us to zones of complicity and, for that matter, of sui generis creativity" (1996:732–733). Nothing could be truer in regard to Spanish politics. When it comes to social class and class consciousness in Spain, Edward LiPuma and Sarah Meltzoff remind us that we need to see classes in Spain themselves as "living, emergent, and constantly transforming categories" (1989:329).

But even more than the changefulness involved: beyond class, and intermingled with categories of politics, sex, region, and generation, there is the enduring concept of community in the broader sense: a timeless parochialism of place of which the national Great Tradition is the most obvious ingredient.

What the discrepant sentiments of carnival coplas suggest is that this enhanced sensitivity to affective nuance must start with the transcendent, primordial sentiments that define and nourish the group *at the same time* that they promote dissent.[4] It is this dialectic of culture and counterculture that endlessly renegotiates tradition.

In this regard, Bakhtin (1984:11) argues that popular inversive rituals are never purely parodies, for the popular imagination is never bare nor unambiguous; the spirit of carnival "denies, but it revives and renews at the same time. Bare negation is completely alien to folk culture." In Spain, the conceptual reversals are restorations of noncarnival norms, especially of Great Tradition notions of Christian charity; they contrast with the persecution and mockery of the subversive and comic genres. In carnival negation is never completed, but displaced "in time," and the object is reclaimed through tropes of affirmation: "The non-being of an object is its 'other face,' its inside out. . . . The object that has been destroyed remains in the world but in a new form of being in time and space; it becomes the 'other side' of the new object that has taken its place" (Bakhtin 1984:410).

Comparing content in the songs about women, for example, one is immediately struck by the anomalously positive images of woman and the robust moral identification with woman as victim of a universal fate in the scholars' ditties, which stands so strikingly in contrast to the malicious misogyny of the comedians. The scholar-bards, whose identification with the object is often reflected in the technique of cross-sexual soliloquy, enact a reversal of the persecutory poesis of carnival by taking the position of the woman in their role as upholders of traditions of romantic love. These Janus-faced poets reclaim standard Castilian notions of chivalry, charity, and compassion, but in a renewed form, stressing egalitarianism and the unity of the sexes over formalism and hierarchy. The serious poets do not victimize the deviant woman as the satirists do, but rather celebrate the unity of mankind by emphasizing conditions that unite rather than divide: suffering, old age, loneliness, fate. Like the Middle Eastern genres described by Stokes, which similarly stress the unity of the sexes before an implacable fate, the sexual ambiguity of the Andalusian carnival voice leads to "merging markers of gender identity" (1992:122) in common experience.

Also, instead of dwelling on the parochialism of local gossip, the scholars focus on the world beyond, in praise of a broader conception of brotherhood, and appeal not to an alienating retributive justice but to an incorporative fraternal mutualism. Like the poets who mourn their mothers and their boyhood, their tone is elegiac and philosophical and their moral messages uplifting, merciful, redemptive, in keeping with the Catholic epistemology of compassion. In a typical carnivalesque paradox, the scholar-minstrels balance the anticlerical subversion of the comedians with a proletarian appropriation of elite and nationalist doctrine.

The comedians denigrate femininity, sometimes maliciously, but their counterparts, the scholars, reinvent women as vulnerable and pure: threatened rather than threatening, life affirming rather than life denying, victimized rather than transgressing. Carnival polyphony points to the "central contradiction in gender relations" (Kaeppler 1993:495): the tension of male ambivalence about female sexuality — woman imagined as both madonna and whore (Giovannini 1981; Saunders 1981). This tension transcends class and time, stemming from the male identification with the "female other" as an inevitable psychic residue of the childhood symbiosis with the mother, combined with the culturally necessary male repudiation of femininity during adolescence in patriarchal societies (Ingham 1986).

Hence men's empathy (otherwise taboo) with women, which is mirrored in the mother's powerful identification with the son, finds expression in sentimental pleas for Christian mercy and forgiveness. The poets often couch the pleas in the feminine first person, taking the woman's voice and assuming her identity. Rather than as object of disgrace, the fallen woman emerges as a tragic figure eliciting sympathy (and empathy), as an existentially human, rather than female, object for whom the maestro acts as mouthpiece. If the chirigotas encourage persecution of female deviance, and thus promote the expression of aggressive feelings and the consequent social alienation or ostracism of the shamed girl, the serious songs reverse the rejection through reincorporation and moral restitution or, perhaps more accurately, masculine guilt. As Mitchell (1988:86) puts it, the positive side of such persecutory folk rituals in Spain represents "the introjection of persecutory feelings (guilt) initially aroused by one's own retrograde desires or deeds."[5]

Paradoxically, then, given its popular and proletarian roots, Andalusian carnival incorporates and ratifies elements of the Spanish Great Tradition, with all its nationalistic pieties and obscurantist longings. As we have seen, for dogmatic Marxist observers, carnival is always a political movement, because culture and politics are always "dynamically related" (Cohen 1993:154). From such a single point of view, observers often interpret carnival simply as "an oppositional description of society" (Le Roy Ladurie 1979:316). In Spain a Marxist class model is plausible and useful up to a point — at one level it captures the Andalusian "revolutionary situation" and the hatred of the "small for the mighty" (Le Roy Ladurie 1979:33, 105). I have described this oppositional and class-conscious aspect of the festival elsewhere time and time again. But using a model of class conflict here to explain the scholars' traditionalism and patriotism returns us to a dated ritual-of-rebellion thesis originated by Max Gluckman, with its baggage of mystification and false consciousness. Who is to say what is false and what not? One might just as logically argue that the workers' left-revolutionism is "false consciousness" and their conservative leanings "true consciousness." It is only a matter of special pleading either way — in other words, of observer bias. As we have seen, some of the composers were politically reactionary, others revolutionary, others apolitical or apathetic.

In classic Marxist epistemology (see Kertzer 1988), carnival lyricism is a sublimation of class struggle, ritual resistance to elite hegemony, nothing much more; although of course sexual perversity has to be acknowledged even by the ideologically pure. In a dogmatically Marxist approach, for example, Abner Cohen sees carnival as always a "contested event" and regards class conflict as "the very essence of the celebration" (1993:153, 131). Le Roy Ladurie (1979:290) regards the sixteenth-century carnival in Romans to be a "nearly perfect example of class struggle." Although their interpretations are richer than these lines might indicate when taken out of context, the general view that carnival shows opposition to and negation of elite values stems from a widespread — and rarely questioned — Gramscian view about cultural hegemony and its relation to Marxist epistemology. Discussing proletarian class consciousness as a counterhegemonic phenomenon, Gramsci (1929–35:273) writes, in a representative sentence: "The lower classes, historically on the defensive, can only achieve self-awareness via a series of negations." The view deriving from such an article of faith — that carnival is a simple negation or inversion of bourgeois ideology — colors the work of most old-fashioned Marxist scholars who deal with cultural issues and ritual. Yet most sophisticated Marxists, Le Roy Ladurie and Cohen included, realize that carnival imagery is more complicated than mere negation or class rebellion and that its symbolism encompasses "contradictory meanings" and psychic tensions inherent in the human spirit. Most of the theorists admit that it is futile to try to explain, or explain away, the cultural "in terms of the political" (Cohen 1993: 120). Useful only up to a point, Gramsci helps very little when it comes to the counterrevolutionary moral tendencies of Spanish festival.

Obviously, a simple class model cannot do justice to the richness of such inconsistent expressions. The embrace of "elite" values; praise for aristocrats, Church charities, and the Civil Guard; and the matriolatry of the poets cannot be explained away simply as "compliance" or "camouflage" (Cohen 1993: 130, 132), that is, as the false consciousness of a subject population. Rather, these elements of the Great Tradition represent active *appropriations* of national culture in the construction of complex proletarian moral systems that have a nationalistic side.

Maurice Bloch (1982, 1985, 1992), another sophisticated Marxist, argues the very flexibility of ideology, its "vagueness and a-logicality," provides the disorienting effects in the ritualization of affect. Thus ideology can "both affirm and deny at the same time" (Bloch 1985:40–41). The carnivalesque allows the denial of "time" as well as the social order; and politicized rituals like carnival superimpose contradictory affects, leading to further confusion and tension. For Cohen (1993:154) either carnival is revolutionary theater or else it gets "co-opted" by the dominant culture and transformed into an "opiate of the masses." For Spain, perhaps the "sherry of the masses" would be a better phrase if we are to take this insight seriously. But I think it is more fruitful to abandon such stilted Marxist dogma and to look at carnival as expressing contradictions both *within* and *between* classes — at least in Spain — as Bloch seems to suggest.

Carnival thus has many faces, many voices; it contains multitudes. Its political economy is multivalent, multiphasic, a counterpoint, a study in what can only be called ambivalence without ambiguity. In summing up his survey of carnivals and other similar rituals, Kertzer notes that popular festivities are at the same time conservative and convulsive: "Popular rites of community solidarity, with their well-developed symbolism, their legacy of emotional fervor, and the power that comes with sharing with others in regular ritual performances, have the power that comes from the communal effervescence. . . . It is indeed a power that can be used to deflect social tensions, but it can be used for quite different purposes" (1988:150). This collective release of tension, with its riotous "upside-downings," as Natalie Zemon Davis calls the playful inversions of carnival, is only part of a dialectic of punishment and forgiveness "used for quite different purposes" (1978:188). The concept of ritual order itself thus takes on a more fluid, more kinetic meaning. As the critic Linda Hutcheon puts it in her study of popular parodic comedy (1986:112), the "aesthetic appropriation" of standard reality in the carnivalesque represents not only a denial of reality, but also the denial of the denial, or the "authorization" of the folk text as equivalent to the elite, not just its opposite. Like dreamwork as Freud described it (that is, the mental process through which repressed emotions are transformed into visual images during sleep), carnival condenses and superimposes all extremes of feeling into colorful visual imagery and verbal chaos.

Carnival is now changing in Andalusia, as it is throughout contemporary Spain. Some of its piquancy has mellowed; its coplas are shifting toward the exploration of the promiscuous sexuality of the 1990s and other self-absorbed, narcissistic concerns. Growing equality between the sexes will eventually tear down many of the remaining barriers that separate men and women in the small pueblos. In some big cities like Cadiz, younger women are beginning to find a voice in the carnival discourse by participating in song recitals (Mintz 1997:200). In the twenty-first century everything that I have written about will doubtless end or change greatly. Yet the underlying themes of the *carnaval del pueblo,* sex and status, will remain the same. These transcendent themes represent concerns that are more than parochial Spanish, or Andalusian; they express the central dilemma of all human life, for male and female, rich and poor. Such concerns stem from the inevitable: whatever we wish for we also fear; whatever we fear we also wish. Like carnival, all of us are multivalent: right-side-up and upside-down, male and female, high and low, good and bad, pure and polluted all at once. Parodic and praiseful, derisive and reverent, misogynist and matriolatrous, magical and mundane, spiritual and carnal, carnival goes on.

Notes

Chapter 1: Introduction

1. Jerome Mintz's book *Carnival Song and Society* (1997) was in press and unavailable as the present volume was entering its final stages. Unfortunately, therefore, I was unable to incorporate his numerous insights and excellent data into my work here except in the most cursory way. Mintz's work provides an excellent complementary view of carnival as it is practiced in the neighboring province of Cadiz, both in the capital city and in some villages and towns. The major differences between the two provincial celebrations are these: first, in Cadiz the *estudiantil* tradition appears to be less well established; second, more emphasis is placed in Cadiz on contests and competitions among bands and poets. While such *concursos* and *desafíos* (as they are called) occur in the Seville area, they have a shallower history than in Cadiz. Finally, it is only in Seville that the post-Franco carnival has become an almost entirely nocturnal event.

2. Checa's (1992:68) actual words are: "La copla de carnaval es una terapía colectiva para alcanzar bienestar." Mintz reports the terms *cuplé* and *cuarteto,* as well as the more familiar *copla,* for carnival songs in Cadiz Province, but I have never heard these terms used except by intellectuals in Seville or Cordoba Provinces. There are no fixed rules governing structure, rhythm, or versification in carnival poems.

3. See, for example, Castle (1984:912) and Lindley (1996:18). For recent reviews of postmodern use and misuse of Bakhtin, see Hirschkop and Shepherd (1989) and Lindley (1996). For a less enthusiastic assessment of Bakhtin by a literary critic, see Gardiner (1992:180), who describes Bakhtin's exaltation of carnival humor as "at times . . . embarrassingly fulsome and naive."

Chapter 2: Carnival in Spain

1. According to Mintz (1997:xxxiii n. 27) *sardina* had nothing to do with sardines, but rather, as one might expect, with pork. He writes: "The word derives from *cerdo, cerdito* (pig, pig remains) which accounts for the confusion of terms. During the days of Lent, it was forbidden to eat the meat of a pig. The *vientre* (guts) of the pig, called *cerdito,* is the only part remaining after the pig is slaughtered and prepared for eating. These remains are buried."

2. Another possible origin is *currus navalis,* stemming from an ancient Roman masque featuring boats (Caro Baroja 1965:28). However, *carne levare,* with its evocation of carnality, seems a better bet.

3. For a useful discussion on Franco's suppression of carnival and on its inconsistencies in the province of Cadiz, see Mintz (1997:xxii–xxv). For more on this, see Schrauf (1998).

4. For more on the carnival of Cadiz, which along with that of Valencia is the most famous big-city festival in Spain, see Ramos-Santana (1985), Solís Llorente (1988), and Schrauf (1998).

5. The original Spanish phrases I recorded are "lo que moleste a la gente" and "qualquiera cosa que le da la lata a la gente."

6. As Mintz (1982:83) writes: "Social controls in rural Andalusia were achieved not through government regulation and police surveillance but, rather, through social sanctions that were enforced by gossip and by various forms of criticism and public censure. At carnival questionable conduct was trumpeted to the public in song." For more on negative sanctions, scapegoating, and social control in Andalusia, see Pitt-Rivers (1971), Brandes (1980b), Gilmore (1987), and Mitchell (1988, 1991).

7. Mintz (1997:43) notes that one such "serious" carnival band in the town of Benalup (Cadiz Province) in 1966 bore the odd name Los Llorones, or the Weepers, attesting to its formal tragic intentions. In certain parts of rural Cadiz a distinction between a comic *murga* or *chirigota* band and a semi-serious *comparsa* variety seems equivalent to the *chirigota-estudiantil* division in the Seville-Cordoba area—see Schrauf (1998). This dichotomy is, however, nowhere formalized in Spain.

8. The only evidence I have ever encountered of a women's singing group in a rural carnival is in a 1982 film, *Carnival del Pueblo,* made by Jerome Mintz. In this video, people in the village of Benalup (Cadiz Province) are heard saying that some girls performed a few songs as a group in 1980 but that, as the songs were not "spicy," the performance was a major flop and was never repeated. For women's partial participation in the carnival of the capital city of Cadiz since 1984, however, see Mintz (1997:200).

9. The last two lines are obscure. I have asked numerous Spanish speakers, including experts on the period in question, and not a one has come up with an adequate explanation. The meaning has something to do with male and female and about either burning or grilling, and hills or hillocks, but the precise meaning remains vague.

10. The mask itself is called the *disfraz,* pronounced "di'fráh" in the Andalusian accent.

11. See Linger (1992:5). A Spanish ethnographer (Rodríguez Becerra 1992:13), speaking about carnival in rural Seville Province, notes that the central theme of the festival is aggression falling just short of actual physical abuse: "tossing people and animals in blankets, the ill treatment and destruction of effigies, casual attacks on passersby; hurling

water, eggs, stones, rotten fruit, flour, salt, and other disagreeable substances, overturning and throwing objects; injuring, verbally abusing, and generally annoying people of the community and neighbors."

12. Caro Baroja (1965) devotes a whole chapter to the history of the agravios, and another to the *luchas* (battles) of Spanish carnival. For more on carnival aggression, see Rodríguez Becerra (1985, 1992).

13. Part of a copla composed by José Siria, ca. 1984, Fuentes de Andalucía.

14. Writing about the small city of São Luís in northern Brazil, Daniel Linger (1992) speaks of a patterned form of street fight, the *briga,* involving two individuals with guns, knives, or fists, often ending in violent death. He notes (1992:45) that carnival provides a pretext for such fighting and this pattern is common in Brazilian cities: "And in São Luís, as everywhere in urban Brazil, Carnival is accompanied by violence." In contrast, in Andalusia, festival violence, though equally pervasive, is almost always of a symbolic nature (Gilmore 1987; Mitchell 1988).

15. For other views of Brazilian carnival, see Rector (1984), DaMatta (1991), and Parker (1991).

Chapter 3: Carnival, Ritual, and the Anthropologists

1. A good discussion of the history of anthropological thought on ritual since Durkheim appears in Kertzer (1988: chaps. 3, 4).

2. See Sider (1986) for a somewhat forced empirical example of this notion of counterhegemony. Curiously, Sider finds modern Newfoundland, Canada, a hotbed of class struggle.

3. Recently, the role of gender has become a focus in ritual and performance studies and often supplants the previous Marxist emphasis on class politics. See Morris (1995).

4. For a useful survey of recent social-science literature on ritual, performance, theater and spectacle see Beeman (1993).

Chapter 4: Woman Degraded

1. The foremost ethnographer of Andalusia, Salvador Rodríguez Becerra, characterizes the Andalusian carnivalesque in these words: "Carnival fulfills social and psychological functions that no other festival can match. It demolishes the social order, puts social classes at loggerheads, unleashes the instincts, does away with repression. All these functions are realized through the use of costuming, inversions of hierarchy, indulgence in food and drink, irony, satires, and, in sum, giving free rein to fantasy and license" (1981:81).

2. Composed in the 1950s by "Marín" (no other information available), and sung by the troupe led by Juanillo "El Gato."

3. This connection between food and sex is strongly drawn out in a description of carnival in southern Italy (Calabria): "The desire for meat to eat and sexual desire went together, and that appears to confirm why the robust man, since he had eaten meat, was considered also handsome and erotic. Abundance and quality of food, fatness, height, the capacity to work, sexual performance, all stem from the same dietary concepts of the popular classes. The model, to which Bachtin [*sic*] drew attention when examining the work of Rabelais, is that of the 'Carnival body'" (Teti 1995:15).

4. Composed by Juanillo "El Gato," ca. 1960.

5. Composed by Félix "El de La Gazpacha," ca. 1967.

6. For interesting discussions of women's "domination" of men through control over food in Mediterranean societies, see Pitkin (1985:214) and Counihan (1987:52–54).

7. The food metaphor for the sexual organs is widespread in carnival versification throughout Andalusia, as Mintz notes (1997:154 n.2). He provides a compendium of such symbolism, in which some favorite representations for the male organ are *banano* (banana), *berejena* (eggplant), *nabo* (beet root), *chorizo* (sausage); and for the female: *almeja* (clam), *conejo* (rabbit), *higo* (fig), *queso* (cheese), and *papo* (dewlap).

8. Composed by Juan "El de La Harina," in the 1930s.

9. Composed by Félix "El de La Gazpacha," date unknown.

10. The author of this ditty, dating from the 1950s, is unknown. My thanks go to Antonio Siria, José M. Lora Sánchez, and Sebastián Lora Sánchez for their help in reconstructing the verses.

11. Composed by Francisco Caro "El Quico," and sung by Los Eligidos, ca. 1969.

12. Composed by Luís "El de La Gamerita," year unknown, probably around 1970.

13. Composed by Juanillo "El Gato," ca. 1961.

14. Composed by Marcelino Lora, ca. 1970.

15. Composed by Juanillo "El Gato" and his son, Manuel Benítez, ca. 1963.

16. Composed by Marcelino Lora, ca. 1965.

17. Composed by Marcelino Lora, ca. 1970.

18. Although, as I stressed earlier, women do not compose or perform carnival coplas, this is not to say that women in Andalusia do not write poetry for both aesthetic and social purposes. Both Brandes (1985) and Mintz (1997: chap. 8) provide examples of women's poetry in Andalusia, which is, however, rarely shared with men. The themes of this poetry are often women's loneliness and the rigors of childbearing and motherhood. In southern Spain, love poetry or burlesque verse by women is a true rarity.

Chapter 5: Woman Redeemed

1. Composed by Marcelino Lora, ca. 1963.

2. Composed by Marcelino Lora, ca. 1959.

3. Composed by Juanillo "El Gato," ca. 1960.

4. Composed by Marcelino Lora, ca. 1954.

5. Composed by Luís "El de La Gamerita," year unknown.

6. Composed by Juanillo "El Gato," ca. 1954.

7. Written by Luís "El de La Gamerita," year unknown.

8. Composed by Marcelino Lora, ca. 1956.

Chapter 6: Macho Man and Matriarch

1. I am grateful to my former student Sarah C. Uhl for sharing her field data from Montemayor (Uhl 1985, 1991). Her material dates from the period of 1983–1984. I also acknowledge her contributions to the data concerning women and the household in Spain.

2. In a telling critique, Chodorow (1994:26) remarks: "It is hard to separate male wish-

fulfillment from an objective description of the female psyche when Freud tells us that 'a mother is only brought to unlimited satisfaction by her relation to her son; that is altogether the most perfect, the most free from ambivalence of all human relationships.' "

3. For opposing views on Hispanic machismo from a fashionable *viriphobic* point of view see Gutmann (1996, 1997) and Vale de Almeida (1996). By "viriphobia," I mean the hatred and fear of heterosexual masculinity.

Chapter 7: Who Wears the Pants?

1. Like many of my Spanish sources, Carlos showed a Shakespearian comic flair, here even echoing unwittingly Helena's line about her rival Hermia in *Midsummer Night's Dream* (III. ii, 338): "Though she be but little, she is fierce."

2. Lyrics by Juanito "El Chocho," ca. 1960.

3. From a carnival poem by Juanillo "El Gato," ca. 1961.

4. Composed by Francisco Caro "El Quico," date unknown.

5. "Working, working, working night and day" is from the poem by Juanillo "El Gato" and his son Manolo, ca. 1963.

6. These, and others, are reported by Jeanine Fribourg (1993:231–232).

7. Female dominance in Spain is even more pronounced in the northern region of Galicia. According to Lisón Tolosana (1979:249), "Not only do women dominate in social life and social relations [in Galicia], but also the man's submission to wife and/or mother in matters of economic, agricultural and domestic decision-making is absolute." In an amusing article, full of songs and ditties, Fribourg (1993) shows how women "get their way" throughout Spain by dominating their husbands and sons-in-law.

8. A more striking example of Iberian matriarchy is found in Jan Brøgger's book (1992) on Nazaré, a fishing village in central Portugal, which he describes as "female dominated." For more on Portuguese matrifocality, see Cole (1991).

Chapter 8: Up and Down

1. To take just one example, consider the King's misogynist soliloquy in *King Lear* (IV, vi): "Down from the waist they are centaurs / Though women all above: / But to the girdle do the gods inherit, / Beneath is all the fiend's; there's hell, there's darkness, / There is the sulphurous pit."

"Belowness" symbolized not only baseness and primitivity in Shakespeare's time but also, in line with contemporary theological homologies, chaos, corruption (the pit), and the Devil.

2. Composed by Juanillo "El Gato," ca. 1968. I am told that "gachón" in this context means "handsome young man or boy" — in other words a gigolo, or male sexual object.

3. Composed by Juanillo "El Gato," ca. 1965.

Chapter 9: Here and There

1. For more on the subject of space, ground rules, and society — the third dimension of social structure — see the following works: Bourdieu (1971, 1977); Buttimer and Seamon (1980); Lawrence (1996); and Low (1996a). Lawrence and Low (1990) provide a fine

summary of the recent literature. For works specifically on gender and space, see Ardener (1981); Callaway (1981); Hirschon (1981a, 1981b); Hirschon and Gold (1982); and Spain (1992). For a recent study on a Hispanic society, see Sabaté et al. (1995).

2. Many anthropologists have examined sexual symbolism in the Mediterranean region in light of various dualisms: left versus right, good versus bad, God versus devil (Campbell 1964); sheep versus goat (Blok 1981); "seed versus soil" (Delaney 1991); "honor versus shame" (Pitt-Rivers 1977); "above versus below" (Gilmore 1977); "activity versus passivity" (Brandes 1980b; Herzfeld 1985b), and so on.

3. Renée Hirschon (1981a:72) refers to this dichotomy as interiority versus exteriority, Herzfeld (1986) as within and without. Many other dualistic rhetorical devices are employed to capture Mediterranean sexual apartheid, almost one per ethnographer.

4. The sexual and anatomical symbolism here is obvious. For an excellent account of the erotic symbolism of the olive harvest, see Brandes (1980). In a later work, Brandes (1992) also provides a superb description of spatial hierarchization in Spanish culture, especially in children's games and adult folklore.

5. There are of course places in the south European countries where this sexual division of space does not appear in rural society, the most striking exceptions being north-central coastal Portugal (Brøgger 1992; Cole 1991) and Spanish Galicia (Lisón Tolosana 1979). But this corner of Iberia is outside the "Mediterranean" ecozone.

6. The title of a recent book edited by Brackette Williams (1996).

7. Compare the symbolic sanctions for sexual trespass in Spain with the violent physical punishments meted out for similar transgressions in New Guinea and South America, where men's huts and sacred cults are off limits to women. In *Tristes Tropiques*, Lévi-Strauss (1961:213–214) tells us that Bororo women may be raped for venturing too near the men's house and clubbed to death for so much as looking at the men's sacred bull-roarer.

8. Composed by Manolo Benítez and Los Andaluces, ca. 1981.

9. *Invita,* normally a verb, is used here as a noun, as in English slang ("I received an invite"). The semantically correct *invitación* (invitation) sounds too formal and is not used.

Chapter 10: *The Mayete as Carnival Caricature*

1. During the Franco period, when carnival was technically banned (1937–1967), the poets had to watch what they said in public or face arrest. Before the Franco years, the maestros had had to submit their lyrics to the local authorities for censorship. Despite the bans and the repression, many poets still voiced subversive opinions, although direct attacks on the local authorities and the government were rare. For a fuller discussion of the censorship, see Mintz (1997:27–30).

2. I have written about this town before (Gilmore 1980, 1987). Here I end the common ethnographic practice of using a pseudonym ("Fuenmayor" previously) to disguise the place. With nothing more to fear from the Franco police, my informants have so requested. In keeping with people's wishes, though, I continue to use made-up names for individuals.

3. Roux (1991:336–337) speaks of the persistence of the inefficient minifundio as late as the 1980s in Andalusia. He estimates that about 90 percent of the total number of

agrarian enterprises fell into this category, and more than 50 percent of the total cultivated land.

4. For insightful remarks on this issue, see Rodríguez Becerra (1985) and Moreno
Navarro (1989). See Luque Baena (1981) for a review of literature.

5. Some commentators suggested that "mayete" may derive from "mayo," the month
of May, because the farmers began their wheat harvests at that time ("los hombres de
mayo" are "mayetes"). This seems far-fetched. Others were as puzzled as I was about the
derivation of this curious term. *Labrador,* meaning sizable farmer, was reserved for the
big latifundists, who were also called *capitalistas.* For their part, the mayetes sometimes
call the landless workers *talegueros,* after the *talega,* or small bag, in which they carry
their midday meal to the fields. It has a pejorative connotation of a person of lowly status,
a drudge, a "nobody" (see Gilmore 1980). The workers also distinguish between categories of mayetes, based on the size of their holdings, so there are "mayetes chicos" (little
mayetes); "mayetes medianos" (medium-sized mayetes); and "mayetes-mayetes," also
called "mayetes fuertes" (big, or powerful, mayetes).

6. Composed by Francisco Caro "El Quico."

7. Composed by Juanillo "El Gato."

8. Composed by Juanillo "El Gato."

9. Composed by Marcelino Lora.

10. Composed by Marcelino Lora.

11. Composed by Féliz "El de La Gazpacha."

12. Composed by Juan "El de La Harina" and El Maestro "Sajones."

13. Composed by Juanillo "El Gato."

Chapter 11: Copla Politics

1. One example of this synthetic approach outside of Iberia is the work on the Turkish
arabesk and *mevlûd* song genres by Nancy and Richard Tapper (1987) and Martin Stokes
(1992). They show that these lyrics, which are composed by workers and peasants sometimes as protest and sometimes not, transcend Turkish class and political divisions and
cannot be "confined to any one level of discourse" (Stokes 1992:13).

2. In a recent study of class and culture in Aracena (Huelva Province), Richard
Maddox (1993:143) speaks of the "differences of opinion" and "tensions" that have
characterized working-class political culture in Andalusia in the twentieth century, but he
does not elaborate. For more on working-class religiosity and traditionalism in Spain, see
Mitchell (1990) and Christian (1996).

3. This song probably originated in the town of Marchena, which claims the credit for
its composition. It was sung, with variations, throughout the province during the Republic. The politicians mentioned are as follows: the conservative prime minister Antonio
Maura y Montener (1853–1925), whose regime coincided with the deadly anticlerical
riots of Tragic Week in Barcelona (1909); Segismundo Moret (1838–1913), whose name
is here apparently deformed, and who ineffectually succeeded Maura; José Cañalejas
(1854–1912), a liberal who ruled from 1910 to 1912; and Juan de la Cierva y Peñafiel
(1864–1938), a conservative minister in the Maura administration who orchestrated the
savage police repressions after Tragic Week.

4. Lyrics by Francisco Caro, "El Quico," ca. late 1950s.

5. The author of these lyrics is unknown but the murga band was led by Pepe Mangara. The copla seems to depict the disaster at Annual in 1921, when the Spanish legion was destroyed by Moroccan rebels. For more on this sorry episode in Spanish colonial history, see Woolman (1968).

6. This song probably dates from 1926 or 1927. The author is Antonio Calleja.

7. Mintz (1997, chap. 3) provides numerous examples of coplas commenting on the police killings of anarchists in 1933 during a famous uprising in the town of Casas Viejas. These songs joined the chorus of public outcry over the massacre, and the poet's sentiments came to the attention of a wide audience throughout Spain.

8. Author unknown. The song dates from the early 1930s.

9. Written by Los Andaluces under the direction of Antonio Benítez, 1981. Antonio Galán was a congressman from Andalusia and a local hero.

10. Probably from 1932 or 1933. Composed by Juan "El de La Harina." I could locate no further information on this poet, except that he was a worker who wrote comic songs as well as serious political commentary.

11. The author of this ditty is unknown. It derives either from Fuentes or La Campana, and is still sung in both pueblos. This song was previously published in Gilmore (1987:97).

12. As Mintz (1997:252) notes in his book on the Cadiz carnival, the underlying motive in carnival derision and criticism was not exclusively opposition to existing hierarchies but "to put things right and to hasten a return to traditional, righteous ways." This backward-looking, traditionalist thread in carnival has been ignored by Marxist and postmodern theorists because of their a priori suppositions.

13. Written by Luís "El de La Gamerita," and sung by him along with (all nicknames) "Patricio," "El Albiro," "Vinagre," and "El Lili del Albiro," among others.

14. Author unknown.

15. One verse Mintz (1997:9) cites from a longer poem:

Fue madre y fue protectora	She was mother and protector
De todo el pueblo en general	Of the whole town in general
Porque toda su vida fue	Because all her life consisted
Sacrificio y caridad.	Of sacrifice and charity.

The woman in question, Ana Barca, a member of the principal landowning family in the town of Benalup, was said to always have a pot of food cooking on her stove for the poor.

16. Composed by Marcelino Lora, ca. 1950. Lines 16 through 20, beginning with "El periodista" and ending with "le dió vida," are reported as printed. These lines are as incomprehensible to me as they have been to all of my informants and to potential translators, because the meaning of the allusion to "the journalist as miracle" has been lost. It may be to some forgotten incident reported in the press at the time. I have rendered the English according to what my local sources *believe* they mean.

17. Composed by Marcelino Lora, ca. 1956, and sung by the murga group Alegría Fontaniega.

Chapter 12: Bars, Bards, and Bawds

1. Naturally, I do not mean to imply that women and girls have no parallel forms of material exchange. I limit my discussion here to male transactions, however, because they

are public, and because being a man myself, I was able to compile useful data from observation and participation only on men's activities. Women in Andalusia, especially neighbors, engage in networks of commodity exchange involving household items, food-stuffs, small domestic appliances, babysitting services, and so on (Uhl 1985, 1991). This subject is worthy of separate study. Despite what overly sanguine ethnographers have said about the narrowing "gender gap" in Hispanic societies (J. Gregory 1984), it is still problematic for male fieldworkers to enter the female world, especially in rural Andalusia.

2. Written by Francisco Caro "El Quico," and sung by Los Elegidos.

3. Composed by Juanillo "El Gato."

4. Composed by one José "Jincapiedra" (no other information available).

5. A charming account of drink and tobacco exchange, and of recent changes in these customs, is found in the second edition of Aguilera's delightful monograph on Almonaster, Huelva Province (Aguilera 1990). For comprehensive reviews of the ethnographic literature on Andalusia, see Luque Baena (1981) and Rodríguez Becerra (1984). For an eccentric look at "what is wrong" with all this literature from an extreme leftist viewpoint, see Moreno Navarro (1984). The best works in English on father-son relations are Michael Murphy's articles on Seville city (1983a, 1983b).

Chapter 13: Carnival Evolving

1. For comparative purposes, see Mintz's (1997:238–239) brief discussion of recent changes in the carnival of Trebujena, a similar farming pueblo near the city of Cadiz. In Trebujena a similar emphasis has been placed on song and costume contests and on children's participation. But Mintz does not mention the shift I found in Seville Province from a daytime to a nocturnal schedule.

2. As I have noted before (Gilmore 1987:99–100), I have found no solid explanation for why the local authorities in Fuentes, to a greater extent than in most other pueblos, ignored the festival and tacitly permitted people to take to the streets. One interpretation, which people repeated to me in the town but for which I have no real confirmation, was the following. The rather autocratic mayor during this period was an outsider who was apparently at odds with the local elite and who enjoyed disconcerting his local rivals by permitting a celebration that he knew annoyed them.

3. A fascinating discussion of the connection between food and carnival in Calabria, Italy, can be found in an article by Vito Teti (1995:13–18). Teti writes: "It has not been sufficiently understood, in my opinion, that Carnival celebrations, at least in some areas of Calabria, were above all food celebrations. Food, drinking and eating appear as central to the core of complex rituals which served a variety of functions" (16). The same might be said of the Spanish festivities.

4. Composed by "Micaelo." No other information available.

5. Composed by Manolo Benítez and Los Andaluces.

6. Composed by Los Raspandurri.

7. Composed by Los Raspandurri.

8. Again, there is evidence of growing female participation in carnival in the major Andalusian cities, especially Cadiz (Mintz 1997).

9. I want to thank Maria del Carmen Medina, who administered the questionnaires for

me during 1995–1996. The test sample was as follows: ages sixty-five and up: twelve women, twelve men; ages thirty-one to sixty-four: fourteen women, fourteen men; ages sixteen to thirty: fourteen women, fourteen men; ages ten to sixteen: ten girls, ten boys. Fifty-eight questionnaires were administered in Fuentes, the rest in the other towns. The respondents were picked at random.

Chapter 14: Conclusions

1. Always attuned to the variety represented in Andalusian carnival lyricism, Mintz (1997:254) makes a similar point in his book about the Cadiz carnival: "Carnival composers reveal both comic and tragic sides of life, setting side by side the serious and the bizarre, and mirroring the realities of daily experience. Art as well as coarseness flourish."

2. Another way to conceptualize carnival behavior is through the use of game theory, as Daniel Linger (1992:228–229) does with great subtlety in his study of Brazilian festivals.

3. See also Linger's interesting discussion of the relevance of Freud's views on "repetition compulsion" and aggressive instinct for an understanding of Brazilian carnival behavior, especially violence and persecution (1992:244–246).

4. This point has been made previously in sociological studies of counter-cultures in American society (Yinger 1982).

5. As Mintz (1977:199–200) notes for carnival in the city of Cadiz: "The participation of men and women in carnival activities mirrors in great measure their place in the social life." Most women, even in that relatively cosmopolitan port city, accept this exclusion from the active role. But Mintz also remarks that in a few cases since 1984, some younger urban women have participated in song performances along with their husbands and boyfriends. He quotes one informant about women's breaking barriers in Cadiz: "Some *chirigotas* are exclusively female and have links with the feminist movement. One of these came out once as widows [*sic*]; another time they ridiculed women who participated in beauty contests." Nothing like this can be reported yet for the small pueblos in the backwater between Seville and Cordoba.

Bibliography

Abrahams, Roger D., and Richard Bauman. 1978. Ranges of festival behavior. In *The reversible world: Symbolic inversion in art and society,* Barbara A. Babcock, ed., pp. 193–208. Ithaca, N.Y.: Cornell University Press.

Abu-Lughod, Lila. 1985. Honor and the sentiments of loss in a Bedouin society. *American Ethnologist* 12:245–261.

——. 1986. *Veiled sentiments: Honor and poetry in a Bedouin society.* Berkeley: University of California Press.

——. 1990. The romance of resistance: Tracing transformation of power through Bedouin women. *American Ethnologist* 17:41–55.

——. 1993. *Writing women's worlds: Bedouin stories.* Berkeley: University of California Press.

Aceves, Joseph, et al., eds. 1976. *Economic transformation and steady-state values.* New York: Queens College Press.

Aguilera, Francisco E. 1990. *Santa Eulalia's people.* 2d ed. Prospect Heights, Ill.: Waveland Press.

Amezcua, Manuel. 1995. Moros y cristianos en Alcalá la Real: La "Fiesta del Arrabal," o la búsqueda de la identidad perdida. *Demófilo* 14:135–150.

Appadurai, Arjun. 1986. Introduction: Commodities and the politics of value. In *The social life of things,* Arjun Appadurai, ed., pp. 3–63. Cambridge: Cambridge University Press.

Ardener, Edwin. 1975. Belief and the problem of women. In *Perceiving women,* Shirley Ardener, ed., pp. 1–27. London: Malaby Press.

Ardener, Shirley. 1981. Ground rules and social maps for women: An introduction. In *Women and space: Ground rules and social maps,* Shirley Ardener, ed., pp. 11–34. New York: St. Martin's.

Arlow, Jacob, and Charles Brenner. 1963. *Psychoanalytic concepts and the structural theory.* New York: International Universities Press.

Artola, Miguel, Antonio-M. Bernal, and José Contreras. 1979. *Los Latifundios, Siglos XVII–XX.* Madrid: Ministerio de Agricultura.

Babcock, Barbara A. 1978. Introduction. In *The reversible world: Symbolic inversion in art and society,* Barbara A. Babcock, ed., pp. 13–38. Ithaca, N.Y.: Cornell University Press.

Bakhtin, Mikhail. 1984. *Rabelais and his world,* Hélène Iswolsky, trans. Bloomington: Indiana University Press.

Barthes, Roland. 1976. *The pleasure of the text,* Richard Miller, trans. London: Cape.

Bastien, Joseph. 1985. Qollahuaya-Andean body concepts: A topographical-hydraulic model of physiology. *American Anthropologist* 87:595–611.

Bauman, Richard. 1975. Verbal art as performance. *American Anthropologist* 77:290–311.

———. 1977. *Verbal art as performance.* Prospect Heights, Ill.: Waveland Press.

———. 1986. *Story, performance, and event.* Cambridge: Cambridge University Press.

Bauman, Richard, and Charles L. Briggs. 1990. Poetics and performance as critical perspectives on language and social life. *Annual Review of Anthropology* 19:59–88.

Beeman, William O. 1993. The anthropology of theater and spectacle. *Annual Review of Anthropology* 22:369–393.

Behar, Ruth. 1990. The struggle for the Church: Popular anticlericalism and religiosity in post-Franco Spain. In *Religious orthodoxy and popular faith in European society,* Ellen Badone, ed., pp. 76–112. Princeton, N.J.: Princeton University Press.

Bem, Sandra L. 1983. Gender schema theory and its implications for child development. *Signs* 8:598–616.

Bennassar, Bartolomé. 1979. *The Spanish character: Attitudes and mentalities from the sixteenth to the nineteenth century,* Benjamin Keen, trans. Berkeley: University of California Press.

Bercé, Yves-Marie. 1976. *Fête et révolution: Des mentalités populaires du XVIe au XVIIIe siècles.* Paris: Hachette.

Bernal, Antonio-Miguel. 1974. *La propiedad de la tierra y las luchas agrarias Andaluzas.* Esplugues de Llobregat: Ariel.

Biller, Henry B. 1971. *Father, child and sex role.* Lexington, Mass.: D. C. Heath.

Black-Michaud, Jacob. 1975. *Cohesive force: Feud in the Mediterranean and the Middle East.* New York: St. Martin's.

Blank, Gertrude, and Robin Blank. 1979. *Ego psychology,* vol. 2, *Psychoanalytic developmental psychology.* New York: Columbia University Press.

Bloch, Jean-R. 1920. *Carnaval est mort: Premiers essais pour mieux comprendre mon temps.* Paris: Hachette.

Bloch, Maurice. 1985. *Power and knowledge: Anthropological and sociological approaches.* Edinburgh: Scottish Academic Press.

Blok, Anton. 1981. Rams and billy-goats: A key to the Mediterranean code of honour. *Man* 16:427–440.

Bourdieu, Pierre. 1971. The Berber house, or the world reversed. In *Echanges et communications*, pp. 151–161, 165–169. The Hague: Mouton.

———. 1977. *Outline of a theory of practice*, R. Nice, trans. Cambridge: Cambridge University Press.

———. 1982. The economics of linguistic exchanges. *Social Science Information* 16: 645–668.

Brain, Robert. 1979. *The decorated body.* New York: Harper and Row.

Brandes, Stanley. 1976. The priest as agent of secularization in rural Spain. In *Economic transformation and steady-state values,* Joseph Aceves et al., eds., pp. 22–29. New York: Queens College Press.

———. 1977. Peaceful protest: Spanish political humor in a time of crisis. *Western Folklore* 36:331–346.

———. 1979. Drinking patterns and alcohol control in a Castilian mountain village. *Anthropology* 3:1–15.

———. 1980a. Giants and big-heads: An Andalusian metaphor. In *Symbol as sense,* Mary L. Foster and Stanley H. Brandes, eds., pp. 77–92. New York: Academic Press.

———. 1980b. *Metaphors of masculinity.* Philadelphia: University of Pennsylvania Press.

———. 1981. Like wounded stags: Male sexual identity in an Andalusian town. In *Sexual meanings,* Sherry B. Ortner and Harriet Whitehead, eds., pp. 216–239.

———. 1985. Women of southern Spain: Aspirations, fantasies, realities. *Anthropology* 9:111–128.

———. 1988. *Power and persuasion.* Philadelphia: University of Pennsylvania Press.

———. 1992. Spatial symbolism in southern Spain. In *The psychoanalytic study of society,* vol. 18., L. Bryce Boyer, Ruth M. Boyer, and Stephen M. Sonneberg, eds., pp. 119–135. Hillsdale, N.J.: Analytic Press.

Brenan, Gerald. 1971. *The Spanish labyrinth.* New York: Cambridge University Press.

Bricker, Victoria Reifler. 1973. *Ritual humor in highland Chiapas.* Austin: University of Texas Press.

Briggs, Charles L. 1992. "Since I am a woman I will chastise my relatives": Gender, reported speech, and the (re)production of social relations in Warao ritual wailing. *American Ethnologist* 19:337–361.

———. 1993. Personal sentiments and polyphonic voices in Warao women's ritual wailing: Music and poetics in a critical and collective discourse. *American Anthropologist* 95:929–957.

Bristol, Michael D. 1984. *Carnival and theater: Plebeian culture and the structure of authority in Renaissance England.* New York: Methuen.

Brøgger, Jan. 1992. *Nazaré: Women and men in a prebureaucratic Portuguese fishing village.* New York: Harcourt Brace Jovanovich.

Bronfenbrenner, Urie. 1960. Freudian theories of identification and their derivatives. *Child Development* 31:15–40.

Brown, Donald E. 1988. *Hierarchy, history, and human nature: The social origins of historical consciousness.* Tucson: University of Arizona Press.

Brown, Michael. 1996. On resisting resistance. *American Anthropologist* 98:729–735.

Burke, Kenneth. 1969. *A rhetoric of motives.* Berkeley: University of California Press.

Buttimer, A., and S. Seamon, eds. 1980. *The human experience of space and place.* London: Croom Helm.

Calero, Antonio M. 1976. *Movimientos sociales en Andalucía (1820–1936)*. Madrid: Siglo XXI de España.

Callaway, Helen. 1981. Spatial domains and women's mobility in Yorubaland, Nigeria. In *Women and space: Ground rules and social maps,* Shirley Ardener, ed., pp. 168–186. New York: St. Martin's.

Campbell, John. 1964. *Honour, family, and patronage.* Oxford: Clarendon Press.

Caraveli, Anna. 1986. The bitter wounding: The lament as social protest in rural Greece. In *Gender and power in rural Greece,* Jill Dubisch, ed., pp. 169–194. Princeton, N.J.: Princeton University Press.

Caro Baroja, Julio. 1965. *El carnaval: Análisis histórico-cultural.* Madrid: Taurus.

Carr, Raymond, and Juan P. Fusi. 1981. *Spain: From dictatorship to democracy.* London: Allen and Unwin.

Carrasco, Pedro. 1963. The locality referent in residence terms. *American Anthropologist* 65:133–134.

Carroll, Michael. 1986. *The cult of the Virgin Mary.* Princeton, N.J.: Princeton University Press.

Casselberry, Samuel, and Nancy Valavanes. 1976. Matrifocal Greek peasants and reconsideration of residence terminology. *American Ethnologist* 3:215–226.

Castle, Terry. 1984. The carnivalization of eighteenth-century English narrative. *PMLA* 99:903–916.

Checa, Francisco. 1992. El humor andaluz: Identidad de un pueblo? *El folk-lore andaluz* (Seville) 8:55–84.

Chodorow, Nancy. 1974. Family structure and feminine personality. In *Women, culture, and society,* Michelle Rosaldo and Louise Lamphere, eds., pp. 43–66. Stanford, Calif.: Stanford University Press.

———. 1978. *The reproduction of mothering: Psychoanalysis and the sociology of gender.* Berkeley: University of California Press.

———. 1994. *Femininities, masculinities, and sexualities.* Lexington: University Press of Kentucky.

Christian, William A. 1996. *Visionaries: The Spanish Republic and the reign of Christ.* Berkeley: University of California Press.

Cohen, Abner. 1993. *Masquerade politics.* Berkeley: University of California Press.

Cohen, Anthony P. 1994. Culture, identity and the concept of boundary. *Revista de Antropología Social* 3:49–61.

Cohen, Percy. 1980. Psychoanalysis and cultural symbolization. In *Symbol as sense: New approaches to the analysis of meaning,* Mary LeCron Foster and Stanley H. Brandes, eds., pp. 45–68. New York: Academic Press.

Cole, Sally. 1991. *Women of the Praia: Work and lives in a Portuguese coastal community.* Princeton, N.J.: Princeton University Press.

Collier, George. 1987. *Socialists of rural Andalusia: Unacknowledged revolutionaries of the Second Republic.* Stanford, Calif.: Stanford University Press.

Corbin, John, and M. Corbin. 1984. *Compromising relations: Kith, kin and class in Andalusia.* Aldershot, England: Gower.

———. 1987. *Urbane thought: Culture and class in an Andalusian city.* Aldershot, England: Gower.

Cornelisen, Anne. 1976. *Women of the shadows*. Boston: Little, Brown.

Coser, Lewis. 1956. *The functions of social conflict*. New York: Free Press.

Counihan, Carole. 1987. Transvestism and gender in a Sardinian carnival. *Anthropology* 9:11–24.

Cox, Harvey. 1969. *The feast of fools*. Cambridge, Mass.: Harvard University Press.

DaMatta, Roberto. 1991. *Carnivals, rogues, and heroes: An interpretation of the Brazilian dilemma*, John Drury, trans. Notre Dame, Ind.: University of Notre Dame Press.

D'Andrade, Roy G. 1992. Cognitive anthropology. In *New directions in psychological anthropology*, Theodore Schwartz, Geoffrey M. White, and Catherine A. Lutz, eds., pp. 47–59. Cambridge: Cambridge University Press.

Davis, John. 1973. *Land and family in Pisticci*. London: Athlone Press.

———. 1977. *People of the Mediterranean*. London: Routledge and Kegan Paul.

Davis, Natalie Zemon. 1973. The rites of violence: Religious riot in sixteenth-century France. *Past and Present* 59:51–91.

———. 1975. *Society and culture in early modern France: Eight essays*. Stanford, Calif.: Stanford University Press.

———. 1978. Women on top: Symbolic sexual inversion and political disorder in early modern Europe. In *The reversible world: Symbolic inversion in art and society*, Barbara A. Babcock, ed., pp. 147–190. Ithaca, N.Y.: Cornell University Press.

Delaney, Carol. 1991. *The seed and the soil: Gender and cosmology in Turkish village society*. Berkeley: University of California Press.

Deutsch, Helene. 1945. *The psychology of women*. 2 vols. New York: Grune and Stratton.

Díaz del Moral, Juan. 1969. *Historia de las agitaciones campesinas andaluzas— Córdoba*. Madrid: Alianza.

Dougherty, Janet W. 1978. Salience and relativity in classification. *American Ethnologist* 5:66–80.

Douglas, Mary. 1966. *Purity and danger*. London: Routledge and Kegan Paul.

Douglass, Carrie B. 1984. Toro muerto, vaca es: An interpretation of the Spanish bullfight. *American Ethnologist* 11:242–258.

Douglass, William A. 1969. *Death in Murélaga: Funerary rituals in a Spanish Basque village*. Seattle: University of Washington Press.

Driessen, Henk. 1982. Anthropologists in Andalusia: The use of comparison and history. *Man* 16:451–462.

———. 1983. Male sociability and rituals of masculinity in rural Andalusia. *Anthropological Quarterly* 56:125–133.

Dubisch, Jill. 1986. Introduction. In *Gender and power in rural Greece*, Jill Dubisch, ed., pp. 3–41. Princeton, N.J.: Princeton University Press.

———. 1991. Gender, kinship and religion: Reconstructing the anthropology of Greece. In *Contested identities: Gender and kinship in modern Greece*, Peter Loizos and Evthymios Papataxiarchis, eds., pp. 29–46. Princeton, N.J.: Princeton University Press.

———. 1993. "Foreign chickens" and outsiders: Gender and community in Greece. *American Ethnologist* 20:272–287.

Dumont, Louis. 1972. *Homo hierarchicus: The caste system and its implications*, Mark Sainsbury et al., trans. Chicago: University of Chicago Press.

———. 1979. The anthropological community and ideology. *Social Science and Information* 18:785–817.

Dundes, Alan. 1976. Projection in folklore: A plea for psychoanalytic semiotics. *Modern Language Notes* 91:1530–1533.

Dundes, Alan, Jerry Leach, and Bora Özkök. 1972. The strategy of Turkish duelling rhymes. In *Directions in sociolinguistics,* John J. Gumperz and Dell Hymes, eds., pp. 130–160. New York: Holt, Rinehart, Winston.

Durkheim, Emile. 1915. *The elementary forms of the religious life,* Joseph W. Swain, trans. London: Allen and Unwin.

Duvignaud, Jean. 1977. *Change at Shebika: Report from a North African village,* Frances Frenaye, trans. New York: Pantheon Press.

Eagleton, Terry. 1989. Bakhtin, Schopenhauer, Kundera. In *Bakhtin and cultural theory,* Ken Hirschkop and David Shepherd, eds., pp. 178–188. Manchester, England: Manchester University Press.

Eco, Umberto. 1984. Frames of comic freedom. In *Carnival!* Thomas Sebeok, ed., pp. 1–10. New York: Mouton.

Erikson, Erik H. 1950. *Childhood and society.* New York: Norton.

———. 1972. Play and actuality. In *Play and development,* Maria W. Piers, ed., pp. 127–167. New York: Norton.

Fabian, Johannes. 1983. *Time and the other: How anthropology makes its object.* New York: Columbia University Press.

Faubion, James D. 1993. History in anthropology. *Annual Review of Anthropology* 22:35–54.

Faure, Alain. 1978. *Paris Carême-prenant: Du carnaval à Paris au XIXe siècle.* Paris: Hachette.

Feld, Steven. 1990. *Sound and sentiment: Birds, weeping, poetics, and song in Kaluli expression.* Philadelphia: University of Pennsylvania Press.

Fernandez, James W. 1972. Persuasions and performances: Of the beast in everybody . . . and the metaphor in everyman. *Daedalus* 101:39–60.

———. 1977. *Fang architectonics.* Philadelphia: ISHI Press.

———. 1986. *Persuasions and performances: The play of tropes in culture.* Bloomington: Indiana University Press.

Filippucci, Paolo. 1992. Tradition in action: The carnevale of Bassano, 1824–1989. *Mediterranean Studies* 2:54–66.

Firth, Raymond. 1951. *Elements of social organization.* London: Watts.

Fortes, Meyer, and E. Evans-Pritchard, 1940. *African political systems.* London: Oxford University Press.

Foster, George M. 1961. The dyadic contract: A model for the social structure of a Mexican peasant village. *American Anthropologist* 63:1173–1192.

———. 1979. *Tzintzuntzan: Mexican peasants in a changing world.* New York: Elsevier.

Foucault, Michel. 1980. *Power/knowledge,* Colin Gordon, trans. New York: Pantheon Books.

Freud, Sigmund. [1905] 1950. *Jokes and their relation to the unconscious,* James Strachey, trans. New York: Norton.

———. [1914] 1975. *On narcissism,* James Strachey, ed. and trans., vol. 14, pp. 67–102. Hogarth Press.

———. [1917] 1975. *Mourning and melancholia*, James Strachey, ed. and trans., vol. 14, pp. 237–269. London: Hogarth.

———. [1925] 1975. *Some psychical consequences of the anatomical distinction between the sexes*, James Strachey, ed. and trans., vol. 19, pp. 243–259. London: Hogarth Press.

———. 1931. *Civilization and its discontents*, James Strachey, trans. New York: Norton.

———. 1933. *New introductory lectures*, James Strachey, trans. New York: Norton.

———. [1922] 1948. *Group psychology and the analysis of the ego*, James Strachey, trans. London: Hogarth Press.

———. 1953. Negation. In *Collected Papers*, James Strachey, ed., J. Rivière, trans., vol. 5, pp. 181–185. London: Hogarth Press.

———. [1925] 1959. *Inhibitions, symptoms, and anxiety*. New York: Norton.

Fribourg, Jeanine. 1993. L'homme espagnol, ce "macho." *Cahiers de Littérature Orale* 34:223–238.

Friedl, Ernestine. 1961. *Vasilika*. New York: Holt, Rinehart, Winston.

Gaignebet, Charles. 1974. *Le carnaval: Essais de mythologie populaire*. Paris: Payot.

Galt, Anthony H. 1973. Carnival on the island of Pantilleria. *Ethnology* 12:325–339.

García de Diego, Pilar. 1960. Censura popular. *Revista de Dialectología y Tradiciones Populares* 16:295–331.

Gardiner, Michael. 1992. *The dialogics of critique: M. M. Bakhtin and the theory of ideology*. London: Routledge.

Gatewood, John. 1984. Familiarity, vocabulary size, and recognition ability in four semantic domains. *American Ethnologist* 11:507–527.

Gaylin, Willard. 1992. *The male ego*. New York: Viking.

Geertz, Clifford. 1973. *The interpretation of culture*. New York: Basic Books.

———. 1980. *Negara: The theater state in nineteenth-century Bali*. Princeton, N.J.: Princeton University Press.

———. 1983. *Local knowledge*. New York: Basic Books.

Gell, A. 1986. Newcomers to the world of goods: Consumption among the Muria Gonds. In *The social life of things*, Arjun Appadurai, ed., pp. 110–138. Cambridge: Cambridge University Press.

Gilmore, David D. 1975. Carnival in Fuenmayor. *Journal of Anthropological Research* 31:331–349.

———. 1977. The social organization of space: Class, cognition, and residence in a Spanish town. *American Ethnologist* 4:437–451.

———. 1980. *The people of the plain: Class and community in lower Andalusia*. New York: Columbia University Press.

———. 1983. Sexual ideology in Andalusian oral literature. *Ethnology* 22:241–252.

———. 1987. *Aggression and community: Paradoxes of Andalusian culture*. New Haven, Conn.: Yale University Press.

———. 1988. Politics and ritual: Fifty years of Andalusian carnival. *Iberian Studies* 17:34–49.

———. 1990a. *Manhood in the making: Cultural concepts of masculinity*. New Haven, Conn.: Yale University Press.

———. 1990b. Men and women in southern Spain: "Domestic power" revisited. *American Anthropologist* 92:953–970.

———. 1993. The democratization of ritual: Andalusian carnival after Franco. *Anthropological Quarterly* 66:37–47.

Gilmore, David, and Margaret Gilmore. 1979. Machismo: A psychodynamic approach (Spain). *Journal of Psychoanalytic Anthropology* 2:281–300.

Gilmour, David. 1986. *Transformation of Spain: From Franco's dictatorship to the constitutional monarchy.* London: Quartet Books.

Ginzburg, Carlo. 1976. High and low: The theme of forbidden knowledge in the sixteenth and seventeenth centuries. *Past/Present* 73:28–41.

Giovannini, Maureen J. 1981. Woman: A dominant symbol within the cultural system of a Sicilian town. *Man* 16:408–426.

Gluckman, Max. 1963. Rituals of rebellion in south-east Africa. In *Order and rebellion in tribal Africa: Collected essays,* pp. 110–136. New York: Macmillan.

Gonzalez, Nancie Lurie. 1970. Social functions of carnival in a Dominican city. *Southwestern Journal of Anthropology* 26:328–342.

González Troyano, Alberto, et al. 1983. *Carnaval en Cádiz.* Cádiz: Ayuntamiento de Cádiz.

Gramsci, Antonio. [1929–1935] 1971. *Selections from the prison notebooks.* New York: International Publishers.

Greenson, Ralph. 1968. Dis-identifying from the mother: Its special importance for the boy. *International Journal of Psycho-Analysis* 49:370–375.

Gregor, Thomas. 1985. *Anxious pleasures: The sexual lives of an Amazonian people.* Chicago: University of Chicago Press.

Gregory, C. A. 1982. *Gifts and commodities.* London: Academic Press.

Gregory, James R. 1984. The myth of the male ethnographer and the woman's world. *American Anthropologist* 86:316–327.

Grossman, William I. 1992. Hierarchies, boundaries, and representations in a Freudian model of mental organization. *Journal of the American Psychoanalytical Association* 40:27–62.

Gutmann, Matthew. 1996. *The meanings of macho: Being a man in Mexico City.* Berkeley: University of California Press.

———. 1997. Trafficking in men: The anthropology of masculinity. *Annual Review of Anthropology* 26:385–409.

Hallowell, A. Irving. 1955. *Culture and experience.* Philadelphia: University of Pennsylvania Press.

Hanks, William F. 1987. Discourse genres in a theory of practice. *American Ethnologist* 14:668–692.

———. 1989. Text and textuality. *Annual Review of Anthropology* 18:95–127.

Hansen, Edward C. 1976. Drinking to prosperity: The role of bar culture and coalition formation in the modernization of the Alto Panedés. In *Economic transformation and steady-state values,* Joseph Aceves et al., eds., pp. 43–51. New York: Queens College Press.

Harding, Susan. 1975. Women and words in a Spanish village. In *Toward an anthropology of women,* Reyna R. Reiter, ed., pp. 283–308. New York: Monthly Review Press.

Heath, Deborah. 1994. The politics of appropriateness and appropriation: Recontextualizing women's dance in urban Senegal. *American Ethnologist* 21:88–103.

Herdt, Gilbert H., ed. 1982. *Rituals of manhood.* Berkeley: University of California Press.

————. 1987. *Guardians of the flutes: Idioms of masculinity.* Columbia University Press.

Herzfeld, Michael. 1980. Honour and shame: Some problems in the comparative analysis of moral systems. *Man* 15:339–351.

————. 1984. The horns of the Mediterraneanist dilemma. *American Ethnologist* 11: 439–454.

————. 1985a. Gender pragmatics: Agency, speech, and bride-theft in a Cretan mountain village. *Anthropology* 9:25–44.

————. 1985b. *The poetics of manhood: Contest and identity in a Cretan mountain village.* Princeton, N.J.: Princeton University Press.

————. 1986. Within and without: "The category of female" in the ethnography of modern Greece. In *Gender and power in rural Greece,* Jill Dubisch, ed., pp. 215–233. Princeton, N.J.: Princeton University Press.

————. 1991. Silence, submission, and subversion: Toward a poetics of womanhood. In *Contested Identities,* Peter Loizos and Evthymios Papataxiarchis, eds., pp. 79–97. Princeton, N.J.: Princeton University Press.

————. 1993. In defiance of destiny: The management of time and gender at a Cretan funeral. *American Ethnologist* 20:241–255.

Hillier, Bill, and Julienne Hanson. 1984. *The social logic of space.* New York: Cambridge University Press.

Hirschkop, Ken. 1989. Bakhtin and cultural theory. In *Bakhtin and cultural theory,* Ken Hirschkop and D. Shepherd, eds., pp. 1–39. Manchester: Manchester University Press.

Hirschon, Renée. 1981a. Essential objects and the sacred: Interior and exterior space in an urban Greek locality. In *Women and space: Ground rules and social maps,* Shirley Ardener, ed., pp. 72–87. New York: St. Martin's.

————. 1981b. Open body/closed space: The transformation of female sexuality. In *Defining females,* S. Ardener, ed., pp. 66–88. New York: Wiley.

Hirschon, Renée, and J. Gold. 1982. Territoriality and the home environment in a Greek urban community. *Anthropological Quarterly* 55:63–73.

Hobsbawm, Eric J. 1959. *Primitive rebels: Studies in archaic forms of social movements in the 19th and 20th centuries.* 2d ed. New York: W. W. Norton.

Huizinga, Johan. 1955. *Homo ludens: A study of the play element in culture.* Boston: Beacon Press.

Hunt, Eva. 1977. Ceremonies of confrontation and submission. In *Secular ritual,* Sally F. Moore and B. G. Meyerhoff, eds., pp. 124–147. Assen, The Netherlands: Van Gorcum.

Hutcheon, Linda. 1985. *A theory of parody: The teachings of twentieth-century art forms.* New York: Methuen.

Ingham, John. 1964. The bullfighters. *American Imago* 21:95–102.

————. 1986. *Mary, Michael, and Lucifer.* Austin: University of Texas Press.

Isbell, Billie J. 1985. *To defend ourselves: Ecology and ritual in an Andean village.* Prospect Heights, Ill.: Waveland Press.

Ivanov, Vladimir V. 1984. The semiotic theory of carnival as the inversion of bipolar opposites. In *Carnival!* Thomas Sebeok, ed., pp. 11–37. New York: Mouton.

Kaeppler, Adrienne L. 1993. Poetics and politics of Tongan laments and eulogies. *American Ethnologist* 20:474–501.

Kaplan, Temma. 1977. *Anarchists of Andalusia, 1868–1903.* Princeton, N.J.: Princeton University Press.

——. 1984. Civic rituals and patterns of resistance in Barcelona, 1890–1930. In *The power of the past,* Pat Thane et al., eds., pp. 173–193. Cambridge: Cambridge University Press.

Kelly, John D., and Martha Kaplan. 1990. History, structure, and ritual. *Annual Review of Anthropology* 19:119–150.

Kertzer, David I. 1988. *Ritual, politics, and power.* New Haven, Conn.: Yale University Press.

Keyes, Ralph. 1980. *The height of your life.* New York: Warner Books.

Kris, Ernst. 1952. *Psychoanalytic explorations in art.* New York: International Universities Press.

La Fontaine, Jean. 1985. *Initiation.* Manchester: Manchester University Press.

Lakoff, George, and Mark Johnson. 1980. *Metaphors we live by.* Chicago: University of Chicago Press.

Lawrence, Denise. 1996. Suburbanization of house form and gender relations in a rural Portuguese agro-town. *Architecture and Behavior* 4:197–212.

Lawrence, Denise, and Setha Low. 1990. The built environment and spatial form. *Annual Review of Anthropology* 19:453–505.

Lawrence, Roderick J. 1981. The social classification of domestic space: A cross-cultural study. *Anthropos* 76:649–664.

Leach, Edmund. 1965. *Political systems of highland Burma.* Boston: Beacon Press.

Le Roy Ladurie, Emmanuel. 1979. *Carnival in Romans.* New York: George Braziller.

Levant, Ronald F. (with Gini Kopecky). 1995. *Masculinity reconstructed.* New York: Dutton.

Levine, Robert. 1973. *Culture, behavior, and personality.* Chicago: Aldine.

——. 1982. Gusii funerals: Meanings of life and death in an African community. *Ethos* 10:26–65.

LeVine, Robert A. 1961. Anthropology and the study of conflict. *Journal of Conflict Resolution* 5:3–15.

Lévi-Strauss, Claude. 1961. *Tristes tropiques,* John Russell, trans. New York: Criterion Books.

——. 1962. *The savage mind.* Chicago: University of Chicago Press.

Levy, Robert I. 1971. The community function of Tahitian male transvestism: A hypothesis. *Anthropological Quarterly* 44:12–21.

Lewis, I. M. 1976. *Social anthropology in perspective.* Cambridge: Cambridge University Press.

Lindholm, Charles. 1982. *Generosity and jealousy.* New York: Columbia University Press.

Lindley, Arthur. 1996. *Hyperion and the hobbyhorse: Studies in carnivalesque subversion.* Newark: University of Delaware Press.

Linger, Daniel T. 1992. *Dangerous encounters: Meanings of violence in a Brazilian town.* Stanford, Calif.: Stanford University Press.

LiPuma, Edward, and Sarah K. Meltzoff. 1989. Toward a theory of culture and class: An Iberian example. *American Ethnologist* 16:313–334.

Lisón Tolosana, Carmelo. 1966. *Belmonte de los Caballeros.* Oxford: Oxford University Press.

———. 1979. *Antropología Cultural de Galicia.* Madrid: Akal.

Llobera, Josep R. 1986. Fieldwork in southwestern Europe: Anthropological panacea or epistemological straitjacket? *Critique of Anthropology* 6:25–33.

Lock, Margaret. 1993. Cultivating the body: Anthropology and epistemologies of body practice and knowledge. *Annual Review of Anthropology* 22:133–155.

Loizos, Peter, and Evthymios Papataxiarchis. 1991. Introduction: Gender and kinship in marriage and alternative contexts. In *Contested identities: Gender and kinship in modern Greece,* Peter Loizos and Evthymios Papataxiarchis, eds., pp. 3–25. Princeton, N.J.: Princeton University Press.

Lovejoy, Arthur O. 1960. *The great chain of being.* New York: Harper and Row.

Low, Setha. 1990. Urban public spaces as reflections of culture: The plaza in Costa Rica. In *Urban condition II,* Leonard Duhl, ed., pp. 98–108. Beverly Hills: Sage.

———. 1995. Indigenous architectural representations in the Spanish American plaza in Mesoamerica and the Caribbean. *American Anthropologist* 97:748–762.

———. 1996a. Constructing difference: Spatial boundaries in the plaza. In *Setting boundaries,* Deborah Pellow, ed., pp. 161–178. Amherst, Mass.: Bergin and Garvey.

———. 1996b. Spatializing culture: The social production and social construction of public space in Costa Rica. *American Ethnologist* 23:861–889.

Luque Baena, Enrique. 1974. *Estudio antropológico social de un pueblo del sur.* Madrid: Tecnos.

———. 1981. Perspectivas antropológicas sobre Andalucía. *Papers* 16:12–49 (Barcelona).

Luria, Zella. 1979. Psychosocial determinants of gender identity, role, and orientation. In *Human sexuality,* Herant A. Katchadourian, ed., pp. 163–193. Berkeley: University of California Press.

Maccoby, Eleanor. 1979. Gender identity and sex-role adaptation. In *Human sexuality,* Herant A. Katchadourian, ed., pp. 194–203. Berkeley: University of California Press.

McEwen, William. 1975. *Changing rural society.* New York: Oxford University Press.

Maddox, Richard. 1993. *El Castillo: The politics of tradition in an Andalusian town.* Urbana: University of Illinois Press.

Mahler, Margaret, et al. 1975. *The psychological birth of the human infant.* New York: Basic Books.

Malefakis, Edward. 1970. *Agrarian reform and peasant revolt in Spain.* New Haven, Conn.: Yale University Press.

Marshall, Marshall. 1979. *Weekend warriors.* Palo Alto, Calif.: Mayfield.

Martinez-Alier, Juan. 1971. *Labourers and landowners in southern Spain.* London: Allen and Unwin.

Mauss, Marcel. 1974. *The gift,* Ian Cunnison, trans. London: Cohen and West.

Merton, Robert K. 1976. *Sociological ambivalence.* New York: Free Press.

Mintz, Jerome R. 1982. *The anarchists of Casas Viejas.* Chicago: University of Chicago Press.

———. 1997. *Carnival song and society: Gossip, sexuality and creativity in Andalusia.* Oxford: Berg.

Mitchell, Timothy J. 1988. *Violence and piety in Spanish folklore.* Philadelphia: University of Pennsylvania Press.

———. 1990. *Passional culture: Emotion, religion, and society in southern Spain.* Philadelphia: University of Pennsylvania Press.

———. 1994. *Flamenco deep song.* New Haven, Conn.: Yale University Press.

Money, John, and Anka Ehrhardt. 1972. *Man and woman, boy and girl.* Baltimore, Md.: Johns Hopkins University Press.

Moreno Navarro, Isidoro. 1972. *Propiedad, clases sociales y hermandades en la Baja Andalucía: La estructura social de un pueblo del Aljarafe.* Madrid: Siglo XXI de España.

———. 1984. La antropología cultural en Andalucía: Estado actual y perspectiva de futuro. In *Antropología Cultural de Andalucía,* Salvador Rodríguez Becerra, ed., pp. 93–107. Seville: Consejería de Cultura de la Junta de Andalucía.

———. 1985. *Cofradías y hermandades andaluzas: Estructura, simbolismo e identidad.* Seville: Andaluzas Unidas.

———. 1989. Cultura del trabajo e ideología: El movimiento campesino anarquista andaluz. In *Actas V, Congreso del Andalucismo Histórico,* pp. 76–93. Cádiz: Diputación Provincial.

Morris, Rosalind C. 1995. All made up: Performance theory and the new anthropology of sex and gender. *Annual Review of Anthropology* 24:567–592.

Mowrer, Orval H. 1950. Identity: A link between learning theory and psychotherapy. In *Learning theory and personality dynamics: Selected papers,* pp. 573–616. New York: Ronald Press.

Munn, Nancy D. 1973. Symbolism in ritual context. In *Handbook of social and cultural anthropology,* John J. Honigmann, ed., pp. 579–612. Chicago: Rand McNally.

Murphy, Michael D. 1978. "Between the virgin and the whore: Local community and nuclear family in Seville, Spain." Ph.D. diss., University of California, San Diego.

———. 1983a. Coming of age in Seville. *Journal of Anthropological Research* 39:376–392.

———. 1983b. Emotional confrontations between sevillano fathers and sons. *American Ethnologist* 10:650–664.

———. 1983c. Masculinity and selective homophobia: A case from Spain. Paper read at the 82d annual meeting of the American Anthropological Association, Chicago, Nov. 17, 1983.

———. 1994. Class, community, and costume in an Andalusian pilgrimage. *Anthropological Quarterly* 67:49–61.

Nadel, S. F. 1954. *Nupe religion.* London: Routledge and Kegan Paul.

Nieberg, Harold L. 1973. *Culture storm: Politics and the ritual order.* New York: St. Martin's.

Ortiz Nuevo, José L. 1985. *Pensamiento político en el Cante Flamenco.* Sevilla: Biblioteca de la Cultura Andaluza.

Ortner, Sherry, and H. Whitehead, eds. 1981a. Introduction: Accounting for sexual meanings. In *Sexual meanings: The cultural construction of gender and sexuality.* New York: Cambridge University Press.

———. 1981b. *Sexual meanings: The cultural construction of gender and sexuality,* Sherry Ortner and H. Whitehead, eds., pp. 1–28. New York: Cambridge University Press.

Papataxiarchis, Evthymios. 1991. Friends of the heart: Male commensal solidarity, gender, and kinship in Aegean Greece. In *Contested identities,* Peter Loizos and Evthymios Papataxiarchis, eds., pp. 156–179. Princeton, N.J.: Princeton University Press.

Paredes, Américo. 1971. The United States, Mexico, and machismo. *Journal of the Folklore Institute* 8:17–37.

Parker, Richard G. 1991. *Bodies, pleasures, and passions: Sexual culture in contemporary Brazil.* Boston: Beacon Press.

Parker, Seymour, et al. 1975. Father absence and cross-sex identity. *American Ethnologist* 2:687–706.

Parsons, Anne. 1969. *Belief, magic, and anomie.* New York: Free Press.

Payne, Stanley G. 1975. *Basque nationalism.* Reno: University of Nevada Press.

———. 1984. *Spanish Catholicism: An historical overview.* Madison: University of Wisconsin Press.

Pérez-Díaz, Victor M. 1993. *The return of civil society: The emergence of democratic Spain.* Cambridge, Mass.: Harvard University Press.

Peristiany, Jean G., ed. 1965. *Honour and shame: The values of Mediterranean society.* London: Weidenfeld & Nicolson.

Photiades, J. 1965. The position of the coffeehouse in the social structure of the Greek village. *Sociologia Ruralis* 5:45–53.

Piaget, Jean. 1962. *Play, dreams, and imitation in childhood,* C. Gattegno and R. M. Hodgson, trans. New York: Norton.

Pi-Sunyer, Oriol. 1988. Catalan politics and Spanish democracy: An overview of a relationship. *Iberian Studies* 17:1–16.

Pitkin, Donald. 1985. *The house that Giacomo built: History of an Italian family, 1898–1978.* New York: Cambridge University Press.

Pitt-Rivers, Julian. 1971. *The people of the Sierra.* Chicago: University Chicago Press.

———. 1977. *The fate of Shechem: The politics of sex.* Cambridge: Cambridge University Press.

Pratt, Dallas. 1960. The Don Juan myth. *American Imago* 17:321–335.

Press, Irwin. 1979. *The city as context: Urbanism and behavioral constraints in Seville.* Urbana: University of Illinois Press.

Radcliffe-Brown, Alfred R. 1952. *Structure and function in primitive society.* Glencoe: Free Press.

Ramos-Santana, Alberto. 1985. *Historia del carnaval de Cádiz.* Cádiz: INGRASA.

Rebel, Hermann. 1989. Cultural hegemony and class experience. *American Ethnologist* 16:117–136.

Rector, Monica. 1984. The code and message of carnival: Escolas-de-samba. In *Carnival!* Thomas Sebeok, ed., pp. 37–165. New York: Mouton.

Richardson, John. 1991. *A life of Picasso,* vol. 1, 1881–1906. New York: Random House.

Robben, Antonius C. M. G. 1989. *Sons of the sea goddess: Economic practice and discursive conflict in Brazil.* New York: Columbia University Press.

Rochlin, Gregory. 1980. *The masculine dilemma.* Boston: Little, Brown.

Rodriguez, Sylvia. 1991. The Taos matachines: Ritual symbolism and interethnic relations. *American Ethnologist* 18:234–256.

Rodríguez Becerra, Salvador. 1973. *Etnografía de la vivienda: El Aljarafe de Sevilla.* Seville: Semenario de Antropología Americana.

———. 1981. Cultura popular y fiestas en Andalucía. In *Los Andaluces,* pp. 447–494. Madrid: ISTMO Editorial.

———. 1984. La fiesta de moros y cristianos en Andalucía. *Gazeta de Antropología* 3:13–30.

———. 1985. *Las fiestas de Andalucía.* Seville: Biblioteca de la Cultura Andaluza.

———. 1992. El carnaval y lo carnavalesco en las fiestas en Andalucía. In *Actas del Congreso del Carnaval.* Cádiz: Ayuntamiento de Cádiz.

Rodríguez Becerra, Salvador, ed. 1984. *Antropología cultural de Andalucía.* Seville: Instituto de Cultura Andaluza.

Rogers, Susan C. 1975. Female forms of power and the myth of male dominance: A model of female/male interaction in peasant society. *American Ethnologist* 2:727–756.

———. 1985. Gender in southwestern France: The myth of male dominance revisited. *Anthropology* 9:65–86.

Roux, Bernard. 1991. Latifundio y minifundio en Andalucía. In *Etnología de Andalucía Oriental,* D. Provansal and P. Molina, eds., pp. 331–351. Almería, Spain: Anthropos.

Sabaté Martinez, Ana, Juana M. Rodríguez Moy, and María A. Díaz Múñoz. 1995. *Mujeres, espacio, y sociedad: Hacía una geografía del género.* Madrid: Síntesis.

Saunders, George. 1981. Men and women in southern Europe: A review of some aspects of cultural complexity. *Journal of Psychological Anthropology* 4:413–434.

Scheffler, Harold W. 1964. The genesis of conflict and repression of conflict: Choiseul Island. *American Anthropologist* 66:789–804.

Schneider, Jane. 1971. Of vigilance and virgins: Honor, shame and access to resources in Mediterranean societies. *Ethnology* 10:1–24.

Schneider, Jane, and Peter Schneider. 1976. *Culture and political economy in western Sicily.* New York: Academic Press.

Schrauf, Robert W. 1998. La comparsa y el concurso: Andalusian carnival on stage. *Anthropological Quarterly* 71:74–88.

Sciama, Lidia. 1981. The problem of privacy in Mediterranean anthropology. In *Women and space: Ground rules and social maps,* Shirley Ardener, ed., pp. 89–111. New York: St. Martin's.

Scott, James C. 1976. *The moral economy of the peasant.* New Haven, Conn.: Yale University Press.

———. 1985. *Weapons of the weak.* New Haven, Conn.: Yale University Press.

———. 1990. *Dominance and the arts of resistance.* New Haven, Conn.: Yale University Press.

Seremetakis, C. Nadia. 1990. The ethics of antiphony: The social construction of pain, gender, and power in the southern Peloponnese. *Ethos* 18:481–511.

———. 1991. *The last word: Women, death, and divination in Inner Mani.* Chicago: University of Chicago Press.

Shapiro, Warren, and Uli Linke, eds. 1996. *Denying biology.* Lanham, Md.: University Press of America.

Sider, Gerald M. 1986. *Culture and class in anthropology and history: A Newfoundland illustration.* Cambridge: Cambridge University Press.

Simmel, Georg. 1955. *Conflict,* Kurt H. Wolff, trans. Glencoe: Free Press.

Singer, Milton. 1972. *When a great tradition modernizes.* New York: Praeger.

Slater, Candace. 1982. *Stories on a string: The Brazilian literatura de Cordel.* Berkeley: University of California Press.

Soja, Edward. 1971. *The political organization of space.* Washington, D.C.: Association of American Geographers.

Solís Llorente, Ramón. 1988. *Coros y chirigotas: Carnaval en Cádiz.* Madrid: Silex.

Spain, Daphne. 1992. *Gendered spaces.* Chapel Hill: University of North Carolina Press.

Spiro, Melford. 1979. Whatever happened to the id? *American Anthropologist* 81:5–13.

Stokes, Martin. 1992. *The Arabesk debate: Music and musicians in modern Turkey.* Oxford, England: Clarendon Press.

Stoller, Robert J. 1968. *Sex and gender.* New York: Science Books.

———. 1973a. Male transsexualism: Uneasiness. *American Journal of Psychiatry* 130: 536–539.

———. 1973b. Overview: The impact of new advances in sex research on psychoanalytic theory. *American Journal of Psychiatry* 130:241–251.

———. 1976. Gender identity. In *The sexual experience,* Benjamin Sadock and Harold I. Kaplan, eds., pp. 182–196. Baltimore, Md.: Williams and Wilkins.

Suarez-Orozco, Marcelo M., and Alan Dundes. 1984. The *piropo* and the dual image of women in the Spanish-speaking world. *Journal of Latin-American Lore* 10:111–133.

Swartz, Marc, et al., eds. 1966. *Political anthropology.* Chicago: Aldine.

Taggart, James M. 1990. *Enchanted maidens: Gender relations in Spanish folktales of courtship and marriage.* Princeton, N.J.: Princeton University Press.

———. 1992. Gender segregation and cultural constructions of sexuality in two Hispanic societies. *American Ethnologist* 19:75–96.

Tapper, Nancy, and R. Tapper. 1987. The birth of the prophet: Ritual and gender in Turkish Islam. *Man* 22:69–92.

Teti, Vito. 1995. Food and fatness in Calabria, Nicolette James, trans. In *Social aspects of obesity,* Igor de Garine and Nancy Pollock, eds., pp. 3–30. Luxembourg: Gordon and Breach.

Thomas, Nicholas. 1996. Cold fusion. *American Anthropologist* 98:9–16.

Tillion, Germaine. 1983. *The republic of cousins: Women's oppression in Mediterranean society,* Quintin Hoare, trans. London: Al Saqi Books.

Tolbert, Elizabeth. 1990. Magico-religious power and gender in the Karelian lament. In *Music, gender, and culture,* Marcia Herndon and Suzanne Ziegler, eds., pp. 41–56. Berlin: Institute for Comparative Music Studies.

Tuñón de Lara, Manuel. 1978. *Luchas obreras y campesinas en la Andalucía del siglo XX: Jaén (1917–1920), Sevilla (1930–1932).* Madrid: Siglo XXI de España.

Turner, Terence S. 1977. Transformation, hierarchy and transcendence: A reformulation of Van Gennep's model of the structure of rites de passage. In *Secular ritual,* Sally F. Moore and Barbara G. Meyerhoff, eds., pp. 53–70. Amsterdam: Van Gorcum.

Turner, Victor. 1957. *Schism and continuity in an African society.* Ithaca, N.Y.: Cornell University Press.

———. 1968. *The drums of affliction.* Oxford: Clarendon Press.

——. 1969. *The ritual process.* Chicago: Aldine.

——. 1985. *On the edge of the bush.* Tucson: University of Arizona Press.

Uhl, Sarah C. 1985. Special friends: The organization of intersex friendship in Escalona (Andalusia). *Anthropology* 9:129–152.

——. 1991. Forbidden friends: Cultural veils of female friendship in Andalusia. *American Ethnologist* 18:90–105.

Urban, Greg. 1988. Ritual wailing in Amerindian Brazil. *American Anthropologist* 90: 385–400.

Vale de Almeida, Miguel. 1996. *The hegemonic male: Masculinity in a Portuguese town.* Providence, R.I.: Berghahn Press.

Van Gennep, Jan. [1908] 1960. *The rites of passage,* Monika Vizedom and G. Caffee, trans. Chicago: University of Chicago Press.

Vasvari, Louise O. 1991. The battle of flesh and Lent in the "Libro de Arcipreste": Gastro-genital rites of reversal. *La Coronica* 20:1–15.

Wallace, Anthony F. C. 1970. *Culture and personality.* New York: Random House.

Weber, Max. 1946. *From Max Weber: Essays in sociology,* Hans H. Gerth and C. Wright Mills, ed. and trans. New York: Oxford University Press.

Weigert, Andrew J. 1991. *Mixed emotions: Certain steps toward understanding ambivalence.* Albany: State University of New York Press.

Wertheim, Willem F. 1965. *East-West parallels.* Chicago: University of Chicago Press.

Whiting, John W. M., et al. 1958. The function of male initiation rites at puberty. In *Readings in social psychology,* 3d ed., Eleanor Maccoby, ed., pp. 359–370. New York: Holt, Rinehart, Winston.

Williams, Brackette, ed. 1996. *Women out of place: The gender of agency, the race of nationality.* London: Routledge.

Williams, Raymond. 1973. Base and superstructure in Marxist cultural theory. *New Left Review* 82:3–16.

Wills, Clair. 1989. Upsetting the public: Carnival, hysteria, and women's texts. In *Bakhtin and cultural theory,* K. Hirschkop and D. Shepherd, eds., pp. 130–151. Manchester: Manchester University Press.

Wolff, Kurt, ed. 1950. *The sociology of Georg Simmel.* New York: Free Press.

Woolman, David. 1968. *Rebels in the Rif: Abd El Krim and the Rif rebellion.* Stanford, Calif.: Stanford University Press.

Yinger, Milton. 1982. *Countercultures.* New York: Free Press.

Young, Frank W. 1965. *Initiation rites: A cross-cultural study of status dramatization.* Indianapolis, Ind.: Bobbs-Merrill.

Zapperi, Roberto. 1991. *The pregnant man,* Brian Williams, trans. New York: Gordon and Breach.

Zinovieff, Sofia. 1991. Hunters and hunted. In *Contested identities,* Peter Loizos and Evthymios Papataxiarchis, eds., pp. 203–220. Princeton, N.J.: Princeton University Press.

Index